LEIBNIZ' PHILOSOPI OF LOGIC AND LANGUAGE

Second Edition

Hidé Ishiguro

Cambridge University Press
CAMBRIDGE
NEW YORK PORT CHESTER MELBOURNE SYDNEY

Published by the Press Syndicate of the University of Cambridge
The Pitt Building, Trumpington Street, Cambridge CB2 1RP
40 West 20th Street, New York, NY 10011, USA
10 Stamford Road, Oakleigh, Melbourne 3166, Australia

First edition published in 1972 by Duckworth, London, and
Cornell University Press, Ithaca, New York.

Printed in Canada

Library of Congress Cataloging-in-Publication Data

Ishiguro, Hidé
Leibniz's philosophy of logic and language / Hidé Ishiguro. –
2nd. ed.
p. cm
Includes bibliographical references.
ISBN 0–521–37428–6. – ISBN 0–521–37781–1 (pbk.)
1. Leibniz, Gottfried Wilhelm, Freiherr von, 1646–1716 –
Contributions in logic. 2. Leibniz, Gottfried Wilhelm, Freiherr
von, 1646–1716 – Contributions in philosophy of language.
3. Logic, Modern – 17th century. 4. Languages – Philosophy.
I. Title.
B2599.L8I83 1990
160′.92–dc20 89–28814

British Library Cataloguing in Publication Data

Ishiguro, Hidé
Leibniz's philosophy of logic and language. – 2nd. ed.
1. Logic. Theories of Leibniz, Gottfried Wilhelm, 1646–1716
I. Title
160′.92′4

ISBN 0–521–37428–6 hardback
ISBN 0–521–37781–1 paperback

Contents

Preface to the second edition

Since the first edition of this book appeared seventeen years ago, I realized that some of the points I made needed to be clarified and developed. This was especially the case with what I wrote about modality and possible worlds in Chapter VII of the first edition (which has become Chapter IX here). It has therefore been emended and expanded, incorporating views I have expressed elsewhere on these problems. I have also expanded some sections of Chapter V of the first edition (Chapter VII in this edition), "Monads, Attributes, Accidents, and Relations." The passages express responses to some recent debates on the topic, and are related to articles I have written on the subject since the first edition of this book appeared. I hope my explanation of what Leibniz said is now clearer.

Various comments about sections of this book have appeared in reviews, articles, and books during these years. I appreciated the support I received of my reading of various texts of Leibniz, which went against hitherto accepted interpretations of Leibniz's doctrines. But there were important critical comments also. Amongst them were some that made me see the inadequacies of what I said, and made me realize the need to correct and expand some of the original passages, and there were others with which I do not agree but which made me reflect on the ambiguities in my assertions, and see the need to improve the expression of my thoughts. As a consequence of this, Chapter II "The Principle of Substitutivity *Salva Veritate,*" has been rewritten extensively.

Two new chapters have been added. These are on topics directly related to the subjects discussed in the first edition, which occupied my mind after its publication. Chapter V on infinitesimals, a topic closely linked to the principle of substitutivity *salva veritate,* is based on a paper delivered to the Leibniz Society of America at the American Philosophy Association meeting held in Boston in December 1986. A slightly different version in French had been given to a symposium held in Brussels in August 1985, organized by the Gottfried-Wilhelm Leibniz Gesellschaft, Hannover. This was published in *Studia Leibnitiana,* Special Issue, Vol. 15, 1988. Chapter VIII, "Hypothetical Truths," which is on a problem presupposed by Leibniz's discussion of modality, was originally published in *Leibniz: Critical and Interpretative Essays,* edited by Michael Hooker, (©) the University of Minnesota, Minneapolis.

One general methodological point has been raised about this book by Hector Neri Castañeda ("Leibniz's concepts and their coincidence salva veritate," *Nous* 8, 1974), namely that I ignore the developmental aspects of Leibniz's thoughts and treat them timelessly within the Leibniz corpus (an attitude which Professor Castañeda calls Athenian). I plead guilty to having cited passages from works of Leibniz of widely different periods without making clear the dates of the works from which they were cited. In the text itself I have tried to emend this when the dates are relevant. It is, of course, very important at times to keep in mind how Leibniz's thought on a particular subject developed and changed. This is, for example, very much the case with his thinking on infinitesimals discussed in Chapter V, and to a certain degree true about his views on what it is to have ideas. However as Benson Mates has said in his recent book on Leibniz, on many important issues there is an amazing steadfastness in Leibniz thesis in all his voluminous works written over a period of fifty years. Quite often he tries out different answers to the same question in each of the different periods of his life, so that in many areas it can be misleading to engage in what Castañeda calls a Darwinian approach and attempt to trace a linear relation of development.

I have seriously wondered whether a revised second edition of this book warrants publication. Many works on Leibniz have appeared since the first edition was published. Especially, Hans Burkhardt's *Logik und Semiotik in der Philosophie von Leibniz,* Munich, 1980, and Benson Mates' well-researched and thorough *The Philosophy of Leibniz,* New York and Oxford, 1986, cover much of the same area examined in this book. However, enough important disagreement about the interpretation of some of Leibniz's fundamental doctrines remains, between these authors and me – many on issues on which I feel Leibniz has made serious contributions to philosophy – to lead me to believe that the publication of this new edition is perhaps justified.

In preparing this second edition I have been helped by the kindness of Professor Albert Heinekamp, Dr. Gerda Utermöhlen, Dr. R. Finster, and the members of the Leibniz Archive in Hannover where I spent several days. I also was helped enormously for the time and assistance I received in the Wissenschaftskolleg zu Berlin, where I was a fellow from October 1987 to July 1988. I am grateful to Mrs. Filooza Kraft of the institute who typed an enormous portion of the work and to Mrs. Sigrid Goodman of Barnard College, Columbia University, who also helped me with the typing.

New York City
March 1989

Abbreviations

Akademie	*Leibniz, Gottfried Wilhelm, Sämtliche Schriften und Briefe* herausgegeben von der Deutschen Akademie der Wissenschaften zu Berlin. Darmstadt, 1923 ff.; Leipzig, 1938 ff.; Berlin, 1950 ff.
Bodemann *LH*	Bodemann, Eduard, *Die Leibniz Handschriften der königlichen öffentlichen Bibliothek zu Hannover.* Hannover, 1895; reprinted Hildesheim, 1966.
Couturat, *OFI*	Couturat, Louis, ed., *Opuscules et fragments inédits de Leibniz, extraits des manuscrits de la bibliothèque royale de Hanovre.* Paris, 1903; reprinted Hildesheim, 1961.
Dutens	Dutens, Ludovicus, ed. [Leibniz, Gottfried Wilhelm], *Opera omnia, nunc primum collecta,* 6 vols. Geneva, 1768.
Erdmann	*Leibnitii Opera Philosophica quae extant latina gallica germanica omnia.* Edited by J. E. Erdmann. Berlin, 1840.
G. *Math.*	Gerhardt, C. I., ed. [Leibniz, Gottfried Wilhelm], *Mathematischen Schriften,* 7 vols. Berlin-Halle, 1849–63; reprinted Hildesheim, 1971.
G. *Phil.*	Gerhardt, C. I., ed. [Leibniz, Gottfried Wilhelm], *Philosophischen Schriften,* 7 vols. Berlin, 1875–90; reprinted Hildesheim, 1965.
Grua	Grua, G., ed., *Textes inédits d'après de la bibliothèque provinciale de Hanovre,* 2 vols. Paris, 1948; reprinted New York, 1985.

Kauppi	Kauppi, Rauli, *Über die leibnizsche Logik.* Helsinki, 1960.
Loemker	Loemker, Leroy, ed. and trans., *Leibniz's Philosophical Papers and Letters,* 2 vols. Chicago, 1956; 2d ed. in 1 vol., Dordrecht, 1969.
NE	*Nouveaux Essais sur l'Entendement Humain,* 1705, in *Akademie,* 6th series, vol. 6, Berlin, 1962; English translation *New Essays on Human Understanding* by Peter Remnant and Jonathan Bennett. Cambridge, U.K., 1981. (The pagination of this corresponds to the pagination of the *Akademie* edition.)
Parkinson *LLP*	Parkinson, G. H. R., ed. and trans., [Leibniz, Gottfried Wilhelm], *Logical Papers: A Selection.* Oxford, 1966.
Parkinson *LRLM*	Parkinson, G. H. R., *Logic and Reality in Leibniz's Metaphysics.* Oxford, 1965.
Rescher	Rescher, Nicholas, *The Philosophy of Leibniz.* Englewood Cliffs, N.J., 1967.
Russell	Russell, Bertrand Lord, *A Critical Exposition of the Philosophy of Leibniz.* London, 1900; rev. ed., 1937.
Wiener	Wiener, P. P., ed. and trans., *Leibniz: Selections.* New York, 1951.

I. Introduction

> . . . thus a new maxim – which goes completely against the old one – has become necessary; namely, that scholars and students should participate as much as possible in conversation, and be as much as they can with people and in the world. (Memorandum to the Duke of Württemburg, 1668–1669.)[1]

Leibniz (1646–1716) is a philosopher whose reputation has altered radically in this century. Unlike his contemporary Spinoza, who fell into oblivion after his death, to be rescued a hundred years later by two German romantics, Leibniz was never disregarded. His works and those of his followers, such as Wolff, remained standard reading in the universities. But until the twentieth century he was treated merely as a metaphysician who believed in an esoteric doctrine of monadology and in the pre-established harmony, and as a logician whose theories on the relation of truth and concepts and on science had been superseded by those of Kant.

Leibniz was recognized as a genius who shared with Newton the honour of having invented, independently, the differential calculus, and who had made original contributions in an astonishing number of different fields of study. Yet his metaphysical and logical theories were read in a way that made them so obviously false or absurd that their interest could at most be historical. Voltaire's ridicule of Leibnizian philosophy in *Candide* makes us forget that although Leibniz was a theoretician, and even had mystical as well as religious leanings, he was concerned with facts and the application of his theory. His interest in developing probability theory was due to his belief that it rendered intelligible and rational what might appear random in nature. He wrote an important book on geology and invented computing machines which could multiply and divide as well as add and subtract. As he said to Huygens, "I prefer a Leeuwenhoek who tells me what he sees to a Cartesian who tells me what he thinks."[2]

Some have talked as if Leibniz's denial of the philosophical theory of causal interaction meant that, according to his theory, even though water boils if heated, there is no real connection between the heat and water when this happens. Others have claimed that his thesis that in all true propositions the predicate is included in the subject meant that all truths were analytic for him and hence that he could not make any real distinction between necessary and contingent truths. The fact is that both the existence of the laws of nature and their regularity, and the distinction of necessary and contingent truths, were basic tenets of Leibniz's philosophy.

In this book I shall deal exclusively with Leibniz's philosophy of logic and language, which is still gravely misunderstood despite the fact that it is the area of his philosophy which has undergone the greatest reappraisal in this century. I shall not make a detailed exposition of the various logical systems which Leibniz constructed; such can be found in the works of Couturat and Kauppi and an article by Rescher, listed in the bibliography. My interest is rather to investigate the philosophical assumptions and consequences of these systems. Many of the interpretations I give of Leibniz's theories are contrary to accepted views, and I defend my position by argument and textual references. I shall also try to reply to several important criticisms of my views that have appeared since the publication of the first edition, making clear where I think my views have to be amended, and where I think my critics have misunderstood Leibniz. I regret that I have not had room to examine Leibniz's interesting contribution to the logic of probability. This is closely linked with his views on hypothetical truths examined in Chapter VIII, but also with his view on scientific knowledge, and on the mathematical theory of games that was being propounded in his time by Bernouilli, Huygens, and others, and that merits a separate book.

To understand Leibniz's philosophy of logic and language against the background of his diverse, prolific, but fragmentary writings in almost all areas of philosophy, we must first remind ourselves of his attitude to the world. Leibniz and Spinoza can be seen to be at opposite poles in their conception of the philosopher's relation to the world around him. Spinoza tried to remain free of any worldly ties that might endanger his intellectual integrity. To retain this intellectual freedom, he refused a professorship and earned his living as a craftsman polishing lenses. He identified himself with no religious institutions or sects, was excommunicated by orthodox Jewry, and was considered a dangerous atheist by most Christian groups. Leibniz too refused a university chair, which he was offered at the early age of twenty. But his refusal, it seems, reflected not so much a fear of losing his intellectual freedom as a desire to secure a position in which to fulfill his ideals and aspirations. He believed that moral philosophy could best bring about the general good by means of legislation and political influence. Leibniz was highly critical of the university education of his time and of what he called the monkish views of academics; but he did not believe that intellectual honesty was necessarily compromised by tenure of an official position, and so he became a lawyer and a diplomat and aspired to a political career.

What is remarkable about Leibniz is that, far from leading the secluded life of a speculative thinker, he took a keen part in many practical and political activities, which he regarded as the only means of changing the world. And more remarkable still – contrary to the common view that a philosopher's intellectual powers are dissipated if his concerns are with the real world – is the extraordinary originality and strength of Leibniz's achievements in the most speculative and theoretical fields of thought. The breadth and profundity of his investigations make us suspicious of Russell's portrait of him as a man who wasted time and talent in efforts to please the princes. He worked intensively in philosophy, even though he published little.

Leibniz remained four years in Paris, working under Huygens, and it was during this time that he invented the differential calculus. It is interesting to note that he had originally left Mainz in 1692 on a diplomatic mission, to present to Louis XIV a memorandum of his own conception with the aim of preventing France from invading Holland and persuading her instead to attempt a conquest of Egypt. (It is of course deplorable, and rather comical, that Leibniz applied his idea of peace and conciliation only within the confines of Europe.) Leibniz was not successful in his mission, but it shows that he was as interested, to say the least, in the question of maintaining European peace, as he was in working out his various theories in mathematics, logic, and philosophy. Leibniz was convinced that the period in which he lived was critical. In his memoranda on diplomacy or politics, he often resorted to calculation and compromise to avoid giving offense, so as to make those in power carry out policies closest to his own ideals. His claim that "we must accommodate ourselves to the world, for the world will not accommodate itself to us"[3] may evoke scorn or dismay for its seeming cowardice or cynicism; but for Leibniz, brought up in a Germany ravaged by the Thirty Years War, it was a realistic assessment of how best to advance his moral views.

What is important is the fact that Leibniz's intellectual rigour was such that neither the questions he raised in philosophy and mathematics, nor the way he answered them, were corrupted or blunted by a facile concern for 'relevance' or by his various commitments. Thus, though one of the initial slogans of Sartre's Existentialism, "In the case of man existence precedes essence," which was to carry a political message as well, was directed against Leibniz's doctrines on individuals and individual concepts, Leibniz himself was an '*homme engagé*' interested in influencing the political authorities of his time.

Leibniz's other characteristic attitude to the world around him was his pluralism. It is usually wrong to draw a simple analogy between a man's metaphysical doctrines and his practical beliefs. But Leibniz was as firm a believer in the coexistence of distinct institutions, religions, or attitudes, as he was in the metaphysical doctrine that the best of all possible worlds is that in which the greatest number of essences is realised, i.e., in which exists the greatest number of kinds of entities. Leibniz deplored the lack of communication between different groups, whether it resulted from a lack of curiosity or from defensiveness. He was constantly lamenting the bickering and hostility between people who held different views. As far as Christianity was concerned, it is true that his ultimate ideal was reunion rather than coexistence; yet he adamantly refused to be converted to Catholicism. He was a Lutheran who served both at the Catholic court of Mainz and at the court of John Frederick, a Catholic convert, at Hanover. He declined the post of chief librarian at the Vatican on the grounds that such a position would make more difficult the task of advancing the dialogue between the two camps. But he was a Protestant who was able to retain more sympathy with the doctrines of Aristotle and the Scholastics than many of his Catholic contemporaries – and who, apart from a very few lapses (the most suspect being his later attitude to the philosophy of Spinoza), was able to remain intellectually honest and open in a period rife with faction.

His voluminous correspondence contains serious discussions in philosophy, the natural sciences, theology, law, politics, and history, addressed to important thinkers of different countries and different convictions (for example, Newton, Boyle, Halley, Papin, Huygens, Bernouilli, Goldbach, Wren, Wallis, Leeuwenhoek, Bossuet, Malebranche, Arnauld, Bayle). In a period when there were far fewer journals than there are today, serious correspondence was much commoner. Even so the variety of topics which interested him, and the diversity in status of the people with whom he corresponded, remain impressive. He wrote as courteously and conscientiously to the miners of the Harz as he did to Princess Sophie-Charlotte. He wrote to Great Tartar and to Sumatra in quest of anthropological and linguistic information. His letter to Peter the Great of Russia, advising him to have more communication and trade with China, puts us in mind of Bertrand Russell.

Not only was he anxious to communicate with people of different persuasions and nationalities; he was also aware, as only a man qualified in so many different subjects would be, of the importance of curiosity and mutual understanding between men engaged in different academic disciplines. For him, 'one-sidedness' was one of the greatest and most prevalent of vices. Worse was the mutual suspicion and incomprehension of people who considered others to be one-sided. Leibniz criticised philologists who had no understanding of science, mathematicians and scientists who believed that they alone possessed knowledge useful to mankind and were suspected in turn by practical people,[4] scholastic philosophers and theologians who saw themselves in the role of guardians of religion and virtue, and popularisers who knew little beyond elementary arithmetic but believed themselves capable of solving questions involving sophisticated mathematics.[5]

At the same time, he believed in popularisation. It had become necessary, he said, "that scholars and students should participate as much as possible in conversation, and be as much as they can with people in the world." Leibniz even undertook to construct a windmill, of his own invention, for the silver-mines of the Harz. In 1679, surrounded by ill-will and suspicion, he began working obsessively on the project, using pipes filled with compressed air. And after repeated failures and fresh attempts, he admitted defeat only in 1695. What is interesting is his own explanation of his failure, as distinct from that of the mining officials who accused him of believing that "all speculationes mathematicae whatsoever can be applied ad praxim." Leibniz naturally opposed such a facile division of speculation and practice. In an untitled manuscript written during this period he describes a figure which could be read as a caricature of himself constructing windmills:

> A half-baked scientist puffed up by an imaginary science will project machines and constructions which cannot succeed because he does not possess all the theory required. He will understand perhaps the common rules about moving forces, the lever, the wedge, the jackscrew, but he will not understand that part of mechanics which I call the science of resistance or rigidity which has not yet been put sufficiently into rules. . . . When we understand these things we are not exposed so vulnerably.[6]

He therefore concludes that we cannot trust reason alone, and must either have some experience or consult those who have it. This, however, is in order to test and improve our theory. For the scientist he described failed by his inadequate theory, not in the practical application of a correct theory.[7]

Leibniz is often thought of as a conservative, which indeed he was in some respects. He agreed with Grotius that, though people have a right to resist their ruler, the harm that results from revolution is incomparably greater than the harm that provokes it.[8] He believed in natural law, and thought that, if made more rational, constitutional rule with a structure similar to that in mediaeval Europe was preferable to the rule of the absolute monarchs of his time.

But, before concluding these biographical remarks, I would like to point out how radical were many of the criticisms Leibniz made in education and politics. For example, as Meyer has shown, Leibniz believed that a university should be located not in a quiet, isolated college town, but in a residential and commercial centre. Those who think that "young men should not be disturbed at their studies nor in any way distracted from them" have, according to Leibniz, contributed more than anything else to the spirit of pedantry – and "monkish erudition . . . which lacks all experience, activity and reality."[9] Leibniz, though himself a great admirer of Aristotle, was vehemently opposed to the way in which students were made to repeat and memorize Aristotle's formal works. He advocated not only a good mathematical education for all, but constant attempts to maintain a balance between the theoretical and the practical.

In politics, his concern to restrain the arbitrary power of rulers far outweighed his concern for any particular form of government. "Arbitrary power is what is directly opposed to the empire of reason. Thus in this world one must think of laws which can serve to restrain arbitrary power not only in kings, but in the deputies of people's and in judges."[10] Here Leibniz disagreed with Hobbes. Laws were not justified because they were willed by an authorized "representative person" but only for their rationality and probity. Leibniz was convinced that sovereignty could not be absolute. Because he preferred a rational universal authority to competition and arbitrary treaties – such as he saw existing between the sovereign states of his time – some have thought of him as the last of the mediaevalists. But his rational universal authority could as well be a United Nations as the Holy Roman Empire of Thomas Aquinas.

It is strange that for so long this diverse thinker, who was described by Frederick the Great as an "academy in himself" and whose interest even within speculative philosophy was much wider than Kant's, was regarded as a thoroughgoing, if wildly imaginative, system builder with little sense of reality. How could the witty Schopenhauer have written that the chief merit of Kant was that he had delivered us from Leibniz and his subtleties, and had thereby "made philosophy serious"?[11]

In the twentieth century Leibniz's philosophy has undergone four radical reappraisals. The first change was at the turn of the century, when the important role played by logical theories in Leibniz's philosophy as a whole, and the deep insight which he often showed in the philosophy of logic, first became apparent. Husserl, in his *Logische Untersuchungen,* published in 1900, attacked the psychologism which infested contemporary theories of logic. He wrote that his own conception of logic looked back to Leibniz "the great philosopher, whose intuitions speed forward far ahead of their time" and "appear sharply defined and highly admirable to a modern man acquainted with formal mathematics and mathematical logic."[12] The importance of Leibniz as a logician had already been recognised at the end of the nineteenth century by two mathematicians of acute philosophical insight, Frege and Peano. As stated in the Preface to *Opuscules et Fragments Inédits de Leibniz* (1908), Couturat's interest in compiling these unknown logical works of Leibniz was aroused when one of Peano's assistants at Turin drew his attention to the originality to be found in these texts. So prolific was Leibniz that even the seven thick volumes of philosophical works and the seven thick volumes of mathematical works which Gerhardt compiled over some forty years (from 1849 to 1863 and from 1875 to 1890) – to say nothing of the eleven volumes of his historical and political works edited by O. Klopp (1864–84), or of his physical and technological works published by E. Gerland (1906) – contained few of the fragments on logic which were to have such an influence on logicians of this century. In his lifetime Leibniz published several articles but only one philosophical book, the *Theodicy*. He was highly critical of the tendency to publish too much, and most of his writings were "thinking on paper" or discussions with contemporaries.

Though ignorant of many of these logical manuscripts, Bertrand Russell in 1900 published his interesting *The Philosophy of Leibniz*, which attempted to show that the whole of Leibniz's philosophy follows from five premises, three of which are logical. This is a most unlikely conclusion, if we remember that most of Leibniz's voluminous works were attempts to work out diverse problems for himself over a period of fifty years, or letters on a vast number of subjects not intended for publication, and hence not parts of any unitary system of philosophy – as he himself stated so clearly.[13]

Russell's understanding of Leibniz was unworthy of one of the architects of *Principia Mathematica*. He was limited by his adherence to a Kantian line on synthetic and analytic judgments. He also implicitly took 'simples' in Hume's manner. All the same, he saw clearly the importance of logical doctrines in Leibniz's various philosophical theories. Here he was vindicated by a well-documented and well-argued work, *La Logique de Leibniz*, published by Louis Couturat a year later.[14]

Couturat argued that for Leibniz all propositions are ultimately of the subject-predicate form, and that since for Leibniz all truths depend on the predicate term being contained in the subject term, all truths are for him analytic. I hope, however, to show that both the question of the subject-predicate form of propositions and the problem of the 'analyticity' of truths are much more complex than Couturat thought. ('Analyticity' was not a concept which Leibniz used with the post-Kantian meaning which we attach to it.) Couturat also rightly indicated the importance of Leibniz's lifelong attempt to construct a system of formal logic which, because its syntax corresponded to the laws of thought, would provide a procedure to determine the truth-value of every human thought expressed in it.

Some of Leibniz's attempts were inconsistent, and all of them seem to lead to various difficulties. Without the concept of quantifiers, it was difficult for Leibniz to make a proper distinction between first-order and second-order predicates. Couturat thought that the main reason for the limitations of Leibniz's system was his 'intensional' reading of the truth-conditions of propositions. This I will discuss in Chapter IV. Couturat belonged to the generation of logicians who developed set theory, and thought that the whole strength and success of modern logic lay in the extensional approach.

The second reappraisal of Leibniz's thought came about with the new redevelopment of modal and intensional logic. In his *Survey of Symbolic Logic,* 1918, C. I. Lewis remarked that although Leibniz's intensional approach led him into difficulties, it also enabled him to make some important distinctions which had since been forgotten. Since then there have been important developments in intensional logic, and R. Carnap, S. Kripke, S. Kanger, J. Hintikka, and D. Lewis among others have all referred to concepts or distinctions which come from

Leibniz.[15] Leibnizian concepts, such as the concept of possible worlds, or of necessity defined as truth in all possible worlds, have now become part of the widely accepted framework in which the semantics of intensional logic are discussed.

A third reappraisal was made by Hans Reichenbach in 1924, when he extolled the importance of Leibniz's theory of space and time.[16] He went so far as to claim that Kant had turned the clock back by two centuries in philosophy of science. Since then some have disagreed with Reichenbach's reading of Leibniz's doctrine of relative space and time, but no one can ignore Leibniz's view when we discuss the various modern concepts related to space and time.

The fourth reappraisal of Leibniz's thought was carried out more recently by N. Chomsky. In his insistence on innate structures and his polemic against Skinnerism, Chomsky has often referred to Leibniz as a believer in the innate nature of language and, like Chomsky himself, as a critic of the empiricist theory of language-acquisition as represented by Locke. It is true that Leibniz made interesting contributions to the philosophy of language, but not for quite the reason that Chomsky gives. Leibniz did say, rightly, that the concepts we form and learn, not only those of mathematics and logic but also those which apply to empirical facts, manifest what we are capable of learning rather than just the nature of external stimuli; they therefore depend as much on the nature and disposition of our mind as on the effect of the qualities of things given to our senses. But not even Locke would have disputed this. Locke thought that one of the fundamental differences between man and other animals was that man was a language-user. He believed that this difference derived, not from the difference in what was given to the senses, but from the nature of human understanding.

What did distinguish Leibniz's theory from Locke's was his deliberate refusal to separate the question of capacity to think from the question of the structure, and also of the contents and identity, of thought. The identity of numbers, for example, cannot be discussed separately from the structure of our thoughts about them.

Leibniz's interest as a philosopher of language lies above all (1) in his understanding of the necessity of structure and syntax (which will be discussed in Chapter III), (2) in his realisation that the surface grammar of a language does not reflect what he called the philosophical grammar of a language (which will be discussed in Chapter V); he thought that we must ignore some surface grammar which is of no logical significance, or learn rules to convert surface grammar idiosyncratic to a particular language to forms which reflect the philosophical grammar, i.e., the logical form, and (3) in his attempt to make clear the relation between the meaning and truth of simple and complex propositions (which will be discussed in Chapter II) and to find a system of signs which would express this most clearly.

Leibniz was not, as is sometimes said, the first symbolic logician. He was not the first to symbolize terms of arguments by letters (which was done even by Aristotle), or to produce a comprehensive workable deductive system (for he failed to produce one). But he tried to develop Jungius' attempt to build a logic which would treat relational propositions as well as simple subject-predicate propositions, and he also tried to formalize logical relations which are not purely truth-functional, a topic which I will develop in Chapters V and VI. Although many of his contemporaries were concerned with the creation of a universal language,[17] only Leibniz's *Characteristica Universalis* (system of universal signs) which expressed *Ars Combinatoria* (the art of combination of concepts) can rate as an expression of logical atomism. Leibniz alone had any insight into the relation of identity of concepts and truth-conditions. He is the precursor of the Russell of the *Philosophy of Logical Atomism* and the Wittgenstein of the *Tractatus*. Much of the failure of Leibniz's project of *Ars Combinatoria,* it seems to me, is a failure inherent in the programme of logical atomism in general, rather than a result either of a particular limitation in his symbolism (such as the unsatisfactory way in which he expressed what we should now render by quantifiers) or, as many commentators have assumed, of his belief that all propositions can be reduced to subject-predicate ones.

What is the doctrine of logical atomism? There are two aspects of the doctrine as it was developed in this century. The first concerns the problems of how propositions are meaningful and have truth-values, and it says that a sentence or a propositional sign states facts by being a sequence or pattern of signs (each of which names the objects which the facts are about) arranged in a certain way (often with an extra sign added), so as to describe the fact that the objects have certain properties or stand in certain relations. The second concerns the relationship of the meaning and truth-value of simple propositions and other propositions which are constructed out of them by various logical operations.

Although he had interesting views also about the first, it is above all at the second level that Leibniz's thought resembles that of Russell and Wittgenstein. I attempt to show in Chapter II that the so-called substitutivity *salva veritate* principle, which Leibniz claims as his basic principle of logic, is one which defines the identity of a concept expressed in words by the identity of the role the words play in determining the truth-value of propositions. In Chapter III, I investigate Leibniz's logical atomism in greater detail.

The belief held by Leibniz that every proposition of our language must derive its meaning from atomic units of meaning into which it can be analysed is not an extravagant one. When Russell wrote his *Philosophy of Logical Atomism* in 1918, under, as he claimed, the influence of the thought of Wittgenstein, it was seven years later than the completion of *Principia Mathematica,* in which the attempt had been made to carry out such a programme within mathematical language. To take the simplest example, following Peano we can establish that the truth-value of all (or, since Gödel, at least most) statements of arithmetic with its infinitely many numbers can be derived from the definitions, given recursively, of the small number of operation-signs which occur in them. We can also see that all numbers for which these operations are defined can be constructed out of natural numbers, which in turn can all be re-expressed in terms of zero and the concept of a successor. Why should we not be able to carry out a similar analysis of truth-conditions in all propositions of language? In the Introduction to his *Begriffsschrift,* Frege states that his aim is to do exactly this, and he refers to Leibniz as the originator of such an enterprise.

One of the basic tenets of logical atomism is the belief that, by undoing the operations and getting to the truth-grounds of complex propositions, we also analyse the sense of these propositions and arrive at simpler units of sense. Leibniz had realised that a proposition which has no surface complexity can often be shown to be derivable from logically simpler ones. Similarly, Russell writes that many propositions which have as subjects singular terms that seem to refer to a certain entity can be shown to be truth-functions of a set of propositions in which there is no reference to such an entity. He refers to Frege's success in reducing propositions about the cardinal numbers of a set into propositions about sets of sets equinumerous to it and thus getting rid of cardinal numbers as referents. He wishes to carry out similar reductions with propositions in which apparent names occur. Wittgenstein wrote in the *Tractatus* that "the sense of a truth-function of p is a function of the sense of p" (5.2341), and also that "if p follows from q, the sense of 'p' is contained in the sense of 'q' (5.122)." I will try to show that these basic presuppositions of logical atomism were held by Leibniz, and that his *Ars Combinatoria* was based on them. In doing so I will try to show what is right and what is wrong in these presuppositions.

In philosophical circles it has been fashionable for some time to deride verificationism, and to hold in contempt those theories which confuse the bearers of sense and the bearers of truth-values. But there is obviously a close relationship between the sense of a sentence and the truth-conditions of the statement one makes by using it, and it would be even more crude and complacent to deny the link between sense and truth-condition than to identify their bearers. We must examine carefully what the relationship is. Leibniz writes with insight that "concepts are explained through propositions or truths." We will see a contextual theory of concept identity, resembling Frege's contextual theory of meaning (*Bedeutung*). The study of Leibniz's views on the sense and truth-conditions of propositions is not merely of historical interest. It makes us see much more clearly the various unexpected difficulties inherent in the view that "the sense of a truth-function of p is a function of the sense of p." This question will be discussed with reference to one example in Chapter IV.

Unless all these questions are clarified, it is quite meaningless to assert that according to Leibniz all true propositions are analytic. And unless we are clear how we identify subjects and predicates of propositions, it is of little use to claim that for Leibniz all propositions are of the subject-predicate form. Nor can we be sure about what is involved in Leibniz's definition of contingency and necessity, in terms of possible worlds, which is so eagerly adopted by modal logicians today. In Chapter IX, I will examine the problem of modal concepts in Leibniz's philosophy. I will try to show where and why I disagree with some interesting work done in this area in recent years.

My view concerning existential import (or, rather, the lack of existential import) in categorical propositions in Leibniz's logic agrees with Parkinson's, expressed in *Logic and Reality in Leibniz's Metaphysics,* and disagrees with others, such as Couturat's. On the other hand, my interpretation of Leibniz's view of 'non-entity' coincides with Couturat's and diverges from that expressed in an early paper of Benson Mates.[18]

The views I express in Chapter V and Chapter VI, concerning Leibniz's theories of relational predicates and relational properties, are probably those which diverge from traditional interpretations of Leibniz most radically. It has been generally accepted that in Leibniz's philosophy relational properties are not real, and thus that relational predicates can be reduced to monadic predicates, which ascribe non-relational predicates to subjects. I try to show that such a reductionist theory is neither asserted by Leibniz nor entailed by his logical doctrines,[19] and also that Leibniz's view on causation properly understood is much more scientific than has traditionally been thought.

I do not think that it is sheer bias on my part to think that Leibniz's philosophy of logic and language makes far more sense in every aspect than has generally been thought, let alone that his thought is more coherent than Russell allowed. In many respects, it is much less dated than the theories of Locke and Berkeley, and even of Kant. Of course, as I point out, Leibniz makes several errors, and there are inconsistencies in the many fragments that he left us. But very rarely are his arguments as simple-minded or perverse as has often been thought. On the contrary, many of his views contain insights which have been fully articulated only by twentieth-century logicians and philosophers. This is why I try deliberately to consider Leibniz's arguments with reference to logical problems as they are discussed now, rather than just within the setting of the debates of his time. I believe that this enables us to understand better those views of Leibniz which, because they were so much in advance of his time, were so long misunderstood.

II. The principle of substitutivity *salva veritate*

. . . though it does not seem to me that there is need for any other kind of proof than one which depends on the substitution of equivalents. (Letter to Placcius, 16 November 1686.)[1]

1. *Identity of substitutable concepts*

At least three of Leibniz's theories related to identity are referred to and constantly quoted by modern philosophers. The first is what is (misleadingly, I think) called Leibniz's law, which says that if A and B are identical, then everything that is true of A is true of B, or $[A = B \rightarrow (f)(fA \equiv fB)]$. The second, which is the converse of the first, is Leibniz's principle of identity of indiscernibles, namely, that if everything that is true of A is true of B, and vice versa, and hence if there is no discernible difference between A and B, then A is identical with B or $[(f)(fA \equiv fB) \rightarrow A = B]$. The third, which I will discuss in this chapter, is Leibniz's claim that "those terms of which one can be substituted for the other without affecting truth are identical": "*Eadem sunt, quorum unum alteri substitui potest salva veritate.*"[2] This is one of the most basic principles of Leibniz's logic and philosophy of language, and it gives one the link between concept identity and truth-conditions. Concepts are the same if they play the same role; they play the same role if the words that express them are interchangeable without affecting the truth-value of the propositions in which they occur. When we substitute a verbal expression of a concept in a sentence with another expression, it is open whether we are substituting a different concept, or still have the same concept. We only make this clear to ourselves by testing the truth-value of the propositions before and after the substitution.

This principle is very close in spirit to what has been called the Context Principle in Frege and Wittgenstein by contemporary philosophers. Frege wrote (in his *Foundation of Arithmetic* §§ 60, 62, 106) that only in the context of a proposition (*Satz*) does a word have meaning (*Bedeutung*). Wittgenstein reproduces that dictum almost verbatim both in his *Tractatus* (3.3, 3.314) and in the *Philosophical Investigations* (Part I § 49). Whatever this opaque and much discussed sentence means, there is no doubt that it insists on the dependence of word meaning on the contribution that the word makes to the sentence which says something true or false. The *salva veritate* principle is likewise an attempt to determine the identity of concepts expressed by words, not by reference to mental images invoked, or any consideration that we can apply to the words taken in isolation, but by the role they play in determining the truth of the propositions in which they occur. Intersubstitutivity discovers the identity of the role.

Dummett has written that Frege's view that the senses of the subordinate expressions "are connected wholly with the contribution they make to the determination of sentences containing them as true or false was an enormous step forward in the theory of meaning."[3] As we shall see in § 2, Leibniz was not talking about word meaning but about concepts expressed by words. Nevertheless, he had already sought to pick these concepts out through the contribution which these concepts make to the determination of the truth or falsity of the propositions of which (according to Leibniz) they are constituent parts.

This thesis of Leibniz, which I will call the *salva veritate* principle, is often misunderstood and confused with the two other principles related to identity. In the *Grundlagen,* when he refers to Leibniz's *salva veritate* principle and says that he will adopt it as his own definition of identity, Frege seems to be understanding it in the sense of Leibniz's law, which I have given in the last paragraph.[4] From Frege to Quine (e.g., Quine, *From a Logical Point of View,* "Reference and modality"), many discussions on extensionality and intensionality or referential transparency and referential opacity are made by using the *salva veritate* principle in the sense of 'indiscernibility of identicals', and calling it Leibniz's law. But this indiscernibility principle is not one that Leibniz himself expressed. The Leibnizian *salva veritate* principle which occurs mainly in his logical works and in his treatises on conceptual analysis, is not, I suggest, a general definition of identity. It is simply a principle to determine the identity of concepts.

What is the current understanding of "*eadem sunt quorum unum alteri substitui potest salva veritate*?" For instance, in a widely read logic text book, Professor Benson Mates interprets it as saying: "Things are identical if they can be substituted for one another without change of truth-value."[5] It is obvious that if this is what Leibniz said, there is a confusion of use and mention here (as Quine, Mates, and others have pointed out).[6] For what can be substituted for one another are names (or descriptions) of things, and what is or is not identical is the thing that the name names or the description refers to. For example, if I say that Stendhal and the author of Lucien Leuwen are one and the same because every time 'Stendhal' occurs in a sentence I can replace it by "the author of 'Lucien Leuwen' without affecting the truth of the sentence, then what is one and the same is the person named and picked out by the words "Stendhal" and "the author of Lucien Leuwen," and the items that can be substituted for one another *salva veritate* are the words themselves. That thing whose identity can be determined is not the same as that which can be substituted *salva veritate*.

But whether there is such a confusion of use and mention in Leibniz's own formulations is not easy to settle. There are various ways in which Leibniz expresses his principle, but perhaps the clearest are the following:

> Those are 'the same' if one can be substituted for the other without loss of truth, such as 'triangle'

> and 'trilateral,' 'quadrangle' and 'quadrilateral.' ("Specimen of Universal Calculus" 1679, Parkinson, *LLP,* p. 34.)
>
> [Eadem sunt quorum unum in alterius locum substitui potest, salva veritate, ut Triangulum et Trilaterum, Quadrangulum et Quadrilaterum.] (G. *Phil.* 7, p. 219.)

and:

> That A is the same as B means that one can be substituted for the other in any proposition without loss of truth. ("General inquiries about the analysis of concepts and truth:" Parkinson, *LLP,* p. 52.)
>
> [Idem autem esse *A* ipsi *B* significat alterum alteri substitui posse in propositione quacunque salva veritate.] (Couturat, *OFI,* p. 362.)

An almost identical passage occurs in "A study in logical calculus" written in the early 1690s. (*Loemker* p. 371. G. *Phil.* 7. p 236). In these passages it is a *definition* of identity of terms that Leibniz appears to be giving. He is explaining what it means to say that the term *A* is the same as the term *B*. Terms are concepts or ideas which are substituted in propositions and are constituents of propositions. (Leibniz considers propositions themselves to be complex terms, i.e., complex concepts.)

But in another formulation which Leibniz gives of his principle in the same work, it looks as if it is more a *proof* of coincidence or identity of concepts[7] rather than a definition of it with which he is concerned:

> *A* coincides with *B* if the one can be substituted in place of the other without loss of truth, or if, on analysing each of the two by substitution of their values (i.e., of their definitions) in place of the terms, the same appear on both sides. The same I mean formally. (Parkinson *LLP* p. 53.)
>
> [Coincidit *A* ipsi *B* si alterum in alterius locum potest salva veritate seu si resolvendo utrumque per

> substitutionem valorum (seu definitionum) in locum terminorum utrobique prodeunt eadem, eadem inquam formaliter . . .] (Couturat, *OFI,* p. 362.)

The above passage shows that there may be a use-mention confusion involved in Leibniz's notion of being formally identical. In my first edition, in order to avoid this, I had interpreted '*formaliter*' (formally) differently, (and, I now think, wrongly), in another mediaeval sense, to mean what pertains to the things themselves rather than to the idea of the thing. I now think that the adverb refers to the form in which concepts are expressed. Any concept can have many different symbolic expressions. Expressions are formally identical to one another if they not only express identical concepts but are made up of the same symbols or words. If this is the correct reading, then it is confusing of Leibniz to talk of terms or concepts as being formally identical. (We can understand what he intends to say but the way he formulates it does involve the kind of use-mention confusion raised by Mates)

It is moreover true that the word 'term' is at times used ambiguously by Leibniz.[8] As in Aristotle, it seems to mean different things at different times. Terms according to Leibniz are ingredients of propositions (Parkinson, *LLP,* p. 122), or subjects and predicates. This by itself does not make things clear since, as Geach points out, the notions of subject and predicate themselves are traditionally not always clear and can be taken to be verbal entities, or the things referred to by the verbal entities.[9] For example, in the sentence "Peter is tall," the 'Peter' may be considered the subject, or the man Peter. For what is tall, i.e., what the predicate "is tall" is predicated of, is the man and not the name. Again a predicate can be taken as an expression, e.g., the words "is tall" or can be taken as a property ascribed by the predicate expression to the subject.

But, on the whole, Leibniz's use of the word 'term' is much more consistent than that of his predecessors, and means neither a word nor a thing. A 'term' for him is a concept.

> By 'term' I understand not a name, but a concept, i.e. that which is signified by a name; you could also call it a notion, an idea. (Parkinson, *LLP,* p. 39.)
>
> [Per Terminum non intelligo nomen sed conceptum seu id quod nomine significatur; possis et dicere notionem, ideam.] (Couturat, *OFI,* p. 243.)

Even when Leibniz writes carelessly, the examples he uses make it quite clear that he is here talking of concepts expressed by linguistic entities rather than of the linguistic entities themselves. For example, he says that the term 'human being' is identical with the term 'that which has humanity,' and since these are obviously different strings of words, Leibniz could only be saying that the concepts expressed are the same.[10]

People may quite rightly feel that only different entities can be substituted for one another. How can one and the same concept be substituted for itself in a proposition, whether truth is preserved or not? Leibniz's point can perhaps be made clearer by thinking of how concepts which are not identical behave. If there is at least one proposition (which is a complex concept for Leibniz) containing the concept *A,* and which changes truth-value when *B* is substituted for *A,* then *A* and *B* are not identical.

Professor Benson Mates believes that such a defence of Leibniz will lead to difficulties. For,

> if concept *A* is identical with concept *B,* then . . . the result of substituting B for A in proposition P will not be some other proposition that has the same truth value as P, but will be just the proposition P itself. On the other hand, if concept A is different from concept B, and if the concept A is part of the proposition P, then the result of substituting B for A in P will be a different proposition P. So the

> salva veritate clause in the principle would seem entirely superfluous, as would the reference to all propositions. Anyone who can recognise the same proposition twice (when he sees it with his mind's eye) – and anyone who cannot do this is in a poor position to be assessing the truth-values of propositions – could on this basis be given the following simpler criterion: Let A and B be concepts, and let P be a proposition in which A occurs; then A is the same as B if and only if the result of replacing A by B in P is the same as P. In the application of the principle there would be no need to check truth-values.[11]

Now what is it to see a proposition with one's mind's eye? Leibniz would refuse to trust the power of such acts, just as he rejected Descartes' reliance on the power to see clear and distinct ideas. We see a written proposition, we hear a spoken proposition, but we do not often know immediately whether they are the same proposition or not, just as we would not immediately know whether the constituent terms are identical or not. To take Leibniz's own example, we may not know whether 'trilateral' and 'triangle' are the same terms or not. We are familiar with each term. We know that the words are formed of units that mean different things but that is no proof, according to Leibniz, that the concept expressed by one is different from the concept expressed by the other. If the concept is that of a particular geometrical shape and the same shape is expressed by the two different words, then the concept expressed is one and the same. We do not discover this fact by seeing it with our mind's eye in some mysterious direct way. We test it by the truth-value of the propositions in which 'trilateral' occurs, e.g., "A trilateral can be obtained by halving a rectangle by a diagonal line," and those in which we replace it by 'triangle.'

In substituting a different word in a sentence, we may substitute the concept which the original word expressed with a different one or leave the concept unchanged.

Aren't we then substituting *words* that express concepts and establishing, on the other hand, the identity or non-identity of *the concepts* themselves? Aren't we therefore back at the use-mention confusion? The problem is a difficult one, but it is more complex and subtle than one might think. As we shall see in § 1 of the next chapter, not only are we unable, according to Leibniz, to talk about concepts or ideas without words, we cannot even think in concepts or ideas without words or 'characters' (symbols). Thus what we establish, when we determine the identity of concepts is none other than types of use of words or other symbols. On the other hand, we do not identify words or symbols just by the shape of their inscriptions, but by the presumed type of use. (That is why we do not find, e.g., the words 'den' or 'it' in the word 'identity'.) The identity of words or symbols are essentially linked to rules of saying things that are true or false. Thus we substitute a type of word for another type of word (under one criterion of kind of type, namely that of the shape of their inscription) and check whether they are the same type of word under another criterion of kind of type, i.e., whether the rules of what Leibniz calls their combination and coordination are the same or not.[12]

Leibniz's idea that a proposition is a complex concept made up of simple concepts is indeed obscure. But something analogous was held by Frege also when he asserted that the thought or the sense of a sentence is not merely a function of the sense of the component words, but is composed of them.[13] Although Frege emphasized that he comes to the component by analysing thought rather than vice versa and therefore distinguished his work "from the similar inventions of Leibniz and his successors,"[14] for Frege also a thought or the sense of a sentence (*Satz*) was something abstract which was composed of the sense of words *in a certain order.* (As we shall see in greater detail in the next section, there are differences between Leibniz's 'term' or concept and Frege's 'sense'. In the case of predicates like "is a triangle," Leibniz's term or concept expressed by it is closer to Fregean

Bedeutung or reference of the expression, which in this case is the Fregean *Begriff or* concept, an unsaturated entity in the world under which objects fall. And we should not forget that Frege did deny the compositional principle for the reference of expressions and only asserted that the reference of the whole is a function of the reference of the constituents. But at least for the thought expressed by a sentence, which is a concept for Leibniz and the sense of the sentence for Frege, both held a compositional view about it. The Leibnizian propositional concept is made up of concepts, and the Fregean sentential sense is made up of word sense.

Moreover, differing here from Mates, I think, that for Leibniz, a proposition and its constituent concepts do not stand in a simple whole-part relationship. Leibniz does not say they do (unlike the subject concept and the predicate of a true proposition, which he says do stand in a whole-part relationship). In a proposition the constituent concepts need to be ordered in some way. I do not suggest that Leibniz has fully explicated how ordered sequences of concepts form themselves. (We will see later in Chapter VII, §4 & §5, that Leibniz gets into related difficulties in his discussions about predicates ascribing relational properties.) But it is surely possible to think of an abstract entity comprising constituents in a certain order. For Leibniz mathematical series was a good example of this.

Thus I can hardly agree with the moral that Mates draws from his reflections, i.e.:

> an absolutely minimum condition to be satisfied by any plausible interpretation of the Leibnizian criterion is that what are substituted for another in applying the criterion shall not be the same as what are thereby determined to be identical or not identical.[15]

The identity of the types of words we are substituting for one another is not immediately clear – as it is the case with many abstract objects. Let us take an example. We may identify a numeral not by its shape but by the rules that govern its use. We can then ask, e.g., whether '4' is the same numeral as 'IV'. By finding out that they designate the number 4 in the system of natural numbers, we decide that they are the same numeral. Similarly we can ask whether the concept 4 is the same as the concept IV, and then check it by the *salva veritate* principle.

Recent objections raised against the *salva veritate* principle are similar to many raised against Frege's Context Principle of meaning. People have wondered how the meaning of a constituent word can only be determined by the way it contributes to the truth condition of the whole sentence, since one would not understand the truth condition of the whole sentence, let alone how this individual constituent word contributed to it unless one knew the meaning of the word already.

Frege's principle is neither circular nor contradictory, because we often grasp the meaning of the constituent word and the truth condition of the whole sentence together, and because what is said by a whole sentence, i.e., the thought, is much easier to grasp than the meaning of an individual word. And similarly, I suggest, Leibniz's *salva veritate* principle can be looked upon as a non-circular criterion of identity of constituent concepts of a proposition.

We cannot discuss or check the identity of concepts without discussing their symbolic or verbal expression. But all the time the items under investigation are concepts. These are what we understand as we grasp a certain type of use of the words. Leibniz refers to the logical analysis of terms into simple terms as analysis of concepts, and refers to his calculus of terms as a calculus of concepts or ideas. (That is why, in the preface to his first attempt in predicate calculus, i.e., *Begriffsschrift,* Frege wrote of his method of symbolising logical relations of concepts as the continuation of Leibniz's unsuccessful attempt to invent a universal characteristic.)

What is central to Leibniz's doctrine is that identity of concepts cannot be discussed without considering the truth-value of some of the propositions which contain them. The case is the same whether we take an intensional or an extensional approach to logic. The relation of concepts, Leibniz writes, "are explained through propositions or truths."[16]

2. *Concept identity and synonymy*

We can now understand Leibniz's claim that the terms "triangle" and "trilateral" are identical, because they can be substituted *salva veritate*. Many people would claim that the notion of "triangle" and the notion of "trilateral" are different, since if "triangle" means "the shape which has three angles" and "trilateral" means "the shape which has three sides," the meaning of the words and hence the concepts expressed by them may be thought to be different.

For Leibniz, however, the problem of the identity of concepts is not one of the synonymy of the corresponding words. The concept of a triangle or a trilateral is not the meaning of these words which express the concepts. Both concepts are complex, one being a function of the concepts of three and of angle, and the other a function of the concepts of three and of side. A concept may be specified by different expressions with different senses. Even if the meanings of the expressions "triangle" and "trilateral" are different, so long as the meanings are related in such a way that anything that is a triangle is necessarily a trilateral, then the concept of a triangle is the concept of a trilateral.[17] Leibniz writes:

> Those terms are the same or coincident of which either can be substituted for the other whenever we please *salva veritate*, for example triangle and trilateral. For in all the propositions about the triangle proved by Euclid, trilateral can be substituted without loss of truth, and conversely. ("A Study in the calculus of real addition," later than 1690, Parkinson, *LLP*, p. 131; I have however deleted the quotation marks which Parkinson has added in his translation.)

> [Eadem seu coincidentia sunt quorum alterutrum ubilibet potest substitui alteri salva veritate. Exempli gratia, Triangulum et Trilaterum, in omnibus enim propositionibus ab Euclide demonstratis de Triangulo substitui potest Trilaterum, et contra, salva veritate.] (G. *Phil.* 7, p. 236.)

There can thus be "superfluous expressions of ideas." He gives as an example someone who claims that by 'triquetrum' he means a trilateral triangle – suggesting that there could be a triangle which was not a trilateral;[18] whereas 'trilateral triangle' is a pleonasm.

That concept identity does not entail the synonymy of the words which express the concept is shown by the fact that there are special contexts in which the sense of words which make up the expressions of *A* and *B* become relevant and affect the truth-value of the propositions in which they occur, even if an instance of *A* is always an instance of *B*. He writes:

> *A* ∞ *B* means *A* and *B* are identical, or that one can be substituted for the other everywhere. (That is, if it is not prohibited, as in the case where some term is considered in a certain respect. For example, although triangle and trilateral are identical, yet if one were to say that a triangle by its nature as such, has 180 degrees, one cannot substitute trilateral. For in the term [triangle] there is something *material* [intensional]).[19]
>
> [A ∞ *B* significat *A* et *B* esse idem, seu ubique sibi posse substitui. (Nisi prohibeatur, quod fit in iis, ubi terminus aliquis certo respectu considereri ver. g. licet, trilaterum et triangulum sint idem, tamen si dicas triangulum, quatenus tale habet 180 gradui; non potest substitui trilaterum. Est in eo aliquid materiale.)] (Couturat, *OFI,* p. 261.)

Leibniz realized that, here, the intensional context created by the words '*quatenus tale*' ("by its nature as such") makes the propositions "The triangle by its nature as such has 180 degrees" and "The trilateral by its nature as such has 180 degrees" different propositions, because the way we are talking about the concepts 'triangle' and 'trilateral' is not a normal one.

We can think of it as analogous to clauses in indirect speech as analysed by Frege. Frege claimed that in indirect speech, words refer to their ordinary sense, and that the clause as a whole refers to its normal sense, i.e., the thought it expresses, and not to its truth-value.[20] For Leibniz also, in an intentional context, the composition of the word can no longer be ignored. The 'nature' in question is the determination of the concept expressed by the whole word through the concepts expressed by the component parts of the word, i.e., 'three' and 'angle'. This makes substitution by the word 'trilateral' impossible. (In an intentional context, a word is not used just to express a concept, but expresses what component concepts the concept is a function of. Leibniz discusses in another manuscript the identical way in which the designation of the Latin name '*Lucifer*' is determined by the designation of the roots '*lux*' and '*fero*' and the designation of the Greek name '*phosphoros*' by the designation of its roots '*phōs*' and '*phero*'.[21] If a word is made up of different roots, sometimes the concept it expresses cannot be adequately discussed without reference to the concepts expressed by the constituent roots.)

If the concept of triangle and trilateral is one and the same, wouldn't the abnormal occurrence of the concept of triangle *be* the abnormal occurrence of the concept of trilateral?[22] It has been suggested that if we read 'terms' to mean concepts as I do, then accepting that terms behave in abnormal ways in intensional contexts will not give us the distinction between 'triangle' and 'trilateral' in the passage quoted above that Leibniz wants. The answer to this question is related to Leibniz's belief, mentioned earlier, in the essential dependence of concepts on words or symbols. There can be, as if it were, no disembodied occurrence of concepts. The word which expresses a concept can also express how the concept is constructed. In the passage quoted above, one is saying that an instantiation of the concept of triangle, expressed as a function of the concept three and angle, by its nature as such, has internal angle of 180°. One can equally say that an instantiation of the concept of trilateral expressed as a function of the concept three and angle, by its nature as such has 180°. An intensional context is one in which how the concept is expressed is relevant, but the concept can still be held to be identical to one that is expressed in a different way. We will see in more detail in the next two sections how ideas are individuated by Leibniz, but let me briefly try to throw light on this question here by an analogy that is equally hard to grasp but which is much more familiar to philosophers.

Think of someone, who, like Professor Anscombe or Professor Davidson, holds that one and the same action can be intentional under one description and unintentional under another. The action of pumping water into the cistern is the very action of poisoning the water supply of the citizens of a town. Then it would have to be maintained that the action of poisoning the water supply was intentionally done under the description "pumping the water into the cistern." The action of poisoning the water supply *was* done intentionally, although not under the description "poisoning the water."

Leibniz does not always use the very same criterion of identity of concepts. And indeed as Benson Mates has cited,[23] there is even a passage in an unpublished manuscript (LHIV VIII 61 r) where Leibniz says that in a plane a triangle and a trilateral do not differ in fact (*in re*) but in concept (*in conceptu*). Indeed it would be odd if little fragments in tens of thousands of pages, written for himself over a period of more than fifty years, did not contain inconsistent thoughts and different usages of words. We know that he tried out many different strands of argument before he settled down to his better-known positions. Also it would be miraculous if he had not at times made use-mention confusions, given that we, writing after Quine and others, can find ourselves making them. My claim was only that, if the *salva veritate* principle is taken as applying to concepts as Leibniz often claims, it can be stated without use-mention confusions.

One should distinguish a particular shape (say, a triangle) which exists as an individual, and its property (triangularity) which exists only as an abstraction. Correspondingly, we must distinguish the concept of a triangle, and the concept of triangularity. In most of the texts, Leibniz claims that the concepts of triangularity and trilaterality are distinct, though the concept of a triangle and a trilateral is one and the same. For example in the *N.E.* he writes:

> someone who said that the triangle and the trilateral are not the same would be wrong, since if we consider it carefully we find that three sides and three angles always go together. . . . However, one can still say in the abstract that triangularity is not trilaterality.[24]

We can now rephrase the *salva veritate* principle after the discussion of these two sections: the concept expressed by the use of *A* in a symbolic expression of a proposition and the concept expressed by the use of *B* is one and the same, if substituting one by the other does not affect the truth-value of the proposition except in special intensional contexts.

3. *Concepts and capacities*

It is probably important at this point to make clear what Leibniz understands by a concept. We have already seen three important characteristics of concepts: namely, that their relationship to one another is "explained through propositions or truths," that their identity is given by the *salva veritate* principle, and that identical concepts can be expressed by non-synonymous expressions. But what are the kinds of things which satisfy these conditions?

Leibniz does not make the distinction, drawn by many empiricists, between concepts or notions on the one hand, and ideas on the other. For him ideas are not mental images or sensations. Kant was wrong to criticise Leibniz for not making the distinction of the sensible and the intelligible, and for treating the former as a confused form of the latter (*Critique of Pure Reason,* B 62). For Leibniz an idea of red is not a mental image of red: it is a notion which corresponds to an intellectual capacity, just as the notion of justice would. And so the word 'notion' can be applied "to all sorts of ideas or conceptions, to the original as well as to the derived."[25]

In an earlier work, Leibniz claimed that an idea is something in our mind.[26] Ideas or concepts are not, however, to be confused with particular mental acts of thinking or with any mental events. I can be said to have one and the same concept which expresses itself in different acts of thinking, and presumably different people can have the same concept. We can be said "to have an idea of a thing even if we are not thinking about it."[27] On these grounds Leibniz denies that ideas could be traces of brain impressions or some ethereal substance in the brain, nor any structural property of the brain, which enables us to have such thoughts.

This leads him to think that to have a concept or an idea is best described as a faculty or ability of a man. However, Leibniz realizes that to have an idea or concept of *C* cannot be adequately described as the faculty that eventually enables one to think of *C* or to identify a *C*. For if it could, then I would always have all the ideas that I would ever use, whereas Leibniz wants to say that, when I go through the sections of a cone in order, "I am bound to come across a pair of hyperbolas although until I do so, I may have no idea of them."[28] Thus, until the person came across the hyperbolas and saw how to distinguish them from other conic sections, Leibniz would not grant that he had the idea of a hyperbola, even though he had the faculty to discover it.

What distinguishes me when I still have no concept of a hyperbola from when I have one? In my later state, "there must be something in me which not only leads to the thing but also expresses it."[29] Thus, when I have a concept of a hyperbola, I must have the power to use an expression for a hyperbola. Leibniz's claim that "I have something in me" which leads to a hyperbola does not mean that there is a mental image in my mind which guides me to a hyperbola, but rather that I have a capacity in me to learn to identify hyperbolas. Similarly, his claim that "there is something in me which expresses a hyperbola" must mean that I have the capacity in me to express truths about hyperbolas in, e.g., language or graphs. By an expression, which Leibniz elsewhere also calls a representation, Leibniz does not necessarily mean a picture. Things like machines can be expressed by models, landscapes can be expressed by maps, truths can be expressed by words, numbers can be expressed by numerals, figures can be expressed by algebraic equations. Thus to have an expression of a hyperbola is to have a sentence about, or an equation of, or a graph of, a hyperbola. To have them in one's mind is not to carry them around like pictures in one's mind but to have a disposition to use or see these words, maps, equations, etc., as expressions of the corresponding truths, landscapes, figures. To have an idea or concept *C*, then, is to have a disposition to use or understand expressions of *C*.

But does the use of any expression correspond to the possession of a concept? It seems not. For the expressions must be capable of expressing propositions – something true or false – or must be capable of expressing constituents of propositions. To have a concept is to understand, or have the mastery of the use of, expressions which express what is true or false (or expressions which combined with other expressions of their kind express what is true or false). For example, a parrot's uttering words in a regular fashion is not a case of sharing "an expression in the mind" or having a disposition to use expressions. Words are expressions of thoughts for men who understand the conventions governing them, but for parrots they are not expressions. They are mere strings of sounds, and these strings of sounds happen to be expressions of thoughts for men. The ability to use expressions presupposes the ability to see, or hear, expressions as expressions of something.

In his later work *New Essays on Human Understanding* Leibniz writes that ideas or concepts are of possibles,[30] and that they are internal objects of thought.[31] To have them is, however, not to have a particular mental state or act. It is to have a disposition or ability to think about them. This was indeed his main point of contention about Locke's argument for the denial of innate ideas.

Frege said, "I call a thought something for which the question of truth arises."[32] A concept for Leibniz would be something for which the question of truth arises, or which combines with other concepts to become something for which the question of truth arises. He did not make the *Sinn* and *Bedeutung* distinction for concept words as Frege did, but we are made to realize that Frege's own distinction was not as clear and convincing as some have thought it is.

The originality of Leibniz's view of concepts is to have discussed it with reference to the capacity to use expressions. Hence, according to Leibniz, the identity of concepts can never be discussed without referring to the expressions – whether written sentences or human gestures – which we see as expressing these concepts.

4. *Propositional identity*

Terms, then, are concepts for Leibniz, and the identity or difference of terms, t, t', depends on whether t and t' contribute in the same way to the truth-value of the propositions in which they figure. This is also the case with propositions. Leibniz thinks that his substitutivity *salva veritate* criterion applies also to propositions, which he treats as complex terms. If "one proposition can be substituted for another without affecting the truth-value" (in all contexts in which they occur) or if "they entail each other reciprocally," then the propositions are said to coincide.[33] (What this 'entailment' amounts to will be discussed later.) In other words, when this obtains, the propositions or complex concepts are identical.

The example he gives of coincident propositions is the proposition L and the proposition "L is true." (Again, there is no simple confusion of use and mention here since the proposition L is a concept or a thought (of a fact), and what is true for Leibniz is the concept, not the sentence. In saying *L*, or "*L* is true," we are *using* a sentence *L* to express the concept.) What you assert by saying of a proposition that it is true is no more nor less than what you do by asserting the proposition itself. However, Leibniz is not claiming that the proposition *L* which he calls *'enuntiatio directa,'* and the proposition "*L* is true" which he calls *'enuntiatio reflexiva'* are expressed by words of the same meaning. Similarly, we shall see in Chapter VI § 1, that he believes that certain relational propositions expressed by a sentence in which two names occur can be re-expressed by a set of two sentences (each of which contains only one name), and a connective giving the logical relation between the two sentences. But he does not believe that the meaning of the original sentence corresponds to the meaning of the rewritten set of sentences. What he says is that the original proposition can be reduced (*reducitur*) to the set of the analysed propositions and the connective, and also that the relation expressed in the original proposition supervenes (*supervenit*) on the truths about the two subjects.

The *salva veritate* criterion of propositional identity may appear to have many unfortunate consequences. Some have even thought that, according to this criterion, all propositions which happen to have the same truth-value, i.e., which are materially equivalent, would become identical. This is clearly not the case since, as we shall see in Chapter VII, Leibniz believed that propositions can be treated as either 'essential' or 'existential' ones, and in the former case the truth conditions are determined by what would hold in all possible worlds, and not only in the actual world. Thus two materially equivalent propositions such as "Snow is white" and "Blood is red" would not have the same truth-value in all possible worlds, and hence they would not be coincident.

Propositions which are logically equivalent (i.e., which necessarily have the same truth-value) pose a more difficult problem for anyone who holds a *salva veritate* criterion of propositional identity. Would not "Three is bigger than two" and "Four is even" have the same truth-value in all possible worlds? If this is so, would not substituting one for the other in all contexts "preserve truth" and make them the same for Leibniz?

I do not think that this is so. For example, in contexts of the form "*A* believes that three is bigger than two," we cannot substitute the proposition in the subordinate clause and assert "*A* believes that four is even" without affecting the truth-value. For even if "Three is bigger than two" and "Four is even" mutually entail each other, *A* may not know that they do. However, for any proposition *L*, it must always be the case that "*A* believes that *L*" and "*A* believes that *L* is true" have the same truth-value, since belief in a proposition presupposes the understanding of what it is for a proposition to be true and vice versa. Thus Leibniz's claim that *L* and "*L* is true" are coincident can be maintained even if we consider them in belief contexts and other intensional contexts.

When we consider belief contexts in general, it is quite clear that the mutual substitution of logically equivalent propositions will affect the truth-value of all propositions in which they are embedded.

In the case of subject-concepts or predicate-concepts which are not propositions, failure to satisfy the substitutivity *salva veritate* criterion in special intensional contexts, in which reference is made to the meanings of words, did not by itself prove the non-identity of the concepts in question. But the failure of substitutivity for propositions in belief contexts does demonstrate the non-identity of the propositions. This is because belief contexts are not about the meaning of words but quite properly about the concepts expressed. Thus although Leibniz leaves many questions unanswered about propositional identity, his theory need not lead him to the position that all logically equivalent propositions are identical. They fail the *salva veritate* criterion in belief contexts.

5. Entity and non-entity

Even if it is clear that for Leibniz a term is not a linguistic entity, it might still be thought to be the thing referred to by the word or expression. For example, it is often said that the whole point of making identity claims such as "Cicero is Tully" is to state the identity of the referents of the names. What is identical is the thing referred to by the names. Are these not the 'terms' of Leibniz's logical calculus? Leibniz does write in the "General Enquiries" "term (by which I understand both entity and non entity)."[34]

Does this passage not show that Leibniz meant by 'terms' things and non-existent things? But what exactly would non-existent things be? It would be a mistake (and one which Leibniz does not make) to think that a non-existent thing is a kind of thing, or that non-entity is a kind of entity. We can have concepts of things that do not exist or conceive of things that cannot exist: what is at issue are the concepts. Nevertheless, 'term' here seems to be understood in a narrower sense than concepts in general.

Leibniz begins "General Enquiries" by stating that all the terms discussed should be understood to be terms of concrete things. Terms are clearly not always of things in the world, for he says that he understands by 'term' *both* entity *and* non-entity. 'Entity' itself is a more comprehensive notion than 'an existent' or 'an individual'. An existent is an actual thing whereas an entity is a possibility. The concept 'entity' is different also from the concept 'individual' since they are identified in different ways. Leibniz explains that even if every entity or being is an individual, by defining an entity we define either a concept which is of any individual of a certain kind, or a concept which is of a particular determinate individual. An entity which corresponds to the concept 'man' or 'any man' is any individual who partakes of human nature, but if I designate an individual as 'this man' by pointing or by giving further distinguishing features, I am talking about one particular individual who instantiates an individual concept.

It seems then that the distinction of entities corresponds to the distinction of internal objects of thought. To each distinct intensional object corresponds a distinct entity. (Although Leibniz does not write in any detail about how an entity is to be individuated, we can see that to each entity there corresponds a distinct property of properties. For example, to the entity 'a man' corresponds the property which any property *f* has if and only if some man has *f*, and to the entity Peter the property which any property *f* has, if, and only if, Peter has *f*. An entity *e* and an entity *e′* are different entities if, and only if, the corresponding second-order properties differ.)[35]

It is even more difficult to grasp what Leibniz means by a non-entity. In one passage he writes that 'non-entity' is the same as 'impossible'.[36] Thus if one thinks of a round square when 'round square' is a concept which cannot be instantiated, then one is thinking of a non-entity. We will discuss Leibniz's distinction of essential propositions and existential propositions in Chapter IX § 3 in greater detail. Here I will merely say that, according to Leibniz, the very same sentence can be understood as expressing an essential proposition which ranges over all possibles or an existential proposition which ranges only over actuals. 'Non-ens' expressed by essential propositions are concepts of impossible things. Only when we are thinking of what Leibniz calls an existential proposition, can a concept which merely happens not to be instantiated in this world, such as 'Pegasus', be considered a non-entity. Whereas a concept such that nothing could be an instantiation of it is always a concept of a non-entity, in any context, existential or essential.

At this point we should remind ourselves that Leibniz never held the view, ascribed to him by Russell as well as by several recent commentators, that a substance or a thing is the sum of its predicates. An individual concept or an individual term is a concept of an individual, and such a concept is made up of the sum of all the predicates that are true of the individual. The individual *has* all the properties which these predicates ascribe to him, but is not a sum of the properties. Properties cannot exist on their own, not even as a conglomeration. Leibniz thought that Aristotle's notion of individual substance had much that was of value which was missing in the views of many of his contemporaries.

A concept of an individual such as that of Cicero or of the planet Venus is, we shall see, according to Leibniz an infinitely complex concept – a concept of an instantiation of an infinitely long list of predicates. It might be asked how we could ever claim of such concepts that they are distinct, or identical concepts. The answer is that it is possible to know empirically that concepts are of the same individual, and hence that whatever is a true predicate of the individual is contained in both concepts. Thus we can claim that the infinitely complex concepts of Tully and of Cicero are necessarily coincident, when we know that the man who is the instantiation of one is the man who is the instantiation of the other, without having to commit ourselves to the view that the senses of the two names are identical, or to the view that the names have any sense apart from that of expressing a concept of a particular man. (Recall how we could establish the identity of the concept of triangle and trilateral while maintaining the difference of the sense of the words that express them.)

We shall see in Chapter V that the problem of the identity of individual concepts is intricately related to the principle of the identity of indiscernibles, although it is not identical with it. Even with his principle of the identity of indiscernibles, we shall see in the next chapter that Leibniz gets into difficulty where certain expressions are concerned.

6. *Concluding remarks about the substitutivity principle*

Some commentators on the first edition of this book thought that I had not argued [enough?] for my claim that the *salva veritate* principle is a principle about concept identity, and not, as it is generally thought to be, a general definition of identity expressed with *systematic* confusion of use and mention.[37]

There is no question but that Leibniz introduces this principle as one of term identity, and he also clearly states that terms are concepts. But as I have said, there are some passages among his vast unpublished papers and drafts in which Leibniz is ambiguous as to what he means by 'terms' and there is a passage from an unpublished paper quoted by Benson Mates[38] which seems to indicate that Leibniz is writing confusedly that an egg can be substituted for another if everything that can be said of one can be said of another.

I must therefore explain why, after inspecting the texts I know where Leibniz discusses the *salva veritate* principle, and after reading a great number of passages in which Leibniz talks of 'terms,' I still think that, on the whole, my reading of the *salva veritate* principle is the closest to Leibniz's intended claim.

First, the many passages in which the *salva veritate* principle occurs are all logical works, where Leibniz is writing on logical deduction (or what he calls logical calculus), and of the analysis of propositions and their constituent terms. These are works on methods of conceptual analysis, since both propositions and terms are concepts for Leibniz. Not only does he state that this is so and give, for example, as an example of 'coincident terms' "the concept of a triangle which coincides with the concept of trilateral,"[39] he goes on to explain that the "scholastics speak of 'terms' in a different way because they are considering not concepts but instances subsumed under universal concepts."[40] Moreover the *salva veritate* principle, unlike the identity of indiscernibles, does not occur in his many works that discuss metaphysical principles such as the criterion of identity of substances about which he wrote all his life.

Second, the examples he gives of identical terms when he talks of the *salva veritate* principle are given by general words such as the pair 'triangle' and 'trilateral', the pair 'quadrangle' and 'quadilateral', or the pair 'human being' and 'rational animal'. It seems odd to choose such examples if he was discussing the identity of things. Obviously not every particular triangle is identical with every particular trilateral: we have to know further which triangle, or which trilateral it is. Whereas if we are talking about concepts which an individual figure falls under – i.e., an instantiation of concepts, as we do in geometrical proof when we write "Let the triangle *A* be included in the circle *B*," then we can substitute (not only the word 'triangle' with the word 'trilateral') but the concept triangle with the concept trilateral, without affecting truth. Leibniz is saying that if this is always the case, then the concept triangle and trilateral should be considered one and the same.

As we have mentioned, the concept of triangle or trilateral under which many particular figures fall, is distinct for Leibniz from the concepts of triangularity or of trilaterality which is that of the properties considered in abstract. "One can still say in the abstract that triangularity is not trilaterality. . . . They are different aspects of one and the same thing."[41] This is asserted in a context where Leibniz is arguing against Locke's view (shared by Professor Mates) that whether idea *A* and idea *B* are identical or are different is evident to the thinker who has the ideas. Leibniz's view is that, for many ideas, only after exploring in depth can we discover that what seemed to be different is one and the same.[42] I take it that the explanation in depth involves checking whether the substitutivity *salva veritate* criterion holds or not.

Thus we cannot use these passages as support for the claim that for Leibniz the concept of a triangle is not identical with the concept of a trilateral. On the contrary, Leibniz is defending his view that they are identical. We may disagree with Leibniz that the idea of the abstract property of triangularity is distinct from the idea of a triangle, but as this distinction is still seriously discussed by philosophers of logic, especially with reference to quantification over properties, what Leibniz says is not to be lightly dismissed.

If by the *salva veritate* principle, Leibniz was indeed talking about what is now called Leibniz's law, i.e., substitutivity *salva veritate* of names of identical things, then one would expect him to use as examples not general words but proper names, which is better suited for his purpose. He does not, however, use examples such as 'Tully' and 'Cicero,' or 'Phosphorus' and 'Hesperus.' This is why, all told, it is more natural to take Leibniz at his word and take the *salva veritate* principle as giving a criterion of identity of concepts or ideas.

To summarize the main points of what has been said in this chapter:

1. Leibniz's *salva veritate* principle must be distinguished from two other principles related to identity, i.e. from his identity of indiscernibles principle – to which it has logical connection – and from Leibniz's law.

2. The *salva veritate* principle is related to the criterion of identity of concepts or notions – which is not always the same as the question of the synonymy of words that are used in expressing the concept. One can be helped by such a criterion, since the identity of concepts that are expressed in different words is not always evident and can be discovered only by the exploration of various truths formed by them.

3. The *salva veritate* principle is in fact a form of what is called since Frege the Context Principle. It is a theory which equates concept-identity with the identity of roles the words expressing them play in propositions. (We shall see later in Chapter V how this principle works in Leibniz's definition of the notion of infinitesimals.)

4. What is often called Leibniz's law, which spells out the consequence of two expressions designating one and the same thing, is different from Leibniz's formulation of the *salva veritate* principle. The antecedent and consequent are reversed.

It is interesting to note that Frege writes: "I agree that Leibniz's explanation '*eadem sunt unum potest substitui alteri salva veritate*' does not deserve to be called a definition; my reasons, however, are different from Husserl's.[43] Since any definition is an identity, identity itself cannot be defined. This explanation of Leibniz's could be called an axiom that brings out the nature of the relation of identity: as such it is fundamentally important."[44] What Frege says is all the more true if we take the *salva veritate* principle as one that brings out the nature of the identity of concepts.[45]

III. *Ars Combinatoria*

> No one should fear that the contemplation of signs will lead us away from the things in themselves; on the contrary, it leads us into the interior of things. We often have confused notions today because the signs are badly arranged, but then with the aid of signs we will easily have the most distinct notions, for we will have at hand a mechanical thread of meditation, as it were, with whose aid we can easily resolve any idea whatever into those of which it is composed (Letter to Tchirnhaus, May 1678.)[1]

1. Thought and signs

Now that we have made clear how the identity of concepts or terms is defined, we must see how concepts are combined or analysed. Leibniz was convinced that signs were necessary for thinking. We do most of our thinking in words, but even when words are not used, some other kinds of signs or diagrams or pictures are. "Ask yourself whether you can perform any arithmetical calculation without making use of any number-signs," he writes.[2] The question then is, how should we construct the correct syntax of our sign language, so that every well-formed formula would express a possible thought, and every provable formula expresses true thoughts? The *Ars Combinatoria,* the first version of which was an expansion of a dissertation presented to the University of Leipzig (in 1666 when Leibniz was nineteen years old and published in the same year),[3] was to be such a system of formal logic more comprehensive than that of Aristotle. Not only would it enable one to see whether or not a proposition followed from other propositions; it would enable one to see how a proposition which appeared simple could be analysed into simpler constituent concepts on which both the meaning and the truth of the proposition were based. Leibniz believed that if the 'alphabet' or the basic simple concepts of human thought could be given, then all other concepts and propositions could be seen to be logical complexes of these simple notions.[4] Thus, if we gave 'characters' or signs to these simple concepts, all other concepts could be expressed as a result of operations based on them. "There will be no equivocations or amphibolies, and everything which will be said intelligibly in that language will be said with propriety."[5] We will no longer need to have different signs to express every different thought we have. We will be enabled to see the logical relation of concepts by contemplating the signs alone. We will have a mechanical way of checking whether we have a clear and precise grasp of the complex concepts we are considering. We will be able to see beneath the surface grammar of propositions, while introducing a mechanical precision into our reasoning.

Leibniz believed that he had made the great discovery that categorical propositions and hypothetical propositions have the same truth-conditions.[6] According to him, the truth-value of both categorical propositions of the form "*S* is *P*" and hypothetical propositions of the form "If *p*, then *q*" could be explained by the inclusion of one concept in another concept. "*S* is *P*" is true when the notion of *P* is included in the notion of *S*. (In Leibniz's terminology, the concept of genus is included in the concept of species, or the concept of a species contains the concept of a genus, not vice versa.) "A dog is an animal" is true because the notion of animal is included in the notion of dog. Similarly, for a hypothetical proposition "If p then q" to be true, the notion expressed by the antecedent proposition *p* must include the notion expressed by the consequent *q*. The "if then" does not correspond to what logicians now call material implication, since the proposition "A dog is a stone" or "If *x* is a dog, then *x* is a stone" does not become true just by there being no dogs in this world. What is asserted is rather that, if something were a dog, then it would be a stone, which is evidently false.

The truth-conditions of Leibniz's hypothetical propositions are, however, not those of strict implication either. For if "The greatest number is even" is logically identical with "If *X* is the greatest number, *X* is even," then, because of the impossibility of the antecedent ever obtaining, the proposition would be true if interpreted as a strict implication; whereas, as we shall see in detail in Chapter VII, Leibniz wanted to say that a proposition with an impossible subject is always false. Moreover as it will be argued in Chapter VII, all propositions, categorical or hypothetical, can be read as either ranging over all possible entities, or only over all actual entities. The former is called essential propositions, the latter existential propositions. This means that some hypotheticals can be taken as ranging only over entities in this world. In contrast, when we read a hypothetical as an essential proposition then "*A* is *B*" can be analysed as "There are *A*s in some worlds, and in all worlds, if anything is an *A*, it is a *B*."

When Leibniz talks of 'wholes' containing 'parts' in his logical deduction, it is, as he himself writes, different from what the scholastic logicians meant by those expressions; they meant class and sub-class relation of the extension of the concepts. Leibniz admits that the traditional method "which considers not concepts but instances subsumed under universal concepts" could also serve as basis of a logical system, as one could then proceed by doing the inverse of the Leibnizian analysis and calculus. One could say that the concept of metal has larger extension than the concept of gold because it contains gold as well as other species. Leibniz explains why he does not follow this (the extensional) method. He prefers to "consider universal concepts or ideas and their composition, for these do not depend on the existence of individuals."[7] One can thus think of possible worlds as well as the actual one.

In other words, Leibniz seemed to have realised that if we consider possibles as well as actuals, his logic based on the inclusion relation of concepts will not be the complete inverse of extensional logic. For example, if one considers the truth-condition of "Men not liable to sin are rational" extensionally, one would have to see whether the class of actual men not liable to sin is a subset of the class of rational beings. Since, for Leibniz, the class of actual men not liable to sin is empty, one would either make the proposition trivially true, or perhaps assign no truth-value to it, neither of which would have been desirable for Leibniz. Leibniz wanted to distinguish the truth-value of "Men not liable to sin are rational" from, say, the truth-value of "Men not liable to sin have horns," which cannot be distinguished by the extensional approach.

If the intensional approach of Leibniz was simply the inverse of the ordinary logic of classes, then, as Michael Dummett has so rightly pointed out,[8] there would be little point in claiming that here is a different approach to logic. One would simply have a logic equally based on the relation of the extension of concepts. What distinguishes Leibniz's approach is that in standard logical contexts, one considers propositions as essential propositions, i.e., as ranging over all possibles. This means that not only universal propositions of the form "All *f* is *g*," but also particular propositions of the form "Some *f* is *g*," lack existential import. "All *f* is *g*" is the same as "If anything is an *f*, then it is *g*," and "Some *f* is *g*" is the same as "If there were *f*, then some of them would be *g*." As long as we inspect the inclusion relation of concepts, we would not be bound by how things happen to be in this world.[9] Leibniz does also consider systems of logic in which particular propositions do carry existential import.[10] But his central concern is with propositions which range over possibles as well as actuals.

2. *The inclusion of concepts*

What is it for a concept *A* to include another concept *B*? Although Leibniz uses expressions like 'part' and 'whole', the inclusion is not a spatial relationship since concepts have no spatial existence. "*A* includes *B*" cannot merely mean the inverse of the extensional relation (of the extension of concept *B* including the extension of concept *A*). Leibniz expresses "*A* includes *B*" also as "*A* involves *B*."[11] This means that since the concept *B* is a part of the concept *A*, something being an instantiation of *A* entails it being an instantiation of *B*. One can see then that the inclusion of concepts is not a metaphysical fact which explains the entailment relationship of propositions. It is a picturesque way of expressing the connection of concepts, which is nothing other than the entailment relation of propositions in which the concepts occur. Indeed Leibniz's view seems to be akin to the thesis of *Tractatus* 5.1222, which says that if *p* follows from *q*, then the sense of *p* is contained in the sense of *q*.

It is therefore no wonder that Leibniz constantly uses class interpretation of his system, despite the fact that he intends an intensional approach to logic. The class determined by a concept is, however, not always the class of individuals which instantiate the concept in this world. According to the kind of proposition one is asserting, it is the class of individuals which instantiate the concept in any possible world. Thus Leibniz's class interpretation of his system does not render him an extensionalist logician, as we shall see in Chapter IX, § 1.

How does one discover that the concept *A* involves the concept *B*, or that *A* entails *B*? Rescher has suggested that we can do this by taking 'terms' to be a set of properties.[12] On this interpretation "A man is an animal" is true if the set of properties which all animals have is a subset of the set of properties which all men have. This does indeed seem to correspond to what Leibniz says about concept inclusion in universal affirmative propositions. However, it does not fit in with what he says about universal negative propositions or particular affirmative propositions. For example, according to Leibniz, "No gold is silver" is true because the concepts 'gold' and 'silver' are 'disparate', that is to say, neither concept is "contained in the other"; whereas if we think of the set of properties which gold has, and the set of properties which silver has, they have much in common – for example, the property of being metal. The sets of properties overlap, as Dummett has pointed out, and we do not get a universal negative proposition under Rescher's interpretation.

Leibniz, on the other hand, acknowledges that the concepts 'silver' and 'gold' have constituent concepts in common, and yet clearly says that neither is included in the other. Thus, to say of concepts *A* and *B* that they are disparate cannot mean that the class of properties which all *A*s have, and the class of properties which all *B*s have, do not have members in common.[13]

When Leibniz discovers that the concepts *A* and *B* are 'disparate' by finding that neither *A* contains *B* nor *B* contains *A*, he does not do this by examining whether a thing which has any of the properties which define *A* has any of the properties which define *B* or not. Leibniz investigates the inclusion relationship by thinking of the class of possible things that are *A* and examining whether any of those things are *B*, and by thinking of the class of things that are *B* and examining whether any of those things could be *A*:

> That A includes B, is that B the predicate is affirmed universally of A. . . . For example 'the wise man includes the just man' is that every wise man is just.[14]

In other words, the inclusion relation of concepts, which Couturat calls an intensional relation, is examined extensionally. What makes Leibniz's method not just extensional is the fact that in these standard cases, he thinks not only of the actual class of things which are *A* and *B*, but the class of all possible things which could be *A* and *B*, as well as the actual ones. For, as we have seen in Chapter II § 5, '*ens*' for Leibniz means in most contexts not only the existents in the actual world but all possibles.[15] Only when particular context makes us treat the proposition as an existential one, do we limit our consideration to existents.

One point remains. We have seen in Chapter II that, if *C* and *C′* are two expressions, to say that the concept expressed by *C* includes the concept expressed by *C′* is not necessarily to say that the expression *C* and *C′* are synonymous. The concept 'triangle' includes the concept 'trilateral' since if anything is a triangle it would necessarily be a trilateral. Being a triangle entails being a trilateral and vice versa. But it does not follow from this that the expressions 'triangle' and 'trilateral' are synonymous, although they express concepts which include each other and hence are identical.

For Leibniz, the validity of logical inference as well as truths of propositions (necessary *and* contingent) therefore show themselves as the inclusion relation of concepts. He writes: "This promises a wonderful ease in my symbolism and analysis of concepts, and will be of the greatest importance."[16] The analysis of truths into their constituent propositions, and the relations of the truths of the latter to the truths of the former, become the basis of all analysis of concepts. In the course of analysis one should eventually arrive at a certain number of absolutely simple irreducible concepts, or what Leibniz calls primitive ones, although, as matter of fact, we may not be able to carry out such an analysis.[17] If we can, however, arrive at concepts which are "primary according to us," or which we cannot further analyse, none of them would be definable in terms of others, and so they are independent of each other. Thus they can all be placed in one class (or in one order).[18] They can, therefore, be expressed by arbitrarily chosen signs. Once, however, we assign characters to these simple concepts, the characters by which we should express the complex terms will be determined.[19]

3. Logical simples

Now most of the notions we have can be seen to be compositions of simpler notions. That is why we can even think of impossible things such as "the impossible chimeras, the maximum speed, the greatest number . . ."[20] But there must be simple concepts which we have not constructed, although we may not discover them, and although we may not have to analyse our concepts into that level in order to carry out the proofs we need:[21]

> I therefore discovered that there are certain primitive terms which can be posited if not absolutely, at

least relatively to us, and all the results of reasoning can be determined in numerical fashion.[22]

Leibniz's position here may appear to be close to that which Russell was to express 230 years later in *Principia Mathematica*. Russell claimed that what he called individuals were the logically lowest type of entity, and thus the logically simplest propositions were 'elementary propositions' which are values of (predicative) functions which take only individuals as arguments. However, what kind of entities individuals are, or what are examples of elementary propositions, are not problems for logic. The relevant question for logical calculus is to distinguish individuals and entities made by quantifications over predicates and to distinguish individuals and classes of individuals. An individual is what is named by an argument of a function in a given context. In other contexts, it may be expressed as a value of a function.[23] In his *Introduction to Mathematical Philosophy* (1919), Russell uses 'individuals' in an absolute sense. He writes that by analysis of propositions, we are led to the conception of terms which, when they occur in propositions, can occur only as subjects and never in any other way. This, he explains, "is part of the old scholastic definition of substance."

However, simple examination tells us how different Leibniz's simple terms are from Russell's individuals. For Leibniz's term is, as we have seen, a concept, and any individual concept is a complex concept containing an infinite number of concepts – that is to say, all the predicates that are true of the individual. Thus individual concepts are certainly not simple terms. The criterion, then, of a word's expressing a simple concept does not consist in its always standing in the subject-position of a proposition. Nor can it consist in our awareness of the clarity and distinctness of an idea, as it did for Descartes. For, Leibniz says, we often believe we have a clear idea of something when the idea is actually mistaken. Therefore the Cartesian criterion must be at least supported by another criterion – if we do not want to fall into psychologism.[24] This criterion must have formal features which are publicly manifest. To doubt, as Leibniz says in a letter to Bernouilli, is one thing, to demand a proof is another.[25]

The criterion of a word's expressing a simple concept is the impossibility of finding a logically equivalent paraphrase. By paraphrase, I understand "an expression in other words, usually fuller and clearer of the sense of any passage . . ." as the OUD says. Obviously, not any phrase which gives a sentence of the same truth-value (at every possible word) when it is used to replace the original word, is a paraphrase. As Professor Fred Feldman has rightly pointed out, unless I can make clearer conditions about what is to count as a paraphrase, it will be possible to find mechanical ways of constructing logically equivalent paraphrase for any word, and hence will not be possible to claim of any word that it expresses a simple concept. Our interpretation of Leibniz must therefore be supported by some argument why these logically equivalent phrases artificially manufactured by the aid of logical connectives are not paraphrases.[26] Something more than the *salva veritate* principle discussed in Chapter II is required. Leibniz used the word 'definition' rather than 'paraphrase', and what he is trying to capture seems intuitively clear. Concepts that are used in definitions, but which themselves cannot be further defined, he says are simple concepts. Since Leibniz has no successful formal criterion of a simple concept, and as I have been unsuccessful in giving any that is precise enough to do the job, we should try to see his point better by examining the analogy he uses. Leibniz compares simple ideas with prime numbers. A number may be expressed as a product in different ways, but there is a unique way of expressing it as a product of primes. (For example, 60 can be expressed as 6×10, 4×15, 2×30, etc., but uniquely as a product of primes $2 \times 2 \times 3 \times 5$.)

To obtain simple ideas, if we are given a concept, we proceed by asking what predicates are true of the thing which is the instantiation of the concept. Moreover, Leibniz seems to think for some reason that, given a predicate, one should find all its possible subjects in order to analyse the predicate. To give an example of his procedure he considers the proposition "Every multiple of 30 is a multiple of 2." But why the search of all possible subjects of "is a multiple of 2" should give the analysis of the concept of being a multiple of 2, I do not see. One might equate the predicate with the disjunction of all its possible subjects – but then it will be an extensional identity rather than an intensional analysis.

Whatever Leibniz's thoughts were about the analysis of predicates, his general view is that analysis consists in replacing an apparently simple expression or sign expressing a complex concept by a paraphrase which by definition designates the same concept. This is the "principle of substitution of equivalents" which is for him the only fundamental principle of logic. What then are the simple concepts which one arrives at by such a method of analysis?

In an article entitled "Simpler terms,"[27] Leibniz writes that it is important to enumerate the simplest terms (concepts) by which other terms can be defined. He suggests that all concepts can be ultimately reduced to the (constituents of the) concise definition, whatever that may be, of the following terms: entity, substance, attribute, positive entity, absolute, the same, one, successor, prior, posterior, such, how much, that which is included (*quod inest*), number, having a position, change, acting on, being acted on (*patiens*), intending to act (*acturiens*), position (*situs*), to be still (*quiescere*), to intend or aim (*tendere seu conari*), power or capacity (*vis seu potentia*). These, then, were the most basic notions for Leibniz, as far as he could go, and so the simplest concepts would be those needed to define the above notions. We should get nearer to the simplest concepts by asking ourselves how we could grasp truths about what the concepts are of e.g., the concept of a successor, or being the same, or number.

We now realise that Leibniz's simple concepts are not only very different from concepts of individual substances, or of Russell's 'individuals', i.e., from the referents of Russell's logically proper names, but also very different from Locke's or Hume's simple ideas. It is not surprising then that Russell misunderstands Leibniz's theories about logical simples in his book. There have been other more recent works in which Leibniz's analysis of terms is taken to be an analysis of language into names of the simplest discriminable entities of the world,[28] whereas, as I have said, for Leibniz the simplest entities were monads, but the concept of an individual monad was infinitely complex.

4. Independence of simple terms

In addition to having no further paraphrase, simple terms were thought by Leibniz to be characterized by their logical independence – that is to say, their being mutually compatible with all other simples. He writes:

> In the elements of symbolic logic are simple thoughts, and simple forms are the source of things. I maintain that all the simple forms are mutually compatible. This is a proposition of which I cannot give the proof without explaining the basis of my symbolic logic [*charactéristiques*] thoroughly.[29]

By examining why his theories of symbolic logic necessitate simples that are mutually compatible, we shall perhaps understand better why Leibniz (like Wittgenstein of the *Tractatus* and Russell) required that there should be logical simples which are independent. We have already seen that Leibniz wanted to construct a formal language with a syntax which reflected the logical relation of concepts. We will then be able to reason correctly without having to think of the interpretation of the signs (i.e., what the signs stand for or mean), but only by thinking of the rules of combining and transforming and substituting signs.

But if we want to construct a logical system in which the logical syntax can be established without mention of the interpretation of the signs, we are compelled to have a set of signs which are logically independent of each other. For example, think of a system of propositional calculus. We can lay down the syntactical rules for any proposition *p, q, r* in connection with the logical constants of the system such as '*v*' and '¬'. Then by pure syntax alone we will know that '*vpv*' is nonsense, and that *pvq* is a truth function of *p* and *q*. The axioms and rules of inference will tell us what are the theorems. But if the signs *p* and *q, r,* etc., are to stand for any arbitrary proposition, there is no way of showing that *p* is incompatible with *q* or that *r* is logically equivalent to *s* unless *p, q, r, s* are further defined by other signs which express their mutual relation or unless one takes into account the meaning of these propositions. If, therefore *p* and *q* are given as signs which have no further definition, one would have either to make them logically independent of each other or to permit extra-syntactical stipulations. That is why Leibniz, who wanted to consider logic as a pure art of combination of characters, had to postulate simple terms which were mutually compatible.

Here is another reason why ideas of colour, heat, sound, etc., are obviously not simple for Leibniz, since, e.g., an idea of a particular colour is clearly incompatible with an idea of another particular colour. We shall discuss this question more fully in the next chapter.

We have already seen that it is not necessary to get to the simplest terms in order to prove a proposition. As long as a partial analysis of the subject shows that it comprehends the predicate, the proof of the proposition is complete. "It is very difficult to complete an analysis of something, but it is not difficult," he writes, "to come to the end of the analysis that one needs. The reason is that an analysis of a truth is completed when one has found a proof of it, and it is not always necessary to complete the analysis of the subject or predicate in order to find the proof of the proposition."[30] His *termini simpliciores* then were required, not so much for the justification of proofs, as for the basis of meaning of our language – a demand to discover the alphabet of human thinking. Whether the catalogue of simple concepts can be arrived at and be exhaustively given, Leibniz (like the

Wittgenstein of the *Tractatus*) refrains from judging.[31] Leibniz merely indicated the direction in which it could be found. But given any language, it was a de jure requirement that what it expressed should be reducible to these simple concepts.

It is important to remind ourselves that even in the most elementary propositions – for example, in the axioms of the various logical systems which Leibniz constructed (in which the non-logical constants are uninterpreted) and in definitions which give us the connection of our basic concepts which cannot be proved – negation can occur as well as the simple ideas. These are what Leibniz calls negative identicals. For example, a definition may be of the form "*A* contains not-B."[32]

Russell wrote that since all simple ideas are mutually compatible for Leibniz, "any collection of simple ideas would be compatible, and therefore any complex idea would be possible."[33] Leibniz himself was acutely worried about precisely this. "Until now," he says, "nobody has known where the incompossibility of different terms comes from, or how different essences compete with one another for realization. For all terms which are purely positive would seem to have to be compatible with one another."[34]

Leibniz came upon his solution in the *New Essays* – that there is no reason "why we could not say that there are privative ideas, as there are negative truths."[35] Elsewhere in the same book he cites the idea of 'rest' as the denial of motion as an example.[36] A complex idea is not a mere collection of simple ideas as a heap may be a collection of sand. A complex idea is a construct obtained by logical operations on simple ideas. The logical operation involved may be that of denial. Thus there are complex ideas of impossible things as well as complex ideas which are incompatible with other complex ideas.

5. Principle of contradiction (or identity)

Leibniz believed that any *Ars Combinatoria,* or in fact any language, was based on the Principle of Identity or Principle of Contradiction which says that "A is A" or "A is not not-A."[37] All proofs proceed by reducing propositions to identities (in the weak sense given by Leibniz) or contradictions.

Leibniz imagined that people might fail to see the importance of this and "say that we are amusing ourselves with frivolous statements, and that all identical truths are useless."[38] (This was indeed the attitude of many commentators, including Russell.) Leibniz declares that such a person will make such a judgment only "for want of having thought sufficiently upon these matters."

The Principle of Identity expresses a law shared by ideas and signs. We can express the identity of concepts by the identity of signs which we immediately perceive. This is what permits us to carry out a completely formalist treatment of signs and yet to follow the correct laws of our thinking. Shapes of signs are perceivable and identifiable by anyone. For Leibniz it is this which makes a formal logic such as his *Ars Combinatoria* so much more reliable than any system dependent at each step on Cartesian intuition of clear and distinct ideas.

The very possibility of carrying out a proof rests on the immediacy of the Principle of Identity. A proof, Leibniz ruled, was to be a sequence of signs, each line expressing a proposition, where the first line is the proposition to be proved and the lines below are derivable from lines above by the rule of 'substitution of equivalents'. If the last line expresses an identity in which we can see that the same sign occurs on both sides of the identity sign, the premiss is thereby proved. If we have a sign on one side, and the negation of it on the other, we have an indirect proof of the falsity of the premiss. A proof will then depend on a correct algorithm accessible to all persons leading to an identity or contradiction, rather than on any inner light given to some one individual mind. "By the combination of the letters of this alphabet, and by the analysis of the words formed by these letters, one can discover all, and submit all to analysis."[39]

Leibniz has been accused of sometimes confusing the Principle of Contradiction (or Identity) with the Law of

Excluded Middle.[40] But this is not quite right. Leibniz never questioned the Law of Excluded Middle, which can be expressed as "It is impossible for a proposition to be neither true nor false." For Leibniz, negation was defined in terms of falsity[41] and he thus did not distinguish the principle of bivalence from the Law of Excluded Middle. All of his logical systems presupposed bivalence. This is understandable, since for Leibniz false meant not true.[42] If a proposition were not true, then it would be false. Thus, for example, since the proposition "The greatest number is even" is not true, it is false, and this does not of course imply that the greatest number is odd.

However, Leibniz thinks that there is more in the Principle of Contradiction than this principle of bivalence. In the *New Essays* he explicitly says that the Principle of Contradiction contains two true statements.[43] One is the principle of bivalence given above, and the other says that truth and falsity are incompatible in a single proposition, of that "propositions cannot be true and false at once." He expresses this elsewhere as "If an affirmation is true, the negation is false, if a negation is true, the affirmation is false."[44] The Principle of Contradiction understood in the way Leibniz understands it entails the principle of bivalence, but is not identical with it.

6. *Sense and reference*

There is, however, a feature of Leibniz's views on identity of concepts examined in Chapter II which leads to a fundamental difficulty or limitation in his algorithmic method of *Ars Combinatoria*.

We have already seen that the identity of the concepts C and C' does not entail the synonymy of the expressions 'C' and 'C.'' A concept C contains all the predicates which are necessarily true of an object which instantiates C. It is thus that the concept 'triangle' contains the concept 'trilateral' and vice versa. Does this mean that *Ars Combinatoria* is only applicable to essential propositions? Leibniz wrote in his early *Dissertatio de Arte Combinatoria* that "warning must be given that the whole of this art of complications is directed to theorems or to propositions that are eternal truths. . . ." and claims that there can be no deductions for singular propositions and universal propositions which are contingent and empirical such as "Augustus was emperor of Rome" or "All European adults have a knowledge of God." These, he says, cannot be proved by *Ars Combinatoria* but only by induction.[45]

But surely, we would want to say, if *pvp* or *p&q* are truth-functions of *p* and of *q*, we can work out the truth-value of these complex propositions so long as we know the truth-values of *p* and of *q*, and it is quite indifferent whether *p&q* expresses empirical truths or eternal truths. If *p* and *q* are contingent truths, *pvq* and *p&q* would express contingent truths as well. So why could we not carry out a logical analysis of complex propositions expressing contingent truths by the methods of *Ars Combinatoria*?

Leibniz had to exclude empirical propositions from his *Ars Combinatoria* because there is no guarantee that in the case of empirical propositions a given sentence type uniquely determines the proposition which it expresses. The same sentence may express different propositions on different occasions.

The most evident cases are sentences containing token reflexive expressions like 'you' or 'I'. I assert "You are tall." This sentence expresses a true proposition if the predicate "is tall" is part of the (concept of the) subject. But the concept which is the subject of the proposition is not the meaning of the word 'you', but an individual concept which includes all the predicates that are true of the person referred to by the word 'you'. That is to say, the subject-concept is determined not only by the sense of the word, but also by the context of its use.

This means that we have to look at the world each time a sentence is used before we can proceed with any analysis of the proposition expressed by the sentence, and so the whole purpose of the algorithmic and formalist method of the *Ars Combinatoria* breaks down. This difficulty arises not only with sentences containing words which, like the ones quoted, are evidently token reflexive, but with all sentences involving general words or definite descriptions when they are understood as expressing contingent propositions. The sentence "The president of France is tall" expresses a different proposition when uttered in 1968 and 1972, and thus has a different logical analysis on the two occasions if we abide by Leibniz's criterion of concept identity.

In the next chapter, therefore, we shall examine in detail Leibniz's analysis of one kind of contingent proposition, those involving the ideas of sensible qualities.

IV. Ideas of sensible qualities

> Consequently I believe that where objects of the senses are concerned the true criterion is the linking together of phenomena, i.e., the connectedness of what happens at different times and places and in the experience of different men with men themselves being phenomena to one another, and very important ones so far as this present matter is concerned. (*New Essays on Human Understanding,* Bk. 4, Chap. 2,§14.)[1]

1. Logic and epistemology

In the last chapter I indicated that Leibniz's general theory about the analysis of concepts or ideas ran into special problems with reference to ideas of sensible qualities.[2]

Leibniz's *Ars Combinatoria* shows that he shares with Locke and Hume the interest in simple and complex ideas and the mutual relation they have in determining the meaning of words. But whereas for Locke and Hume simple ideas corresponded to what was given in experience, and primarily consisted in those of sensible qualities, for Leibniz ideas of sensible qualities were clear but not distinct "because we cannot distinguish their contents."[3] Thus, although Leibniz says at one point that he does not mind calling them simple ideas, so long as we remember that they are not logically simple, his own view was that they are complex and confused ideas. (For Leibniz, ideas which are not distinct are confused. Thus it is possible to have "ideas clear but confused in themselves." Simple ideas or concepts were postulated as an end product of the analysis of the propositions rather than as a starting point.

Why are ideas of heat or red or softness not simple for Leibniz, as they were for many empiricists? It is because Leibniz believed that in principle these ideas could always be further analysed.[4] By this, we have seen that he meant logical analysis, or a redescription of the same idea by a combination of other words, each of which has a more general use. Since Leibniz held that the logically complex is usually given first in our experience, epistemological priority could not count for him as any sort of guarantee of the logical primitiveness of ideas. To grasp that something was gold logically presupposed, whether it was understood distinctly or confusedly, grasping that it was metal. Logical analysis should reveal the constituents of the concept 'gold,' including that of being metal. In general, logical analysis depends on the intension or content of concepts (although we shall see that this relation of dependence is a very complicated one) and is quite independent of the existence of individuals which fall under them. Nevertheless, in many cases we are guided by what we grasp through our experience. Given any object and experience, the identifying of the object as a so-and-so presupposes a concept. And if this concept is not a simple one, it presupposes the simple concepts out of which it is built up, even if we refer to the object by a single general word.

But, it might be asked, how could our identifying an object as red presuppose, even without our knowing it, our possession of any other concept? And how could we come to understand anything about sensible qualities except through our senses? According to Leibniz, the senses give us a quick but confused knowledge of sensible qualities. "We use the external senses as, to use the comparison of one of the ancients, a blind man does a stick."[5] The senses make us know "their proper objects which are colours, sounds, odours, flavours and the qualities of touch, but they do not make us know what these sensible qualities are, nor in what they consist."[6]

We might be inclined to protest and say that the senses do tell us what these sensible qualities are, and nothing else can tell us what they are. What we learn by means other than our senses cannot be features of the sensible qualities themselves. Leibniz thinks not, since for him sensible qualities, or what we learn by our senses, are properties of objects or phenomena, not properties of our experiences. There is therefore no a priori reason why we should not learn about these properties by means other than our senses as well. "For example," he writes, "whether red is the revolving of certain small globules which it is claimed cause light; whether heat is the whirling of a very fine dust; whether sound is made in the air as circles in the water when a stone is thrown into it. . . . This is what we do not see."[7]

Russell criticised Leibniz saying that he had no right to think that an idea of objects given by sense, such as colour or heat, was the idea of the cause of these objects. But is Russell's criticism justified? It seems to me that we can very easily understand the distinction between a sensation like pain and its cause – say, a stab by a knife. They are two things which stand in a causal relation to each other. But in the case of colour or sound, the question is not so easy. After all, even for Locke, secondary qualities like colours, smell, or heat were powers in the objects to produce ideas in us.

For Leibniz the idea of colour or sound is not an idea of a particular sensation, but the idea of a property of phenomena, or even of phenomena themselves. And in saying that the idea of a colour might one day be found to be the idea of whirling globules of a certain kind, Leibniz is saying that one may have good reasons for assuming that they are ideas of identical phenomena. For example, every time one says, "There is something red," one can say, "There is the whirling of . . . ," and if the truth-value of the two propositions is always the same, then, according to Leibniz's substitutivity *salva veritate* principle, 'red' and "the whirling of . . ." are identical terms. (Of course, intensional contexts must be excluded from the general consideration as was shown in Chapter II § 2.) Sensible qualities may appear simple: "we are not aware of any divisions within them; but we must carry out their analysis by means of further experiments and by our reason, as we go on rendering them more intelligible."[8]

As the example of whirling globules is too bizarre for us today, let us reformulate another example which Leibniz gives that "colours are reflected from polished surfaces of opaque bodies."[9] One might say, for instance, that colour is what we ascribe to a body by saying that the surface reflects light waves of a certain wavelength. Recently, too, the theory that colours are objectively specifiable properties of objects has been countered with many arguments: for example, the argument that "the *quale*" we see also depends on the idiosyncrasies of the human eye and nervous system; or the argument that "the *quale*" not only depends on the wavelength of the light reflected from the object, but also on light coming from the background. Although these arguments are supposed to refute the claim that colour is a physical property of the object, they do not so long as it makes sense to say of an object, "It is red, say, but looks purple against that background," or "It looks orange in that light." Leibniz realised this when he said "So from the fact that something does not always appear the same it does not follow that it is not a quality of the object."[10] We could still claim that ". . . is red" and ". . . reflects light waves of a certain long wavelength" ascribe identical properties to things. This raises various problems about property-identity, but it is not based on any simple confusion between the idea of a certain property and the idea of the cause of the property.

Leibniz did not believe, of course, that understanding the explanation of the phenomenon which makes us have colour perceptions or sensations of heat makes us have the perception or sensation itself. He writes:

> Imagine a land where men do not know the sun and fire and have blood which is cold, not warm; surely they cannot be made to understand what heat is merely by describing it, for, even if someone were to explain to them the innermost secrets of nature and even interpret the cause of heat, they would still not recognise heat from this description if it were presented to them, for they could not know that this peculiar sensation which they perceived in their minds is excited by this particular motion,

> since we cannot notice distinctly what arises in our mind and what in our organs.[11]

There is some confusion in what Leibniz writes here. We do not perceive a sensation when we touch a hot object. We have a sensation of heat, and we perceive that the object is hot. But his point is clear. The heat of an object about which we can have an idea causes us to have a certain sensation, or an experience. We can learn to identify the heat, i.e., the fact that the object is hot, by having that sensation. But whenever an object is hot its constituent molecules might be in a particular state of motion of which we can learn in other ways, and predicates expressing such states of the object will be a part of the concept or idea of heat. Learning such predicates of hot objects will not by itself enable us to tell that a sensation we have is that of heat or that it is not, but from this it does not follow that these predicates are not constituents of the concept of heat. On the contrary, we would have a fuller concept of heat if we not merely identified it as a phenomenon which is there when we have a particular kind of sensation, but learned that the phenomenon which makes us have that kind of sensation has various properties which other people (who have no such sensations) will be able to detect as well.

2. *Essence and constitution*

Perhaps it is important here to remind ourselves of Leibniz's view of essences. Locke tried to distinguish real and nominal essences. Real essences correspond to the constitutional differences of species which exist in nature; nominal essence is the feature we ascribe to objects which we group together for some purpose or convenience of our own and call by a general name. Leibniz criticises Locke, and says that there may be a point in distinguishing nominal definitions and real definitions. But there could be no distinction between real and nominal essences. If there are essences – the nature of things – then they are all real. We may falsely ascribe wrong essences to them, but if things have any essences at all, then these cannot but be real.

For example, he says "the essence of gold is what constitutes it and *which gives it* its sensible qualities." So in perceiving the sensible qualities of gold – in looking at its shiny yellow colour, feeling its weight – we are perceiving the essence or nature of gold, although not distinctly. Gold can be nominally defined in many ways – corresponding to the different ways in which people perceive its difference from other objects. According to the knowledge of Leibniz's period, it was defined as the heaviest of all metals, that which is the most malleable, and that which is easily melted and resists all acids except *aqua regia*. But it was a contingent fact about men's experience until then that these features distinguished gold from all other bodies. We could always have found an element heavier than gold (which we have done), or more malleable, and so on. If, however, we can grasp or conceive the real essence of gold, then it will be that which distinguishes gold from every other substance, and by coming to grasp such a 'structure' we should also see how they must have these qualities.[12]

The concept 'gold', according to Leibniz, does not contain only those features which the speaker knows of it – for example, something yellow and very heavy – but also what he does not know, and which another may know, i.e., a body endowed with an internal constitution from which flows colour and weight, and from which spring still other properties admitted to be known by experts.[13] One can apply the same arguments to sensible qualities like yellow since these qualities exist in the world also. A person may apply a colour word like 'yellow' on the basis of what he sees, but the concept of yellow would include the necessary and sufficient conditions of the constitution which any object has which appears in that shade under normal conditions. The constitution will then have a non-contingent relation with the idea of yellow, although at the same time the experiences of seeing the colour yellow may have a causal, or (since, strictly speaking, Leibniz did not believe in causal interaction) an isomorphic, relation with the constitution. That is to say, Leibniz suggests that we can both hold that a certain perception (say, a perception of yellow) is caused by a certain constitution of things, and also that the idea of the quality perceived – say, yellow – is identical with the idea of the constitution.[14] Leibniz writes that when the qualities of objects are perceived as sensible we call them secondary qualities, but when the *same* qualities are "distinctly explained" and made intelligible we call them primary qualities.[15]

It is important to notice that in his discussion of essences, Leibniz is not claiming that the internal constitution of objects is something which, in principle, is not observable. He says in the passage previously quoted that even if a man does not know it, another man might. Thus the kind of argument which Berkeley raised against Locke's representative theory of ideas (or which some have raised against Lenin's theory of knowledge)[16] cannot be raised against it. Leibniz is not arguing for the resemblance or non-resemblance, or even for a functional relationship, between two terms one of which can never be identified. The constitution might be observable – as we may observe patterns under electron microscopes. And hence any claims about the constitution of objects would be based on induction and might be corrigible, as claims about the malleability or weight of a metal might be. But, if we arrive at a right theory about the constitution of the object, we will understand what makes objects of that kind distinct from objects of other kinds. We will also be able to explain all the other disparate sensible qualities the object has in a general way – even if the theory of the constitution itself is based on some observation. The patterns we observe there can be seen to follow a regularity of a more general kind than other observed qualities, and what seemed to be random variations in other observable features could be explained by correlating them with these regular patterns. We can, then, identify the sensible quality as that of the objects having these constitutional features. It is more like explaining the various symptoms of, say, leukemia by the change that occurs in blood cells. Both are observable and so our correlating of the two is synthetic. Nevertheless, leukemia, which is the state of a man's having a set of various symptoms, can be said to be identical with the state of a man who has a certain change in the blood cells.

Thus, for Leibniz, an idea of any sensible quality contains truths about the constitution of objects that are – as a matter of fact – unperceived by us, but which we may one day perceive by improved senses or instrumental aid. But with the aid of theories we may identify them without actually perceiving them. A person can use the concept of sensible qualities in many ways. He will know the truth-conditions of many propositions in which the word standing for a sensible quality, like colour, occurs. And for Leibniz the use of concepts is an intellectual faculty, even when the concept is that of an object given in the senses. (This problem will be discussed further in Chapter VI, §§ 4 and 5.) The concept is not the sensation itself. To have a single term to express the property 'red' is necessary insofar as one does not know a definite description which distinguishes red from other properties. But it can be expressed by a combination of more general and simple ideas and is not needed for the minimum vocabulary required to describe all our experience.

One could not of course have referred to red as what we see when something reflects light waves of such and such frequency, without the requisite knowledge, and thus it was necessary to have a word to describe red objects. Once we possessed a description which made all the discriminations involved in the use of the word 'red,' we could dispense with the word. Of course, at some stage one must learn by extralinguistic means the meaning of the constituent words which make up the description, but this does not mean that we have to correlate them individually with certain sensations corresponding to each of them.

Leibniz would have to admit that *if* a blind man could never learn to distinguish the category of colour from other categories – in any context – *then* he would not be able to acquire the major use of the expressions which express colour. Leibniz nevertheless writes, "I do not doubt that a blind person can speak aptly about colours and make a speech in praise of the light without being acquainted with it."[17] What is important is that this is not a question which can be settled a priori, for there is no reason why a man could not learn to distinguish the same category by other than visual means.

3. Property identity

It is now important to examine the problem of property-identity in general. For Leibniz's view on the idea of sensible qualities is not just of historical interest. It seems to indicate the right direction in which the solution to the problem of how one is to identify property lies.

Our arguments in Chapter II § 2 show that if '*f*' and '*g*' are predicates which ascribe properties to the entity denoted by the expression which takes the blank place, then to say of any '*f*' and '*g*' that they ascribe the same property is *not* necessarily to say that the expressions '*f*' and '*g*' have the same meaning. The property of being a triangle and of being trilateral were claimed to be identical although the words 'triangle' and 'trilateral' clearly had different meanings. Thus when Leibniz asserts that ". . . is red" and ". . . is the revolving of small globules" ascribe the same property, it is no refutation merely to say that the predicates have different meanings. We can very well understand what it would be for the words "is red" and the words "has the colour of pillar-boxes in England" to ascribe the same properties, and yet we would have no temptation whatsoever to think that the words have the same meaning.

The question which we are discussing, then, is not one of synonymy of predicates. We begin with a rather inarticulated and intuitive hunch about properties. If things and events in the world have properties, it seems clear on the one hand that one can refer to the properties or identify them by different descriptions. Furthermore, since everything has more than one property, the fact that the very same objects have properties P and P_1 seems no guarantee that the properties are identical. But if P_1 and P_2 are the same property, a thing which has the property P_1 has the property P_2.

Leibniz believed, on the one hand (almost as Quine and Goodman do), that in some sense individual objects or substances are the only basic existents. Universals or facts do not exist over and above individuals. He writes early on in the *Preface to Nizolius* that the nominalists following Ockham had "deduced the rule that everything in the world can be explained without any reference to universals and real forms,"[18] a rule with which Leibniz firmly agrees. On the other hand, Leibniz attacks Hobbes' and Locke's version of nominalism. Locke claims that what is called general and universal does not belong to the "existence of things" but is the work of the understanding, and hence claims that the essence of each species is only an abstract idea. Leibniz retorts that "generality consists in the resemblances of separate things among themselves, and this resemblance is a reality." Leibniz goes on to remark that we may at times be unaware of certain internal resemblances of things, but this does not make the resemblances exist any less in nature. Resemblances do not just depend on our awareness.[19]

We can see the truth of Leibniz's remark by thinking of the fact that until the Renaissance whales were thought to be fish. They were nevertheless always mammals and had the essential properties which we now know to be common to all mammals. Similarly, Leibniz said in opposition to Locke that although colours are not substances such as extracted dyes, it does not follow that colours are imaginary.[20]

Wherein does the reality of these resemblances or properties consist? If they are real, they should naturally have their criterion of identity, but how are we to settle it?

The condition of the predicates '$\phi\chi$' and '$\psi\chi$' expressing identical properties cannot be their coextensiveness. For then the property of being nineteen years of age and the property of being nineteen years of age or being 1,000 years of age would be the same (assuming there are no people who are 1,000 years of age). Or, again, as Leibniz writes, in a particular time of the year being a hill and being a green hill would be the same.[21] Coextensiveness is not enough. One might rule this counter-example out by some theory of logical simplicity of predicates, namely that they include no truth-functional connectives, etc. But we can think of properties like that of having one heart and that of having one liver which may well be coextensive but are certainly not the same property. We are made to realize that there might be something after all in Leibniz's dictum "Given a predicate, find all its possible subjects." We should be interested not only in the things to which the predicate applies in this world, but in all possible worlds. This shows *how* we identify the properties in *this* world when we ascribe predicates to things.

One reason why properties play a role in explanation comes out when we think of reduction statements. As H. Putnam said, the property of being water and the property of being water or being a unicorn are coextensive because the class of unicorns is empty. Now water may be identical with aggregates of molecules of H_2O, but one would not for this reason say that the property of being H_2O is identical with the property of being water or a unicorn. One could make a reduction statement of water into H_2O – because we think that there is a scientific law which explains something being water as also being H_2O. But there is no natural law which explains the relation between water or unicorns and aggregates of H_2O. In other words, natural laws make us see the necessity of water being H_2O but not the necessity of water or unicorns being H_2O. Thus we seem to be able to think of worlds inhabited by unicorns, in which the two properties would not be shared by the same objects, and surely this seems to indicate that they are not the same properties.

As we have seen, Leibniz seems to want to say that 'triangle' and 'trilateral' are the same concepts, or being a triangle and being trilateral are the same properties, because an object which is a triangle is necessarily also a trilateral, and vice versa. It would seem that if we take this view, then to say of two predicates '*f*' and '*g*' that they ascribe the same property to an object is to say at least that '*f*' and '*g*' are logically equivalent, or in other words that in every possible world anything that has the property *f* has the property *g*. If *f* and *g* are identical properties, it is not possible for anything to have the property *f* without having the property *g* and vice versa.

But how does one account for the necessity in virtue of which certain predicates are coextensive in all possible worlds? It may be possible to deduce from the meaning of 'triangle,' *together with the most basic geometrical concepts,* that any object which has the property of being triangular is trilateral as well. Supplementary geometrical or logical concepts, however, are not enough to deduce that "is hot" is logically equivalent to "has a molecular energy of above. . . ." Are these predicates necessarily coextensive in virtue of the laws of nature? If so, they will be coextensive in any world which has the same natural laws as ours. Does this adequately express the necessity involved in claims of property identity? We have seen that the truth-condition of categorical propositions for Leibniz (apart from special cases we will discuss in Chapter VII) did depend on things which are the instantiation of the subject-concept in all possible worlds.

In a similar vein, it has recently been suggested that two names of properties t_1 and t_2 name the same property if the property which t_1 names in this world, and the property which t_2 names in this world, are coextensive in all possible worlds.[22] Although this might seem to be a plausible definition in the spirit of Leibniz, it is difficult to see how we are to decide that the property named by t_1 in our world belongs to exactly the same thing in any possible world as the property named by t_2 in our world. Presumably if we can in some sense imagine or describe a world in which a thing can have the property we name by t_1 but not have the property named by t_2 in this world, we have a negative proof that t_1 and

t_2 do *not* name the same property. But how is our power of coherent description of possible worlds to be guided? Can we describe a world in which colours have nothing to do with wavelengths of light or even with vision? Is it to follow a Hume-like hunch about imaginability and separability? We cannot of course rely on any assumed criterion of property-identity, because we are trying to describe these possible worlds in order to provide such a criterion. And if, as a contemporary logician said, "a property is identified when, and only when, we have specified exactly which things have in it every possible world,"[23] we cannot *use* any assumption about property-identity in deciding which things have it in all possible worlds.

However, we are made to realize that we can only describe a possible world by using concepts that are available to us. The identity of these concepts is determined by the way they contribute towards the truth-conditions of the propositions we state in this world, and, it seems, also by the truth-values we attach to conditionals, including counter-factual conditionals. Leibniz writes that we cannot assign arbitrary truth-values to conditionals – even counter-factual ones. The possibility or impossibility of the combination of concepts, or the necessity of certain propositions, "is not a chimera which we create, since all that we do is to recognize them, in spite of ourselves and in a constant manner."[24]

And so the entailments that hold of *our* concepts hold in any possible world we describe by using our concepts. We may identify red in all sorts of ways. We cannot rule a priori that we will identify it only by normal visual means. And much that we learn of red by other means will become a part of the concept of red as well. That is to say, we can find out by other than visual means what must necessarily be true of an object in order that it have the property which is visually distinguishable as red.

That is why we can sympathize with Leibniz who seems to want to say that, among the features which we discover about red, at least those which involve the structural properties of objects in this world and our laws of nature become part of our concept of red, and carry over to all the things that are describable as red in any possible world. This makes "χ is red" logically equivalent to "χ reflects lightwaves of wavelength λ" and the pair of predicates are said to ascribe the same property to things.

4. Physical necessity and logical necessity

Would this not be contrary to Leibniz's apparent belief that it is possible to have worlds in which different laws of nature hold and that the necessity of physical truths is at most "hypothetical necessity" depending on how the world was created? Leibniz did write that "although all the facts of the universe are determined in themselves. . . it does not follow that their connection is always truly necessary; that is to say, that the truth which pronounces that one fact follows another is necessary."[25]

Would it then not be possible to conceive of a world in which things which have surface structures identical to those which red things have in our world reflect light waves of the shortest wavelength rather than the longest wavelength? We can surely conceive of identifying structural properties independently of dispositional properties such as that of reflecting or absorbing light waves of a certain kind. Would this not prove that the property of having a certain colour could not be identical with the structural property of an object, as Leibniz seems to think?

Again, it seems possible to think of a world in which Boyle-Charles' Law did not hold. The product of the pressure and volume of a given gas is not proportionate to its absolute temperature. However much we raise the temperature without any change in the pressure, the volume of gas does not increase in that world. But if the mean kinetic energy of molecules does not correspond to heat in such a world, then Leibniz's claim that the idea of heat is *identical* with certain kinetic properties of molecules ("the whirling of fine dust") would cease to be a valid one. For the predicates are not coextensive in all possible worlds. But are we still using our concept of heat in such a world? What would we feel when we came in contact with a gas in which there was no increase in kinetic energy? How would our thermometers work in such a world?

It may indeed be possible to describe a world in which some of our natural laws do not operate and others do. If we can still use our concepts to describe this possible world, we know where we stand. But where the natural laws diverge from those of our world, we must work out fully the consequences it has in individuating the entities and properties in that world.

It is not obvious that any predicate can be meaningfully ascribed to objects in all possible worlds, including those worlds which have different natural laws from ours. And if assumptions of certain laws of nature are surreptitiously involved in our thoughts about all possible worlds, then to be necessarily coextensive in worlds which share *these* natural laws does indeed collapse into logical equivalence. (What I mean is that if n_1, n_2, n_3 are the assumptions about natural laws involved in our identification of properties in other worlds, "$\Box(n_1$ & n_2 & . . . & $n_n \rightarrow (\chi)\ (\phi\chi \equiv \psi\chi))$" collapses into "$\Box\ (x)\ (\phi\chi \equiv \psi\chi)$." Conversely, the claim that ϕ and ψ are identical if and only if $\Box\ (\chi)\ (\phi\chi \equiv \psi\chi)$ is the same as the seemingly weaker claim that $\Box\ (n_1$ & n_2 . . . $n \rightarrow (\chi)\ (\phi\chi \equiv \psi\chi))$.

We can conceptually distinguish logical necessity ("true in all possible worlds") and physical necessity (or what Leibniz calls hypothetical necessity, necessary given the initial conditions of the world), but their mutual relation is a very complex one. Logical necessity and physical necessity (in the sense given above) are intricately intertwined in our thoughts about possible worlds.

As Leibniz says, we do not individuate things as bundles of accidentally coexisting properties. We individuate things in a world of natural law, and so the criterion of individuation is bound up with our precepts about the regularities of nature. Extensionalists have assumed that the individuation of things, and establishing the satisfaction of predicates, are primitive basic acts. But the individuation of things to which we ascribe predicates depends a great deal on notions of their constitution – for example, that if it is a material object, then it occupies one place and only one place at a particular time, or that it moves following certain laws, or that it expands or diminishes in size according to certain laws, etc. (For Leibniz, an individual substance is above all a unit of action.) The way we identify molecules or cells, or even the way we identify but do *not* individuate elementary particles, could hardly be independent of various physical theories which we have. (What I mean is, the way we can identify but cannot meaningfully re-identify an elementary particle is determined by the theories we have relating to elementary particles.) It follows that all talk of coextensiveness of predicates presupposes identification of entities which have the properties, and the latter is dependent on certain assumptions about nature.

The individuation of properties is even more involved with nomological concepts than is the individuation of things which have properties. Leibniz observed that we ascribe necessity to what we regularly observe when we see regular phenomena as expressing the constitution of things which that particular individual shares with other things. Such assumptions of necessity are involved in the way we come to learn the ascription of predicates which express sensible or other physical properties of things.

Carnap has written, for example,[26] that an intension of a predicate *q* for a speaker X is, roughly speaking, the general condition which an object *y* must fulfill for X to be willing to apply the predicate *q* to *y*. But our judgments about objects fulfilling the same condition presuppose various natural laws.

We know that some stars emit more radiation than others. Some are bigger than others and also some are hotter than others. However, we would not ascribe the predicate "emits more radiation than most stars" just by seeing how bright a star looks in the night sky. We do not arrive at a judgment whether or not the appropriate condition obtained in the star without various assumptions about the laws of nature – for example, how light travels, which would tell us how far the star is. It is not merely an epistemological question how we *find out* the conditions that obtain in the star. The sense of the predicate "emits more radiation" cannot be given independently of various assumptions about laws of nature.

It is probably true that some of our assumptions about laws of nature could be replaced by others without affecting the way we individuate objects, or the way we ascribe many predicates to them. For example, could we not imagine a world in which Newton's first law does not hold and material bodies just changed speed or direction of motion, in the absence of external forces and if all the inertial properties of material bodies were lost? We must realize, however, that such a change would entail a considerable alteration to our notion of mass. Hence all our concepts which depend on the exact notion of mass we do have can no longer be used in individuating properties or defining the conditions under which each of the predicates is to be ascribed in such worlds. Leibniz was describing our framework when he wrote that "the foundation of the laws of nature must be made to consist . . . in this, that the same quantity of active power, still more . . . the same quantity of moving force must be preserved."[27]

Could we retain our method of identifying material bodies if bodies could increase and decrease mass in unexpected ways? Certainly the equations which we accept as expressing our concept of energy do determine how we identify particles. Not even traces in a Wilson chamber or clicks in Geiger counters will make the identification unless we already accept the truth of an enormous set of laws which explain what these apparatuses catch. Even for macroscopic objects, where the individuation of things appears to be more independent of conservation laws which govern their dynamic properties, enough similarity to our laws of dynamics has to be preserved in the alternative laws which we ascribe to possible worlds in order to enable us to use a coherent notion of mass and material bodies.

For Leibniz, properties are not mere correlates of linguistic inventions. The identity of properties or qualities is not determined by the synonymy of predicates which ascribe these properties to objects. Properties exist in the world as resemblances. However, we can also think of properties which nothing actually has but things in different worlds could have. Two different predicates could have the same extension (in this world) and yet be true of different objects in other possible worlds. For Leibniz the identity of properties depended on their being coextensive in all possible worlds in virtue of their definitions; and these definitions seemed not only to involve logical and mathematical truths, but in some cases to involve various assumptions about laws of nature. For example, ideas of sensible qualities such as red or hot were not simple for Leibniz, and hence could be given a definition involving complex assumptions of physical laws which modern philosophers call reduction statements.

This seemed to remove all distinctions between physical and logical necessity, and thus appeared *prima facie* and implausible. However, by realizing that the individuation of objects and the understanding of satisfaction-conditions for predicates already involve a great number of assumptions about laws of nature, we see that we cannot even describe possible worlds which are radically different from our own without making *those* assumptions about laws of nature presupposed in the individuation of objects and ascriptions of predicates. Thus Leibniz's attempts to individuate qualities or predicates of things by predicates which are coextensive in virtue of their definition is not a naive confusion of logical necessity and physical necessity. Some of these definitions involve the assumption of certain laws of nature and appear entirely synthetic in character. But this is only appearance since these laws must hold in *all* possible worlds, either because they are required for the individuation of objects or else for the ascription of predicates in terms of which we describe these worlds.

V. Leibniz's notion of the infinitesimal

. . . every number is finite and specifiable, every line is also finite and specifiable. Infinite [magnitudes] and the infinitely small only signify magnitudes which one can take as big or as small as one wishes, in order to show that the error is smaller than the one that has been specified. (*Theodicy,* "Preliminary discourse on faith and reason, § 70.)

1. Common view of Leibniz's infinitesimals

It is widely thought that Leibniz did not have a rigorous conceptual foundation for differential and integral calculus of which he was one of the two independent inventors. It is believed that until Cauchy or until Weierstrass, or even until Abraham Robinson, what Leibniz and Newton invented worked, but it was not solidly founded. This was because the concept of infinitesimal was seen as being confused.

There has been at least three different lines that people have taken in expressing their somewhat condescending attitude towards Leibniz's view on foundational issues. Firstly, many mathematicians as well as philosophers have claimed that Leibniz did not think that making his methods rigorous was very important, and that he concerned himself more with how the newly established calculus worked. Or they say that rigour in methodological issues concerned Leibniz only insofar as unsatisfactory features in the mathematics – such as the problem he had with higher differentials – made rigour a practical issue. It has even been suggested that Leibniz and his followers were able to develop their calculus more efficiently because they were less preoccupied with rigour than were their English counterparts.[1] This is probably true of Leibniz's followers like Johann Bernouilli, de l'Hospital, or Euler, who were all brilliant mathematicians rather than philosophers, but it is prima facie a strange thing to ascribe to someone who, like Leibniz, was obsessed with general methodological issues, and with the logical analysis of all statements and the well-foundedness of all explanations. We will see moreover that we can discover from the writings of Leibniz that the charges are unfounded.

The second kind of critic acknowledges that Leibniz was interested in foundational questions, but after examination sees basic inconsistencies in his views. He finds that Leibniz equivocates in his basic concepts of infinite and infinitesimals, and ends up making contradictory assertions. John Earman is perhaps one of the most forceful representatives of this kind of view. And Carl Boyer also, in his *History of the Calculus,* writes of the Janus face of Leibniz. Indeed as we shall see, Leibniz did use some signs equivocally, but as far as his basic concepts are concerned, Leibniz was not, I will try to show, inconsistent. It seems clear that in his mature works Leibniz maintained the four following theses: (a), that we have an idea of absolute infinity (by which he meant an infinite as distinct from an indefinitely big finite magnitude), and (b) that there are infinitely many substances and infinitely many numbers in his sense of infinitely many, i.e., actually more than any finite number of them, and not merely potentially more,[2] (c) that any number and any specifiable quantity however big or however small is a finite number and a finite quantity (which means that Leibniz did not think that there should be what we call the cardinality of the set of all things),[3] and (d) that the plurality of infinitely many things is not a totality or a whole in the way that the class of finite things is.[4] It seems to me that one can disagree with any one of those four positions but that one can coherently hold all four of them.

The third kind of critical position about Leibniz's foundational views not only acknowledges considerable rigour in the views, but denies that Leibniz held an incoherent position at any given time. It nevertheless sees Leibniz as having drastically changed his views on infinitesimals at a certain moment. For example, Bos, the historian of mathematics who is one of the most sympathetic interpreters of Leibniz's views on the foundation of analysis and who comments that Leibniz was interested in methods rather than results, writes that Leibniz "faced the problem that his calculus involved infinitely small quantities which were not rigorously defined and hence not quite acceptable in mathematics. He therefore made the radical but rather unfortunate decision to present a quite different concept of the differential which was not infinitely small but which satisfied the same rules."[5] Bos talks (perhaps naturally as a post-Robinsonian) as if it is quite clear what it is for a magnitude to be infinitely small, and that Leibniz first assumed the existence of such things. Therefore Leibniz's mature works in which he defines the differentials and infinitesimals via finite quantities is thought to be a switch from his early position. We will show that Leibniz came to see that the concept of being infinitely small was not at all a clear one and that he tried to make the very same concept more rigorous in his mature years by talk of the existence of certain finite quantities. He developed his earlier views rather than change the direction of his thought.

In what follows, we will try to achieve a better understanding of Leibniz's foundational views by placing them more fully in the context of his view on meaning, truth, and logical analysis than is usually done. Our aim is to suggest that people have misunderstood what Leibniz said about the foundation of calculus through a misunderstanding of his doctrine concerning how ideas are identified, and how words get their meaning, rather than from a misunderstanding of his mathematics. We saw in Chapter II that Leibniz held that ideas were identified through propositions or truths.[6] This led Leibniz to assume a contextual theory of meaning for all expressions somewhat in the manner suggested by Frege with whose doctrines we are familiar: namely that we ascribe to expressions a well-defined sense when we can explain the truth-condition of the sentences to which the expressions belong (*Grundgesetze der Arithmetik* Bd I § 32).

We will see however that for certain expressions like that of 'infinitesimal', Leibniz took a position closer to that of Bertrand Russell in his theory of descriptions, a theory which Russell claimed was a theory of contextual definition. Leibniz also maintained that one can have a rigorous language of infinity and infinitesimal while at the same time considering these expressions as being syncategorematic (in the sense of the Scholastics), i.e., regarding the words as not designating entities but as being well defined in the proposition in which they occur. (Letter to Varignon, 2 February 1702, G. *Math.* 4 93). He gives a contextual definition to the word 'infinitesimal' as well as to the sign for the differential quotient. Therefore one of the reasons Kitcher gives for finding Leibniz's language of differential calculus lacking in rigour, namely that "Symbols have been introduced without any specification of their referent" would not have been a criticism for him. To see this, let us examine some of Leibniz's basic concepts relating to the infinitesimal.

2. *Whether the word 'infinitesimal' designates an entity*

If we look at Felix Klein's famous book recommending revisions in the teaching of analysis (*Elementary Mathematics from an Advanced Standpoint*), we read "the differential dx of the variable x had for [Leibniz] actual existence as an ultimate indivisible part of the axis of an abscissas, as a quantity smaller than any finite quantity and still not zero." Klein acknowledges that Leibniz expressed different views about differentials but nevertheless treats him as the origin of a long tradition in modern mathematics which ascribes actual existence to infinitely small magnitudes. Such an interpretation of Leibnizian infinitesimals has been enhanced by Abraham Robinson's success in vindicating infinitesimals by his non-standard analysis. His success in showing that (1) there are non-standard models of first and higher order analysis that contain non-Archimedean infinitesimal elements, and that

(2) formulae of analysis containing constants for such elements and which are true in such models yield simpler and more direct proofs of standard formulae of analysis than the epsilon-delta proofs, seemed to vindicate Leibnizian infinitesimals. Robinson's results are remarkable, but his belief that, even if Leibniz considered infinitesimals to be an ideal fiction which can be dispensed with, these infinitesimals for Leibniz were fixed entities with non-Archimedean magnitudes, the introduction of which shortens proofs, seems unwarranted. It is the introduction of seemingly ostensibly designating expressions which follow certain sui generis rules that shortens proof. The word 'infinitesimal' does not designate a special kind of magnitude. It does not designate at all.

Robinson's success in introducing infinitesimals into the Weierstrassian analysis seemed to vindicate Leibniz from Berkeley's famous attack, in which Berkeley claimed "to conceive a quantity infinitely small, that is, infinitely less than any sensible or imaginable quantity or any finite quantity however small is, I confess, beyond my capacity." We must remember however that Leibniz wrote also in the *Theodicy* (1710) the only philosophical work he published in his lifetime, "every number is finite and assignable, every line is also finite and assignable. Infinites and infinitely small only signify magnitudes which one can take as big or as small as one wishes, in order to show that the error is smaller than the one that has been assigned" (*Theodicy,* § 70). Leibniz is in effect, it seems, a proto-Cauchy or even a proto-Hilbert rather than a proto-Robinson.

As the *Theodicy* is a very late book (1710), it may be thought that this expresses a later-year shift to finitism brought about by senility. In order to see that this is not the case, let us trace some of the things Leibniz writes on infinitesimals from his early years. In his first published paper on the calculus of 1685, *Nova methodus pro maximis et minimis, itemque tangentibus,* 'differential' is defined without the use of infinitesimals. It is, on the contrary, contextually defined through the proportion of finite line segments, but he uses the adverb, infinitely small, *'infinite parva,'* a neutral concept which was widely in use at his time (e.g., in Pascal or in Cavalieri). Leibniz writes that a tangent is found to be a straight line drawn between two points on a curve of infinitely small distance, or a side of a polygon of infinite angles. However, granted that Leibniz already thought at this time that infinitely many things should not be thought of as a completed whole and that 'infinite' means "more than any finite number of them," infinitely small distances can be thought of as distances that can be taken smaller than any distances that are given. During this period Leibniz makes various different hypotheses about the nature of infinity, revealed most clearly in his Paris notes of 1676 (a selection of which appears in *Loemker*, p. 159). Therefore we cannot be sure what Leibniz may exactly have meant by infinitely small distances; but there is no talk about a special kind of small magnitude.

Ten years later, in 1695, in response to the Nieuwentijt's specific demand to clarify what infinitely small means, Leibniz explains that although he treats (*assumo*) infinitely small lines *dx* and *dy* as true quantities sui generis, as well as their quadrates and cubes as quantities, this is just because he found them useful for reasoning and discovery.[7] I take it that he is treating them as convenient theoretical fictions because using signs which looks as if they stand for quantities sui generis is useful. He likens their status to that of imaginary numbers in a letter to Bernouilli three years later [7 June 1698, (G. *Math.* 3, pp. 499–500)]. In another letter to John Bernouilli written the same year Leibniz writes:

> as concerns infinitesimal terms, it seems not only that we never get to such terms, but that there are none in nature, that is, that they are not possible. Otherwise, as I have already said, I admit that if I could concede their possibility, I should concede their being.[8]

He is not saying that infinitesimals do not exist as physical things though they may exist as mathematical entities. They are impossible and thus not a possible mathematical entity. Leibniz compares their impossibility to that of having an infinitely long straight line bound on both ends.

We should remind ourselves here that this finitist reasoning of Leibniz is not of an empiricist kind like that of Berkeley. The impossibility of a term is not entailed by our inability to have a sensory image of it or our inability to distinguish it by perception. Remember how he argues against Locke in the *New Essays* that although we cannot distinguish the image of a polygon with 999 sides and a polygon with a thousand sides we do distinguish them and have different ideas of them. The impossibility of infinitesimals is not about our failure to perceive them. In yet another letter to John Bernouilli (written the following year on 21 February 1699), although he concedes that there are an infinite plurality of terms, he argues nevertheless:

> since an infinite plurality does not constitute a number or a single whole, it follows that even given infinitely many terms in an infinite series, there need not be an infinitesimal term. The reason is that we can conceive an infinite series consisting merely of finite terms or of terms ordered in a decreasing geometric progression.[9]

After another seven years in a letter to Des Bosses in 1706 he explains that he considers infinitesimals to be "fictions of the mind useful for calculations, of the same order as imaginary roots in algebra," and adds:

> Meanwhile I have shown that these expressions are of great use for the abbreviation of thought and thus for discovery as they cannot lead to error, since it is sufficient to substitute for the infinitely small, as small a thing as one may wish, so that the error may be less than any given amount, hence it follows that there can be no error. R. P. Gouye who objected to this does not seem to have understood me properly.[10]

It seems then that throughout his working life as a mathematician Leibniz did not think of founding the calculus in terms of a special kind of small magnitude.

3. Incomparability

It has been argued – for example by John Earman in 1978 – that although Leibniz did indeed reject the existence of infinitesimals in the sense of intrinsically small quantities, he accepted infinitesimals in the sense of "incomparably small with respect to ordinary magnitudes." Earman's own phrase which he uses to interpret this is that of being "infinitesimally small in an ordinal sense."[11] Since the smallest ordinal is the first one, I am not sure whether I understand what this means, but I find it difficult to understand how a magnitude can be incomparably small with respect to ordinary magnitude without being intrinsically small in some sense. So let us go back to what Leibniz says about incomparably small magnitudes.

One of the most interesting and instructive things that Leibniz wrote about foundational concepts occurs in a letter to the mathematician Varignon in February 1702. Reflecting on what he has already done, he writes:

> my intention was to point out that it is unnecessary to make mathematical analysis depend on metaphysical controversies or to make sure that there are lines in nature which are infinitely small in a rigorous sense in comparison with our ordinary lines, or as a result, that there are lines infinitely greater than our ordinary ones. . . . This is why I believed that in order to avoid subtleties and to make my reasoning clear to everyone, it would suffice here to explain the infinite through the incomparable, that is, to think of quantities incomparably greater or smaller than ours.[12]

Does this passage justify a reading that ascribes to Leibniz the acceptance of a special kind of magnitude that is incomparably small with respect to ordinary magnitudes? That is to say, some kind of magnitude which has a non-Archimedean property (i.e., magnitudes such that there is no number with which you can multiply them so that they would become bigger than any given ordinary magnitude)? No. It seems not, since Leibniz says he wanted to show that it is not necessary to establish whether there are lines infinitely small in comparison with our ordinary lines (*infiniment petites [en] comparaison des nostres*). Moreover, the fact that he is not talking about a special kind of fixed magnitudes becomes clear by what Leibniz goes on to write in the same letter. He says:

> these incomparable magnitudes – are not at all fixed or determined but can be taken to be as small as we wish in our geometrical reasoning and so have the effect of the infinitely small in the rigorous sense. If any opponent tries to contradict this proposition, it follows from our calculus that the error will be less than any possible assignable error since it is in our power to make this incomparably small magnitude small enough for this purpose inasmuch as we can always take a magnitude as small as we wish.

We see that the incomparable magnitude is not an infinitesimal magnitude. It seems that when we make reference to infinitesimals in a proposition, we are not designating a fixed magnitude incomparably smaller than our ordinary magnitudes. Leibniz is saying that whatever small magnitude an opponent may present, one can assert the existence of a smaller magnitude. In other words, we can paraphrase the proposition with a universal proposition with an embedded existential claim. This fact about the existence of smaller and smaller finite magnitudes is supposed to justify certain rules governing the sign '*dx*'.

It is misleading for Leibniz to call these magnitudes incomparably small. What his explanation gives us is rather that a certain truth about the existence of *comparably* smaller magnitudes gives rise to the notion of incomparable magnitudes, not incomparably smaller magnitudes.

If magnitudes are incomparable, they can be neither bigger nor smaller.

Often when Leibniz uses the word 'incomparable', he is (as Bos, Boyer, et al. have pointed out) thinking in the line of the traditional notion of incomparable non-homogeneous quantities. (Boyer refers to the work of Tacquet of 1651, who wrote that geometrical magnitudes are made up only of homogenes.) For example, the length of a line and an area of a plane could not, it was thought, be compared with each other since entities of different dimensions were said not to have homogeneous quantities. Leibniz, in the reply to Nieuwentijt of 1695 cited earlier, also asserts that the magnitude of a line and a point of another line cannot be added, nor can a line be added to a surface, and he says that they are incomparable since only homogeneous quantities are comparable. (Leibniz writes that all homogeneous quantities are comparable in the Archimedean sense.) The homogeneity of quantities in Leibniz, however, seems not to depend on a prior notion of a common dimension as in earlier mathematicians, since Leibniz wanted to free mathematics from geometrical intuitions. The fact that we cannot add or subtract the quantities in question to make one quantity constitutes, it seems, the very criterion of their non-homogeneity and hence of their incomparability. Thus he writes that a quantity which is a differential is not a nothing, but it cannot be compared to the quantity of that of which it is a differential. And indeed, multiplying a length with any (finite) number however big will not get a surface and the quantity of acceleration cannot be compared with the quantity of speed. As we have already mentioned, the unfortunate thing about Leibniz's vocabulary here is that he moves from incomparable to incomparably small or incomparably smaller (*incomparabiliter parva* or *incomparabiliter minor*), when smaller is already a notion involving comparison. As Leibniz writes, adding a line to a surface does not increase the surface, but this is surely not because the line is incomparably smaller than any surface.

It may be believed with Earman that what Leibniz writes in the very same year to the mathematician de l'Hospital, suggests that Leibniz is not talking merely of incomparables but incomparably smaller magnitudes – the kind of notion now made precise by Abraham Robinson. In order to defend the notion that quadratures or any higher order differentials *dxdx* or *ddx* are magnitudes, he ostensibly says that when they are multiplied by an infinite number they will become ordinary magnitudes.[13] It is important to realise however that in this letter Leibniz is using de l'Hospital's own criterion to refute him. De l'Hospital had asserted both that higher differentials are not magnitudes and, if after being multiplied by an infinite number the assumed quantity does not become an ordinary magnitude, then it is not a magnitude at all. It is a nothing. Leibniz responded that if that is what de l'Hospital believes, then he cannot at the same time claim that *ddx* and *dxdx* are not magnitudes, since they would, if multiplied by an infinite number ("*per numerum infinitum sed altiorem seu infinites infinitum*") become ordinary magnitudes. This is, however, *not* Leibniz's *own* criterion, as he does not believe that there is such a thing as an infinite number. He is on the contrary trying to explain what differentials and quadratures are by spelling out the thought that leads to them in terms of finite quantities, finite numbers, and Leibniz's concept of 'infinitely many' and of 'incomparable.' (He points out for example that de l'Hospital is wrong to think that if *dy* is equal, *dx* would also be equal.) One can work out many things about magnitudes that are incomparable.

We must notice that here it is the derivative of a function at a point that is incomparable with the quantity of an interval of two values of a function. Leibniz is not affirming, it seems, the incomparability of a segment joining two points of a curve and of whatever other smaller segment joining two other points of the same curve. Thus the Archimedean incomparability is not used to justify ignoring very small magnitudes in order to obtain the mathematical result that one wishes.

In reading Leibniz we must therefore distinguish two things: the differential of a function which corresponds to the value of the limit and the infinitesimal which is a finite variable quantity which one can take as small as one wishes. As he wrote to Varignon:

> Although it is not at all rigorously true that rest is a kind of motion or that equality is a kind of inequality, any more than it is true that a circle is a kind of regular polygon, it can be said, nevertheless that rest, equality and the circle terminate the motions, the inequalities and the regular polygons which arrive at them by a continuous change and vanish in them. And although these terminating points (*terminaisons*) are excluded, that is, are not included in any rigorous sense in the variables which they limit, they nevertheless have the same properties as if they were included in the series, in accordance with the language of infinites and infinitesimals, which take the circle, for example as a regular polygon with an infinite number of sides.[14]

His use of the word 'arrive' is unfortunate since the very next sentence says that they do not arrive at the limit though they approach it. One can therefore consider the limit as an ideal entity. What is ideal is the limit regarded as being included in the value of variables that it limits. Thus I think Leibniz is misleading when he writes to Varignon that truthfully speaking he himself is not sure whether he shouldn't treat infinitesimals as ideal things or as well-founded fictions.[15] The limit may be a well-founded fiction, but talk of infinitesimals is, as he says, syncategorematic and is actually about "quantities that one takes . . . as small as is necessary in order that the error should be smaller than the given error."[16]

4. *Limit presupposed and defined*

Is it not the case that what Leibniz says in these texts just quoted is lacking in rigour, since he is presupposing the existence of the limit which he does not prove? Obviously Leibniz did not give us any kind of existential proof that Weierstrass or Dedekind was to give us, but we should not thereby think that Leibniz did not trouble himself with the problem or that he did not think that he needed principles to support his concept of limit. He claimed that his mathematical thoughts make use of what he calls the Principle of General Order, a principle which he says has its origin in the infinite and is absolutely necessary for geometry, and which he formulates in the following manner:

> When the difference between two terms can be made less than any magnitude given *in datis* or in what is posited, then what is [the difference between two terms] to be sought or in which is to come must be at least less than any magnitude given; or to talk more colloquially, when the terms (or that which are given) approach one another, the terms that follow (or those that are sought) do the same.[17]

Leibniz says that this principle is based on an even more general principle, "*Datis ordinatis etiam quaesita sunt ordinata*": the order of things that are sought are as the order of things given. We see how the Principle of General Order is close to Cauchy's definition of a sequence converging to a limit, the so-called Cauchy sequence. According to Cauchy the necessary and sufficient condition for a sequence converging to a limit is that the difference between the terms S_p and S_q for any value of p and q greater than n can be made less in absolute value than any assignable magnitude by taking n sufficiently large. (And like Leibniz, Cauchy believed wrongly that the continuity of a function was sufficient for the existence almost everywhere of a derivative.)

What then is the difference between Leibniz's view and that of Cauchy to whom we believe we owe a rigorous concept of limit and thereby a conceptual rigor compatible with the language of infinitesimals as Cauchy himself claimed? It is perfectly true that Cauchy formulated both the condition of being a derivative and that of a sequence having a limit in a clearer language, and Leibniz would be the first to acknowledge that this would of its own be an important step. There was however no basic change in the thoughts about infinitesimals between Leibniz and Cauchy. C. H. Edwards writes, for example, in the *Historical Development of the Calculus:*

> the device that enabled him [Cauchy] to 'reconcile with infinitesimals' was a new definition of infinitesimals that avoided the infinitely small *fixed numbers* of earlier mathematicians. Cauchy defined an infinitesimal or infinitely small quantity to be simply a variable with zero as its limit.[18]

We have seen that Leibniz denied that infinitesimals were fixed magnitudes, and claimed that we were asserting the existence of variable finite magnitudes that we could choose as small as we wished. We could say that Cauchy claimed that limits existed whereas Leibniz wanted to say that they were a well-founded fiction. But is there a substantial difference between their claims? Very little, it seems to me. For both, the existence of a limit follows from the internal properties of the sequence itself. According to Leibniz it is nothing but the understanding of a general rule under which a sequence is generated, which makes one understand the limit when the sequence converges. In Leibniz's words "the rules of the finite are found to succeed in the infinite."[19] It is important to understand that although the limit and the differential may be an ideal entity or a well-founded fiction, the language of infinitesimals or the language of limit is not, according to Leibniz, a fiction. He writes in his letter to Varignon:

> Yet we must not imagine that this explanation debases the science of the infinite and reduces it to fictions, for there always remains a syncategorematic infinite.[20]

In other words, every proposition or equation which makes reference to these ideal entities or fictions can be paraphrased into propositions and equations in which such entities are not designated, which have strict truth-conditions.

5. The importance of the derivative

Before we make our concluding remarks we must examine very briefly the role of the differential quotient in Leibniz's analysis of the language of calculus. It is a general criticism made to Leibniz that he did not understand sufficiently the importance of the concept of derivative, but gave too much weight to the concept of differentials whether they are *dx* or *dy* without according attention to the dependence of the differential *dy* to the differential *dx*.

H. J. M. Bos shows in a very subtle way the difficulties that Leibniz encountered in connection with higher order differentials. I would not like to, nor am I able to, add to these technical explanations, but I would just like to draw attention to Bos's argument where Bos shows that Leibniz defines the derivative contextually through the ratio of fixed finite segments of x and of y.[21] The interpretation given by Bos enables us to defend Leibniz against a criticism often raised against him, viz., that Leibniz in his calculus wants the differential *dx* to function both as a magnitude and as zero which can be ignored.

Let me put this criticism in the form that has been formulated by John Earman.[22] Earman examines the case where Leibniz seeks the tangent to the function $y=x^2/a$, and he proceeds by considering a point $(y+dy,\ x+dx)$ infinitesimally close to the point (y,x). Recall that Earman assumes that *dx* and *dy* are fixed incomparably small magnitudes. Earman continues:

a. $$y + dy = \frac{(x+dx)^2}{a} = \frac{(x^2+2xdx+(dx)^2)}{a}$$

b. $$dy = \frac{(2xdx+(dx)^2)}{a}$$

dividing both sides by *dx:*

c. $$dydx = \frac{(2x+dx)}{a}$$

then Earman says:

"Neglecting the infinitesimal term dx in comparison with the finite $2x$ we arrive at the answer

$$\text{d.}\quad \frac{dy}{dx} = \frac{2x}{a} \text{"}$$

Earman writes, probably expressing the thoughts of many others as well, that if $\frac{dy}{dx}$ is considered to be an infinitesimal quantity, so long as '=' is read as meaning "equality up to an infinitesimal quantity," the step is justified, but if $\frac{dy}{dx}$ is understood as the tangent, then '=' has to be read as strict equality, in which case the elimination is not justified. We therefore, it is claimed, see an equivocation or an incoherence. Bos shows however that in order to understand Leibniz better, one must distinguish his use of dx and dy which [are *variables* whose values] are finite corresponding differences [from a particular y and x], and $(d)x$ which is a finite fixed line segment of x, and $(d)y$ which is defined [contextually] by the proportion:

1. $(d)y : (d)x = dy : dx$ when $dx \neq 0$
2. $(d)y : (d)x = y : \sigma$ when $dx = 0$ and σ is the subtangent.

Thus when $dx \neq 0$, $(d)y : (d)x$ can be substituted for $dy{:}dx$ in the formula expressing the relation between dy and dx. What is interesting is that by this indirect method, $\frac{dy}{dx}$ is well defined for all values of dx, including the case where $dx = 0$. Thus in c. above, both sides of the equation are well formed. We may not know immediately whether the equation is true, but since it is well-formed, it can be examined. Today we use the notion of limit to legitimize the limiting case of $dx = 0$, and justify the elimination of dx from c). For Leibniz it was the Principle of General Order, which we just examined, that justifies it. It is a fiction, according to Leibniz, that dx which ranges over finite differences should include 0 among its values; but it is a well-founded fiction because of this Principle of General Order. As Leibniz confesses, he takes for granted the following postulate: "In any supposed transition, ending in any terminus, it is permissable to institute a general reasoning, in which the final terminus may also be included."[23]

We therefore see how the quotient $\frac{(d)y}{(d)x}$ plays an important role in determining how 'dx' has its rigorously defined use. Bos points out that what was unclear about Leibniz's notion was not so much his ignoring the importance of the quotient or the relation of $(d)x$ and $(d)y$, but rather, his not insisting that dx be taken as an independent variable and dy as a dependent variable. (He did not even exclude the inclining side of his characteristic triangle from being the independent variable.) This affects his definition of higher order differentials the defect of which has been pointed out by many. One cannot, however, like Boyer, criticize Leibniz for being "unable to explain the transition from finite to infinitesimal magnitudes"[24] in his consideration of the ratio between dx and dy. As we saw, there are no actual infinitesimal magnitudes. There are only finite magnitudes which we can take as small as we wish. The quotient $\frac{dy}{dx}$ is defined, nevertheless, for all the values of dx, fictitiously including the limit.

The other infelicitous aspect of Leibniz's language of infinitesimals is the ambiguity in the use of the signs 'dx' and 'dy' (as both Earman and Bos have pointed out). These are variables and yet '$\frac{dy}{dx}$' plays the role of the sign for the differential, the value which the quotient takes at the limit. We must not be misled by this ambiguity.

6. *Leibniz's theory of ideas and contextual definitions*

Let me conclude this chapter by coming back to the feature of Leibniz's theory of ideas and of the meaning of words and signs that express them. That he was so ahead of his time seems to me to be the reason why he was misunderstood for such a long time even about one of his central conceptions of the infinitesimal. We saw that Leibniz believed that his language of infinitesimals was rigorous, although there is only a syncategorematic infinitesimal. This belief depended on his substitutivity *salva veritate* criterion of the identity of ideas examined in Chapter II, namely that ideas are identical if the role they play in contributing to the truth-condition of the propositions in which they occur is the same. This, I suggest, made Leibniz committed to a contextual theory of meaning similar to the one put forward by Frege in the *Foundation of Mathematics (Grundlagen der Arithmetic),* § 60. Let me quote the passage from Frege in full, because there have recently been various reinterpretations of Frege's contextual theory, some of which I find contentious, and because we forget that Frege talks about infinitesimals in the very passage. Think of the word 'infinitesimal' as you read.

> That we can form no representation [*Unvorstellbarkeit*] of its content is therefore no reason for denying any meaning [*Bedeutung*] to a word, or for excluding it from our vocabulary. We are indeed only imposed on by the opposite view because we will, when asking for the meaning of a word, consider it in isolation, which leads us to accept a representation as the meaning. Accordingly, any word for which we can find no corresponding mental picture appears to have no content. But we ought always to keep before our eyes a complete proposition. Only in the proposition have the words really a meaning. . . . It is enough if the proposition taken as a whole has a sense; it is this that confers on its parts also their content. This observation is destined, I believe, to throw light on quite a number of difficult concepts, among them that of the infinitesimal.

Frege puts a footnote by the word 'infinitesimal' and explains

> the problem is not, as might be thought, to produce a segment bounded by two distinct points whose

> length is dx, but rather to define the sense of an identity of the type df(x) = g(x)dx.

Leibniz held a similar view.

We know that Leibniz objected to Locke (and to Molyneux) according to whom a man born blind who regained his sight would not be able to distinguish a cube and a globe before him visually. An idea of the cube is, for Leibniz, not a visual or tactual representation of it, but understanding truths about it. Leibniz's claim that ideas are explained through propositions and truths, has all too often however been examined by his admirers only in the context of his disagreement with the empiricists and ideas of sensible qualities. Whereas it seems to me that this view is also important in understanding his mathematical ideas. Frege's footnote on the infinitesimal could have been given by Leibniz.

The contextual theory of Frege is nevertheless compatible with a position which assigns to each expression in a sentence a unique reference (Bedeutung). Thus although Frege's theory of reference was highly complex and although he thought that the sign for the integral or differential refers to second level functions, his view is different from that of Leibniz, for whom the word 'infinitesimal' does not designate. Moreover although Frege continued to support a contextual theory of meaning in the *Basic Laws of Mathematics (Grundgesetze)* of 1893, where he wrote "One can ask for the reference only where the signs are constituents of sentences which express thoughts,"[25] he criticised contextual definitions of numbers in this book. Therefore to appreciate Leibniz's language of infinitesimals which did not designate a fixed magnitude, we must go to Bertrand Russell for whom contextual definition and the theory of incomplete symbols played an important role in the foundation of mathematics. We all know that for Russell, the true logical form of a proposition whose grammatical subject is a definite description, e.g., "The king of France is bald" or "The greatest number is odd," is not a subject-predicate one. It is, according to him, a conjunction of existential and universal propositions, and that is why it is meaningful and can have truth-value (i.e., false) when there is no king of France or the greatest number. Perhaps not many of us are aware that in explaining that definite descriptions are incomplete symbols, or symbols that do not designate independently but can only be contextually defined, Russell (in the section "Definite descriptions" in the *Principia*) gave the sign for the differential $\frac{d}{dx}$ as his first example of a sign with which we are familiar which has a meaning only contextually.[26]

Likewise in Leibniz's language of the infinitesimal, we do not designate a particular entity. We are saying rather that, given any finite magnitude however small, we can find a smaller magnitude. We therefore do two things. We assert a universal proposition or, more precisely, a proposition with a universal quantifier followed by an existential quantifier. On the other hand, we are also implicitly making an existential claim, we assert the existence of the limit, the unique value which is a well-founded fiction. As we saw, to claim the existence of a limit is nothing more for Leibniz than an admission of "a rule of general reasoning in which the final terminus may also be included." The existence of the limit is therefore constituted by the truth of the universal proposition just given.

There are of course differences between the Leibnizian language of infinitesimals and Russell's theory of descriptions. In Russell's theory one is affirming the unique existence of an entity which falls under the very description given in the original sentence; e.g., that of being the king of France of being the greatest number, in the above example. In the language of infinitesimals, one does not assert the unique existence of an entity which has the property of being infinitely small – which according to Leibniz is impossible (otherwise all our talk of infinitesimals would become false, as the talk of the greatest number was for Russell). One is only indirectly acknowledging the existence of a limit, via the assertion of a universal proposition which claims the existence of a finite magnitude smaller than any given one. The similarity which we find in the two theories lies in the common intention Leibniz and Russell have of understanding a sentence which ostensibly designates a specific entity, as really, in its logical form, being a quantified sentence; i.e., a universal or an existential sentence.

Two points remain to be discussed very briefly. Firstly, why I believe that Leibniz's views on the contextual definition of infinitesimals is different from those of other mathematicians of his own time who sought for operationist definitions for certain mathematical notions. For example, many attempted to define the notion of imaginary numbers in this way. And we saw that Leibniz refers to imaginary numbers as being analogous to his notion of infinitesimals. Many mathematicians then and now do not hesitate to define the signs of '$\sqrt{\ }$', 'i', '+', or negation by the rules of operations which govern them. But often, they do not incorporate this process into their general theory of sense. Not only among Leibniz's contemporaries and in Berkeley, but also in Husserl or even in Hilbert we see a division between proper sense which is based on what is given to the intuition, and formal or ideal sense, which is defined by the rules of operation and formulae. Hilbert even writes that he regards the sign and operation symbols of logical calculi as being abstracted from their sense.[27]

Leibniz, however, like Frege, denied that the notion expressed by *any* word was an image, and thought that we cannot define any notion except through propositions and truths. Thus what he says about infinitesimals constitutes an integral and coherent part of his theory of ideas and of meaning.

The second and final point is a general metaphysical point. The fact that Leibniz thought of all magnitudes and numbers as *entia rationis,* which have a secondary existence dependent on the possible existence of substances, does not in the least diminish the importance that Leibniz attached to his claim that, strictly speaking, there are only finite numbers and magnitudes. One must distinguish what Leibniz called ideal entities, *entia rationis* or *êtres de raison,* on the one hand and fictions, *entia fictitium,* on the other. When we refer to numbers or to relations which are ideal entities, we are referring to something. Even if they correspond to property or properties of possible individuals, or to what reason constructs in correspondence to certain equivalence classes of classes of possible individuals, they are entities that are referred to. Fictions, on the other hand, are not entities to which we refer. They are not abstract entities. They are correlates of ways of speaking which can be reduced to talk about more standard kinds of entities. Reference to mathematical fictions can be paraphrased into talk about standard mathematical entities. One can be a monadologist while remaining a finitist in mathematics, or one could be a realist about infinitesimals and also be a monadologist, believing that monads are the only constituents of the actual world. Even if one took the view that all numbers are *entia rationis,* there are objective truths about *entia rationis* as well as about how talk of fictions can be reduced to talk about them. Frege regarded numbers as classes of classes, and Russell maintained his "no-class theory" in which classes can be reduced to individuals and propositional functions, but, as we saw, both of them were interested in the logical priority of different kinds of numbers and of the problem of the contextual definition of differentials and infinitesimals.

As we have seen, Leibniz's ideas of the infinitesimals have much in common with Russell's views of contextual definition and incomplete symbols. It is therefore singularly ironical that Russell himself misunderstood Leibniz's thoughts on infinitesimals in the traditional manner and attacked Leibniz in *Principles of Mathematics,* Chapter 39, for invoking mysterious entities which are neither finite nor zero.[28]

VI. Subject and predicates (relational and non-relational)

There is no term which is so absolute or detached that it does not involve relations, and is not such that a complete analysis of it would lead to other things and indeed to all other things. (*New Essays*, Book 2, Ch. 25 § 10.)[1]

1. *Surface syntax and logical form*

One of Leibniz's central doctrines is believed by many to be that "every proposition is ultimately reducible to one which attributes a predicate to a subject."[2] But what exactly does this claim mean? Aristotle, Kant, or for that matter most logicians until Frege, talked in terms of subject-predicate propositions when they discussed logic. Is Leibniz supposed to have had a stronger view about subject and predicate form than they had? Or are we meant to criticise Leibniz's failure to do as Frege was to do and treat words expressing relations as many-placed predicates? (Here 'predicates' is used to refer to the linguistic expressions and not, as in Leibniz, to concepts.) But the view that propositions are basically of the subject-predicate form does not by itself rule out the possibility of there being more than one subject in a proposition – or of there being many-placed predicates. Nor does the fact that a property is ascribed to a subject (or to subjects) by a predicate rule out the possibility of the property being a relational one, in the sense in which we will explain later. In some passages, Leibniz says explicitly that relation is to be treated as an accident which is in multiple subjects.[3]

It is true that Leibniz considered that what he called categorical propositions were more basic and were presupposed by other types of propositions, such as modal, hypothetical, or disjunctive propositions.[4] We have already seen in Chapter III, however, that hypothetical propositions were considered to be of the same basic logical form as categorical propositions, and we shall see in Chapter VII why modal propositions presuppose categorical propositions. But again, if Leibniz could be said to have believed in the basic role of categorical propositions, he was in agreement with the main stream of logicians before and after him.

It cannot be seriously maintained that for Leibniz there were no existential propositions, nor any propositions asserting identities. Even Russell dwells on the fact that for Leibniz existential propositions have a distinct feature among propositions: that of being 'synthetic'. (Whether Russell's assertion is correct or not will be discussed in Chapter VII.) As for identities, we have already seen that Leibniz includes among his subject-predicate propositions those of the form "Cicero is Tully."

What then is the doctrine of the subject-predicate form of proposition which people ascribe to Leibniz? One can get a better understanding of the problem, and of people's misunderstanding of the problem, by considering two kinds of proposition which according to Russell cannot be reduced to subject-predicate form and which are supposed to provide a counter-example to Leibniz's theory.

First are propositions of the type "There are three men," which according to Russell "assert plurality of subjects . . ." and "cannot be regarded as a mere sum of subject-predicate propositions. . . ."[5] As Parkinson has pointed out, Leibniz *has* a logical analysis of this type of proposition. Ironically, it is quite close to that which Russell was to produce later.[6] The proposition expressed by "There are three *m*" follows from the proposition expressed by "*A* is *m*, *B* is *m*, *C* is *m*, and *A*, *B*, *C* are disparate (i.e. $A \neq B$, or in Leibniz's words *A* is not *B* and *B* is not *A*, $B \neq C$, $A \neq C$).[7] As a matter of fact, the latter proposition only entails the claim that there are at least three *m*. Further conditions have to be added to indicate that there are at most three *m*. In addition, the latter proposition mentions three particulars and is stronger than the former. The latter cannot therefore be regarded as a paraphrase of the former. But we see the general direction of Leibniz's analysis. Similarly with any number. The proposition "There is one man" would follow from the proposition "*A* is a man and for any *A, B, C* . . . where *A, B, C* . . . is a man, *A* = *B* = *C* . . ."

Russell's argument that the "number only results from the singleness of the proposition and would be absent if these propositions, asserting each the presence of one man, were juxtaposed" is completely unjustified. The question is whether the truth-condition of the original proposition is identical or not identical with that expressed by the rewritten sentence consisting of a conjunction of six sentences, three of them of subject-predicate form and three identities (or rather negation of identities). If the truth-conditions are identical, then, following the *salva veritate* principle, the rewritten proposition *is* identical with the original proposition. Identities can also be taken as subject-predicate propositions and for Leibniz have the basic logical form, i.e. the concept *g* is included in the concept *f,* or whatever *f* is *g*. (In identities proper, it is also true that the concept *f* is included in the concept *g,* or whatever is *g* is *f.* But so long as whatever is *f* is *g* Leibniz calls the proposition "*f* is *g*" an identical proposition in the wide sense.) Thus Leibniz is claiming that propositions of the form "There are *n* number of *m*" can be reduced to a conjunction of propositions of the standard subject-predicate type.

The second kind of proposition which Russell considers cannot be reduced to subject-predicate form and hence provides a counter-example to Leibniz is relational propositions such as "*a* is greater than *b,*" "*a* is a part of *b,*" "*a* is between *b* and *c*." We must therefore examine (1) whether these propositions were subject-predicate propositions for Leibniz, and if not (2) whether Leibniz thought that these propositions could be reduced into a complex of some *simpler* propositions of the subject-predicate form. This second question will be discussed at the end of this chapter in § 7.

Leibniz, like Frege, thought that a proposition could have many different logical analyses. In a letter to Clarke, which I shall quote later, Leibniz explicitly says of a sentence of the form *mRl* that one can take it as ascribing "the accident which philosophers call relation" *either* to *m* or to *l*. *m* is the subject of the accident *Rl*, and *l* is the subject of the accident *mR*.[8] Similarly, the sentence "David is the father of Solomon" can be regarded as ascribing a relational property to David or to Solomon. Thus propositions of the type "*a* is greater than *b*" or "*a* is part of *b*" can at least always be taken as subject-predicate propositions with one subject.

To return to our original question. How do we decide whether a proposition is a subject-predicate proposition or a relational proposition? It is by no means a simple syntactical question – like that of deciding whether predicate expressions contain only one blank place or more than one blank place, or whether a sentence has a direct-object or indirect-object word. For example, is the proposition expressed by the sentence "John has good health" relational or not? The truth-conditions of this sentence are the same as for the sentence "John is healthy," which is not relational. Should we then say that a proposition is relational if it can only be expressed by relational sentences, and that a proposition is not relational if it can be expressed by at least *one* non-relational sentence? At this point it might be suggested that all these difficulties come from talking about 'propositions' over and above sentences. As a matter of fact, Leibniz's talk about propositions and statements (*propositio, enuntiatio*) can be safely expressed in talk about thoughts expressed by sentences – but if even this causes anxiety (as it might to Quine) because of the unclarity about the identity of such thoughts, we can forget the question of propositions and sentences for the moment (we will return to the subject later). We will merely consider the properties ascribed to the subjects by the predicates as we have done in the last chapter.

Is the property ascribed to things by the predicate expression ". . . has good health" relational or not?[9] It is of course easy to say that the predicate expression ". . .

has . . ." is relational because it has two blank places. But what happens when a constant occupies the second blank place, as in ". . . has Jill's cat"? The predicate expression still expresses a relational property in the sense that it ascribes to the subject a property which holds between it and something else. Can we at least say that if a property *can* be expressed by some non-relational predicate expression (which excludes not only predicate expressions in which there are two blank places but also excludes those in which there are words referring to other entities), it is a non-relational property? And since the property ascribed to a being by the expression " . . . has health" is identical with that ascribed to it by the expression ". . . is healthy," should we say that the former ascribes a non-relational property as well? This would mean that predicate expressions which have one blank place, *and* in which there are no words referring to other particulars, ascribe non-relational properties to things. We shall see, however, that to say this is not enough.

2. *Monadic predicates which ascribe relational properties*

What about properties ascribed to things by predicate expressions like ". . . perceives," ". . . is faithful," ". . . is gregarious"? Although the predicate expressions contain no words which refer to other particulars, they conceal what modern logicians call quantification over other particulars. Thus the property ascribed to the subject carries implicit reference to other entities. An animal will not perceive unless there is an object, a phenomenon it perceives. A person is not faithful without there being another person related to him in a certain way to whom he is faithful. A person is not gregarious unless there are other people whose company he seeks. In this sense, these properties depend on some relation of the thing to other things and are, therefore, relational. The question of whether a property is relational or not cannot then be decided by syntactical features of predicate expressions, for the fact that a predicate expression has in it a word which refers to another entity is neither a sufficient nor a necessary condition for its ascribing a relational property to the subject.

Leibniz realized that it is no easy matter to decide when a property ascribed to a thing involves a relation's holding or not. In the *New Essays* Leibniz casts doubt on the distinction of relative terms and absolute terms which Locke had employed in his *Essay Concerning Human Understanding.* According to Locke, words like 'black,' 'merry,' or 'thirsty' are absolute words, since when we denote a man by, for example, the word 'black', "we neither signify nor intimate anything but what does or is supposed really to exist in the man thus denominated." In contrast to this, words like 'father' or 'merrier' are relative, since the words "together with the thing they denominate" imply also something else separate and exterior to the existence of that thing.[10] Thus a father is a father *of someone,* a person who is merrier is merrier *than someone else.*

Locke noticed, therefore, that some words which can occur in a predicate's position ascribe relational properties to the subject. Leibniz goes further and says that although one may distinguish between properties which are intrinsic and those which are relations, it is not possible, strictly speaking, to refer to one without implicitly making reference to the other.

According to a well-known view of Russell, Leibniz's assumption that all propositions are of the subject-predicate form, combined with Leibniz's doctrine of the identity of indiscernibles, leads to the conclusion that for Leibniz, strictly speaking, there were *no relational properties.*[11] Rescher, who sees that Russell is misunderstanding Leibniz, nevertheless claims that for Leibniz any relational property is "reducible in the sense of inhering in predications about the substances" concerned.[12] But what is predication? Is there something basically non-relational about it? Does every monadic predicate expression (a predicate expression with one blank place) ascribe a non-relational property?

3. Intrinsic and extrinsic denomination

Since a statement in the *New Essays,* that there is no "purely extrinsic denomination,"[13] is often quoted to support this reductionist interpretation of Leibniz's theory of subject-predicate propositions, we must here examine what Leibniz and the other philosophers of his time meant by 'extrinsic denomination.' We shall then see what, if anything, could be the distinction between relational and non-relational predicates, and whether every monadic predicate can be called a non-relational predicate.

It is important to remind ourselves that Leibniz not only held that there are no purely extrinsic denominations but also in the same chapter argued the complementary thesis that "there is no term so absolute or so detached that it does not involve relations, and the complete analysis of it would lead to other things and even to all things." Leibniz's general thesis, then, is not so much that there are no purely extrinsic relations as that there is no way of characterizing things without invoking both the relational properties and the non-relational properties of the things in question. The syntactical form of a sentence or a predicate expression offers no simple guidance.

Locke wrote that the peculiarity of a relational denomination like 'father' or 'whiter' is that a thing can change how it is to be characterized by such a relational denomination without any change occurring in itself, e.g., Caius ceasing to be a father by his son's death or ceasing to be whiter because every other object becomes whiter. Thus we must distinguish absolute or non-relative words from relative words. Leibniz says in reply that "that can very well be said if we are guided by the things of which we are aware; but in metaphysical strictness there is no entirely extrinsic denomination because of the real connection of all things."[14]

Leibniz does not define any of the words 'denomination', 'intrinsic', or 'extrinsic'. But he probably uses them in the way the mediaeval logicians did. 'Denomination' was used by mediaeval logicians to mean something close to what Aristotle meant by 'paronymy' in *Categories* I and VIII: "Things that are called in a way which derives from the qualities they have, are said to be paronymously called."[15] Anselm in the *De Grammatico* uses 'denominate' to mean the appellation of an object in terms of a word derived from a word which refers to a quality the object has. An example given by Aristotle of paronymy would be to call a man 'just' (*dikaios*) from the quality of justice (*dikaiosunē*) he has. Similarly, Anselm gives as an example of denomination the way one calls a grammarian '*grammaticus*' (a word derived from the word for grammar).

When Locke and Leibniz talk of 'denominate', they are, I suggest, talking of the characterization or identification of an object by the use of words that are derived from an expression referring to its property. Denomination is intrinsic if the property referred to inheres in the object independently of anything outside it. A denomination is extrinsic if it leads our thought beyond the object which we are characterizing to something distinct from it.

Thus there are three kinds of way in which we use expressions to characterize or identify an object, i.e., three kinds of denomination (*not* three kinds of property):

a. To identify objects by using expressions corresponding to Locke's absolute words, which do not refer to, or imply, anything else but what is in the subject one is characterizing. They express non-relational properties of things. Leibniz's view is that the use of such words also implies that one is referring to relational properties of the thing, as well, a view I will examine later.

b. Using expressions which denote objects by relational properties which are so external that they might be thought not to involve any nature or real properties of the objects. (For example, if I pick up one pebble before another for no particular reason, and call the first one 'that' because it is the one which was chosen by me before the others, I am referring to the pebble by a relational property of a purely external kind, which does not affect or reflect the internal property of the pebble.)

Leibniz thinks that although the use of demonstratives may be thought to be of this kind, we can never refer to things only by pointing to the purely extrinsic relations they have to other things, without at the same time making some reference to the non-relational properties of the thing. (For example, I pick up the pebble thinking of it as grey and hard and call it 'this'.)

c. Using expressions which refer to the property of the thing denoted and also explicitly carry reference to other existent things, for example, "perceives a tree," "is a teacher of somebody else," or "is whiter." For Leibniz, many more uses of expressions than is commonly thought belong to this category.

4. *Denomination by expressions referring to sensible qualities*

Consider our characterization of things as 'black,' 'merry,' and 'thirsty.' For Leibniz none of these denominations is absolute as Locke thought. If we characterize an object by any of these words, we implicitly refer to relations. In thinking of black more fully, reference is made to the property of the object which accounts for how it appears to a perceiver.[16] In identifying a person as merry, we refer to his disposition vis-à-vis certain situations or people; in referring to a person as thirsty we refer to his condition, which not only initiates a certain disposition to act towards other objects but is dependent on a particular causal history involving lack of water, etc.

We will examine the three in turn. Does the identification of the property of being black involve relational properties? We have seen that a sensible quality like black is a property of things or of phenomena, and not of the experience of a perceiver. Why then should it involve any relational property? Leibniz thinks that we might well think of black as a perceptual quality without thinking of the cause of our perceptual experience. But if we obtain a complete knowledge of our perceptions of black we will see how our perceptions are related to objects of certain structures[17] (for example, the structure of a surface which absorbs all light). Thus the idea of black carries reference both to perception and to the cause of perceptions.

If we use the notation of modern quantification theory, "*a* is black" is claimed to be not of the form *fa* but of the form "$(\exists\chi)fa\chi$" – or at least "$(\chi)(g\chi$ and $fa\chi)$". For all human beings χ, *a* will give χ a visual experience of a certain kind under certain conditions. Thus if "$(\exists\chi)fa\chi$" and "$(y)(\exists\chi)f\chi y$" are propositions in which predicates occur ascribing relational properties, then the predicate ". . . is black" also ascribes a relational property. But is Leibniz right?

Leibniz is right in thinking that to refer to a person's perceptions is to refer to a relational fact. He says that perceptions are "representations of the complex, or of that which is outside, in the simple."[18] In other words, to say of a person that he perceives is to say that he has in the mind a representation of phenomena belonging to the outside world. And, quite independently of whether we adopt any talk of 'representation', we can agree with Leibniz that the truth-conditions of statements about perception involve a relation's holding between the perceiver and external objects. Thus although ". . . perceives" and ". . . perceives something" are monadic predicate expressions in the sense that they have only one blank place, they express relational properties.

Similarly, Leibniz believes that to make reference to a perceptible quality is to refer to a relational fact. *If* black *is* a structural property, then things could have it even if no one perceives them, and even when the condition of light is such that black cannot be distinguished from any other colour. It remains nevertheless that, even if secondary qualities are identical with primary qualities, they can be identified as secondary qualities only by beings who perceive, and hence such identifications carry reference to the relational fact of perception.

5. Expressions referring to dispositions

What about the next example Locke gives of absolute terms, namely 'merry'? Could this carry reference to things other than the subject? Does not 'merry' refer to a constitution of a person, which can be specified without reference to anything else?

Leibniz does not discuss this example at all, but elsewhere in the *New Essays* he comments in some detail on the relational feature of dispositions with reference to 'tenderness'. Tenderness, he says, is a quality which renders a lover sensitive to whatever good and harm comes to the beloved, and "generally those who have a tender heart have some disposition to be tender when in love."[19]

The same thing may be said of merriness. A merry person is a gay-tempered person given to laughter. But to be merry is to have a disposition to respond in certain ways in appropriate circumstances. To be in high spirits for no reason at all would not make a person merry. Thus ascribing the property of being merry to a person carries reference, if not to a particular circumstance, at least to an unspecified set of circumstances of a certain kind which occur during a certain period.

Some people may object and say that a person may be merry or tender, and yet the world in which he lives may happen not to provide him with circumstances in which such dispositions can manifest themselves. For example, a merry man may live in a world of utter misery and constant gloom, and he may always have acute pain, and so although it is true that he has a very merry disposition, he may never laugh or may never be gay – just as a courageous man may never come across challenging situations in which he can show his bravery. This, they may say, indicates that predicate expressions like ". . . is courageous" or ". . . is merry" ascribe non-relational properties to a person, which would be true of a person even when the person never finds himself in appropriate circumstances. If we borrow Leibnizian terminology, it would amount to saying that a person may have an essential property of being merry or courageous which would manifest itself in certain ways in any world in which he encountered certain situations, although in *this* world he would never come across these situations.

This, as was pointed out by Dummett,[20] seems to be clearly wrong. When we predicate 'merry' of a person, we are ascribing a disposition or temperament and not physiological grounds for such a disposition, which may or may not manifest itself. If a person never encountered an occasion to manifest the disposition, or the opposite disposition, in this world, then it is not that we cannot tell whether he is merry or not merry, but that he is neither merry nor unmerry in this world. The fact that we cannot assert the contradictory judgment, i.e. that we cannot say of him that he is not merry in this world either, is no ground for saying that he must therefore be either merry or unmerry essentially, and that his merriness would have manifested itself if the world had been different. If this is so, then to use a word to refer to a person's disposition, then, is also to make reference to certain relational facts.

What, then, about the third example from Locke: the expression "is thirsty"? How could this ascribe a relational property to the subject? Surely an animal can be thirsty if it has a special kind of sensation and is in a particular physiological state? To ascribe thirst to it is to say that it is in the particular dehydrated state and has an experience of discomfort caused by it, a characterization which does not carry any reference to other things. Again, when Leibniz argues against Locke, he does not discuss this example in any detail. But in another passage in the *New Essays* he discusses what it is to say of a man that he is hungry.[21] According to Leibniz, "even when one is hungry one does not think of it every moment; but when one thinks about it, one is aware of it." To be hungry is not to have a sensation of a certain kind: it is "a very marked disposition." Leibniz says that when a man is hungry there is a particular reason. (For example, his stomach is empty or he has not eaten for a long time.) These reasons concern causal relations which the man has to other things such as food. Also, if a man can be hungry without constantly having a particular kind of sensation, then being hungry cannot be the state of having a certain sensation when one's stomach is empty. To treat hunger as a disposition is, among other things, to say that when a man is hungry he is disposed to act in certain ways. He seeks food. He is satisfied when he eats food; and this again seems to carry reference to relations. Leibniz writes that our confused ideas of various pleasures and pains can be made a bit more distinct if we consider the "little aids or little releases and imperceptible releases of a thwarted endeavour which finally generate notable pleasure."[22]

It might be objected that seeking food is not a relation between the seeker and the object sought, for an animal may well seek an object that does not exist. Thus a hungry animal may search for food in a world in which there is no food at all.

But to go back to Locke's example, so long as "*X* is thirsty" is not a predicate which indicates a state of dehydration alone but also ascribes a particular kind of disposition to the man who sometimes feels sensations of a special kind, then that disposition can be specified only with reference to certain acts which relate to other things. The sensations of thirst therefore can only be identified relatively to the disposition. Thus in a world in which water has never existed and hence no possible act of taking water exists, one would not be able to identify the experience of thirst. The obvious discomfort produced by dehydration might be dizziness or weakness rather than thirst. If this is so, Leibniz seems to be right to claim that many of these predicate expressions, which Locke calls 'absolute', cannot be ascribed to a subject without implicitly referring to a relational property of the subject or to other objects.

We can see that Leibniz's attitude towards our idea of sensations was quite different from Descartes'. He never thought that they could be characterized just by some qualities which we can 'feel' or 'introspect'. He attacks the numerous thinkers of his day who "believe that our ideas of sense-qualities differ *toto genere* from motions and from all that goes on in objects and are something primary and inexplicable and indeed arbitrary."[23]

6. Concepts involving coordinative definitions and congruence

Many, however, will obviously feel that there are other examples of ways of characterizing things by predicates that carry no reference to other things and will cause greater difficulties for Leibniz's position, and I want to examine two such examples. One is the kind of property ascribed to objects by expressions of the type ". . . is 1 metre long," and the other is the Kantian example (against Leibniz) of predicate expressions of the type 'left-hand' or 'right-hand.' For one might want to say ". . . is 1 metre long" is not relational as, say, ". . . is the same length as . . ." or ". . . is longer than . . ." is. And, even if the expression ". . . is 1 metre long," being meaningful, implies the existence of a definition, a definition is not another entity; so there is no ground for saying that the predicate makes reference to any entity other than itself.

As Leibniz realised, however, the definition of metres or feet carries a reference to some object and to a definition of congruence. He writes. ". . . it is impossible to know what the foot and yard are if there is not available an actually given object applied as a standard to compare objects. What "a foot" is, therefore, cannot be explained completely by a definition, i.e. by one which does not contain a determination of the same sort. For we may always say that a foot consists of 12 inches, but the same question arises again concerning the inch, and we have made no progress."[24] Thus, if I say of a stick that it is a metre long, I am saying that measured against the standard metre in Paris it is of the same length. This is probably why Leibniz believed that all quantitative statements about things, whether it was a question of their length, or their number, were relational statements.

Let us now think of the predicate 'left-hand' or 'right-hand' – one of Kant's examples in his argument against Leibniz's theory of Relative Space. People will no doubt say that ". . . is left-hand" does not express a relational predicate as ". . . is to the left of . . ." does. If I say of a tree that it is to the left of a house, I am making a claim about a relation that holds between the tree and the house, or rather a relation involving the tree, the house, and myself facing a certain way. It might appear that we can say of a glove, in a universe in which nothing else exists, that it is left-hand or right-hand, and that a universe consisting only of the former would be different from a universe consisting only of the latter. Thus, it might be said, 'left-hand' expresses a distinct property of an object which involves no relation to anything else.

Kant argued that although every point in the left-hand glove stands in exactly the same relation to all other parts of the glove as points in a right-hand glove would to all other parts of the glove, the two universes (each with one glove) would *not* be indiscernible. Kant claimed that a left hand and a right hand which are completely alike are nevertheless incongruent, and hence have different properties. In Kant's words they are 'incongruent counterparts'.[25]

Leibniz would probably have said to such an assertion that, although it is perfectly clear that in a world in which there are both left-hand and right-hand gloves one can make the distinction between the two, in a universe which consists solely of a single glove, this is not the case. Whether you can distinguish a universe in which there is a single left-hand one from a universe in which there is a single right-hand one is not a simple question. According to Leibniz, "elements are homogeneous when they can be made similar through a transformation of one into the other."[26] Thus what would count as congruent differs, depending on what kind of things count as continuous transformations. And how are we to think of continuous transformations between *different* universes?

Think of a simpler case: the triangles *a* and *b* on the following page. The triangles are not congruent if we only allow them to be moved, without lifting them out of the plane. However, if one thinks of a line *L* running between *a* and *b*, equidistant from either, and, if we fold the page along the line *L*, *a* will cover *b*. Thus *a* and *b*

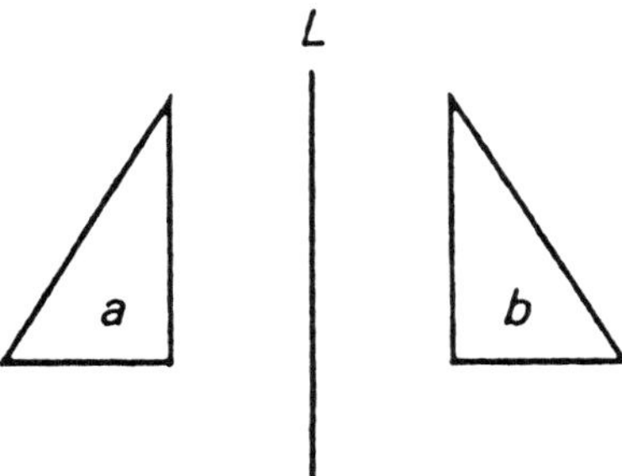

will be congruent if we allow them to be rotated in a three-dimensional space. So long as there are more figures than the triangle *a* (e.g. the triangle *b*) on the plane, one can see the point of distinguishing the triangle *a* from triangles like *b*. And we can always fix a coordinate system which will make one left-oriented and the other right-oriented. But if we are given only the triangle *a* in a plane, it makes no sense to ask in an absolute manner whether the triangle is congruent with another triangle *b* in a different plane or not, and consequently by itself (without any coordinate system) we cannot say of it whether it is right-oriented or left-oriented.

It is the same with a left-hand glove and a right-hand glove. In any world in which both exist, one can say that they cannot be made congruent within a three-dimensional world. But when we think of a world in which there is only one glove, although it may seem at first sight (as it did for Kant) that the glove must either be a left-hand glove or a right-hand glove – as one will fit the different hand from the other – this is not the case. We believe that this is so only by surreptitiously thinking of a world in which there are two bodies each with a single glove on a different hand, and where we can indeed tell the difference between the body with the left-hand glove and the body with the right-hand glove. But without a coordinate system in the three-dimensional world, or without some asymmetric object or point of view external to the glove in the same three-dimensional space, it makes no sense to say of a single glove in the universe that it is left-hand or right-hand. Kant himself makes the distinction of a single right hand or left hand which exists by itself by a counter-factual (i.e., by imagining a human body to be created later by God, to which the hand will be either a left hand or a right hand), which involves the hand standing in relation to another object.

'Left-hand' and 'right-hand,' then, do not ascribe a relational property to a thing in the sense of implying the existence of anything else to which the thing which has the property stands in relation. But nevertheless the use of the predicate expression "is left-hand" carries an implicit reference to, or presupposes, a coordinate system (if not an asymmetric body within the same space to which it is related).

In this attenuated sense, saying of something that it is left-hand and right-hand, like black, which we have already examined, is a way of referring to a property "which carries reference to other things" as Leibniz says. Leibniz seems at least right in attacking Locke's belief in the clear-cut division of 'relative' and 'absolute' terms, and certainly his view is far more subtle than that which makes a simple correspondence between syntactical features of monadic and many-place predicate expressions in ordinary usage and the non-relational and relational properties we are supposed to ascribe to objects by using them.

7. *The logical form of relational propositions*

Why then did Leibniz make attempts to rewrite relational propositions of various kinds? What is the point of rewriting a proposition expressed in a sentence of a certain syntactical structure by sentences of a different structure, if syntactical structure by itself does not indicate the nature of the properties ascribed to a subject in a proposition? We must here distinguish surface syntax from the true logical syntax.

Leibniz believed that certain forms of sentences, or methods of symbolism, reflect the logical form of thought which they expressed better than others. That is to say, they showed their truth-conditions more explicitly. For example, if there is a proposition with a very complex truth-condition but expressed by a sentence with simple surface syntax, it is better if we are shown explicitly all the complex elements of thought which contribute towards the truth-conditions by rewriting the sentence. We would thus see more explicitly various propositions which are logically entailed by the given proposition as well as the multiple truth-grounds of the latter. Russell attempted such a rewriting programme in his theory of descriptions. We have already seen how Leibniz attempted to do this with propositions given by sentences like "There are *n* number of ϕs." Leibniz also carried out rewriting attempts with several kinds of relational propositions in which two particular individuals are mentioned.

Despite their fragmentary character, they are projects which point in interesting directions. In most cases the sentences into which the original sentence is rewritten still describe relational facts, and the rewriting projects do not form any part of a general programme of reduction into propositions in which non-relational attributes are ascribed to the subject. It is rather an attempt to render explicit special logical relations which hold between relational propositions and other relational propositions or between relational propositions and certain non-relational propositions. Leibniz knew they were not catered for by Aristotle's logic. He admired and quoted the fragmentary logic of relation of Jungius, who had tried to show the existence of the valid relational inferences which could *not* be reduced to the traditional syllogism.[27] (Leibniz even thought that Jungius was the greatest mathematician and philosopher of Germany, equalling Aristotle and Descartes.) However, Jungius provided neither explanation nor proof of the soundness of the arguments involving relational propositions which he produced. In the *New Essays,* therefore, Leibniz claims with great passion to expose the logical form of arguments like "David is the father of Solomon, and so without doubt Solomon is the son of David,"[28] an example which appears in Jungius' *Logica Hamburgensis*. He also works on inferences of the type "He learns painting. Painting is an art. Therefore he learns an art."[29] He hoped that his system of universal characteristics would enable one to express such deductions as logical truths.

According to Leibniz, relations are based on either comparison or connection (*comparationis vel connexionis*).[30] The relation of being smaller than would belong to the former, whereas that of co-existing with would belong to the latter. Leibniz apparently did think that *some* propositions expressing relations based on comparisons could be reduced to a conjunction of propositions in which only non-relational predicates occur, or to a set of such propositions with another proposition stating the entailment relationship which these had to one another. For example, Leibniz says that when we claim that "Paul is like Peter" what we claim can be reduced to the conjunction of the propositions "Peter is now *A*" and "Paul is now *A*."[31] To say of two things that they are alike is to attribute a particular property to one of them and to attribute the same property to the other as well.

However, there are other relations based on comparisons from which relational predicates (predicates which seem to attribute relations to the subject and other entities) *cannot* be eliminated. For example, Leibniz attempts to show that propositions expressed by sentences of the type "Titus is wiser than Caius" can be reduced to a pair of propositions and a connective indicating that the propositions stand in a certain *logical* relation to each other – i.e., "Titus is wise and as such (*qua talis*) is superior, to the extent that (*quatenus*) Caius *qua* wise is inferior" (Couturat, *OFI*, p. 280). But note that each of the two resultant propositions, "Titus is wise and as such is superior" and "Caius *qua* wise is inferior," are expressed by sentences which also contain the comparative adjectives 'superior' and 'inferior' which are not eliminated. What we have is not so much a reduction of any relational proposition to a non-relational proposition as an explicit expression of the relational property by a pair of sentences each of which contains a non-relational predicate expression *and a relational* predicate expression (i.e., "is superior" and "is inferior") of the most general form, and in addition a connective which is supposed to express the logical relation of the two relational propositions, e.g., '*quatenus*'. It is true that when we claim that Titus is superior we are not specifying the person to whom Titus is superior. We are merely saying that Titus is superior to someone, or that there is someone to whom Titus is superior. But we have already seen that the fact that one does not name the second term of the relation does not make the property expressed by "is superior" any less relational. Its sense depends on there being another person to whom the subject's ability is compared. (One could also, I suppose, compare the ability of a person at a particular time to the ability of the same person at another time.)

There is a very great difficulty about making clear exactly what logical relation exists between two propositions connected by the connective '*quatenus*', which must be non-extensional and presumably intuitively means something like 'insofar as'. (Material equivalence is no good as an explication. It lets in too much. For example "$2 + 2 = 4 \equiv$ snow is white," but one would not want to say "2 + 2 = 4 *quatenus* snow is white.") On the other hand logical equivalence seems too strong. It seems possible for Titus to be wiser than many other people, without Caius being less wise. Think, for example, of a world in which Titus exists and is wiser than all others and in which Caius does not exist. A certain consequence of Leibniz's mirror thesis, namely that individual concepts can be instantiated in only one world, would make this impossible, but I will not go into details of the problem here.

All that I am anxious to stress is that there is no elimination of relational properties in what is expressed by the rewritten result. Not only is there a relational expression (viz. a comparative) in each of the sentences expressing the constituent propositions: the two propositions are claimed to be related in a non-extensional way. The rewriting nevertheless enables one to deduce, for example, "Caius is less wise than Titus." (It also seems, unfortunately, to allow one to deduce "Titus is wise," which I do not think follows from "Titus is wiser than Caius," unless one means by "Titus is wise" that Titus has some wisdom.)

When we come to relations which are based on connections, the elimination of relational properties – if that were the project – would become even more difficult. In another manuscript, Leibniz writes that "Paris is the lover of Helen" can be logically reduced to "Paris loves, and by that very fact (*eo ipso*) Helen is loved."[32] Again, strictly speaking, this is an expansion rather than a reduction, for as Leibniz remarks, the original proposition is shown up to be logically a 'compendium' of two propositions – this time linked by the logical connection '*eo ipso*'. And each of the two propositions is still a relational proposition in the sense that it is expressed by a sentence that conceals a two-place predicate, since the first means that Paris loves someone, and the second means that Helen is loved by someone. It is part of their truth-condition that there is someone whom Paris loves and someone who loves Helen. Thus although a relational proposition in which two individuals are mentioned has been eliminated, in each of the propositions expressed by the rewritten result relational properties are still ascribed to the subject, relating him to another person. The connective '*eo ipso*' shows, moreover, that the original proposition is *not* a truth-function of the two constituent propositions. The rewriting enables one to see that the original proposition entails the propositions "Helen is loved by Paris," "Helen is loved," and "Paris loves."[33]

It might be objected that I am wrong to equate "Paris loves" with "There is someone whom Paris loves." If Paris is in love with his reflection as was Narcissus, the former proposition will be true but the latter will not.[34] But even if, as a matter of fact, there are complexities about this verb, there is no doubt that Leibniz thought that implicitly, if not explicitly, all predicates carry reference to other existents. It is also quite clear that Leibniz held that relational propositions of the type "*A* is adjacent to *B*" or "*A* precedes *B*" *cannot* be reduced to a 'compendium' of non-relational propositions. As will be shown in the next chapter, even if we paraphrase "*A* preceded *B*" as "*A* existed at t_1 and *B* existed at t_2," times such as t_1 and t_2 are themselves *entia rationis* for Leibniz and logically *derived from* propositions in which relational properties are ascribed to substances and their mutual order is expressed.

Thus Leibniz's project of rewriting certain relational propositions cannot have been part of any general plan for eliminating relational properties. Leibniz was interested in any reduction or paraphrase of irregularities and unnecessary complexities in the grammar of ordinary language which would make language amenable to logical calculus.[35] He wanted to construct a language whose syntax would reflect the truth-functional and other logical relations of all the propositions expressed in it. This he thought was what arithmetic already did. The great advance in mathematics – and the objectivity of mathematics – was for Leibniz inseparably linked with their good syntax.

VII. Monads, attributes, accidents, and relations

> The concept of an individual substance involves all its changes and all its relations, even those which are commonly called extrinsic. (Letter to Arnauld, 14 July 1686.)[1]

1. Leibniz's definition of attributes and accidents

The distinction between relational and non-relational predicates is neither an absolute nor simple one for Leibniz, as we have just seen, and how any predicate expression is to be categorized cannot be discovered from its surface form, nor can the logical form of a given proposition be found just by examining the grammatical form of the sentence which expresses it. Thus the central doctrine of Leibniz's metaphysics, traditionally ascribed to him and accepted by Couturat and Russell – that all propositions are basically of the subject-predicate form and that reality consists of substances and their attributes or accidents which are described by these propositions – must be reexamined.

Monads are the ultimate constituents for Leibniz, and the bearer of infinitely many attributes. But what is an attribute? Is it something essential to a substance as in Spinoza? Is it different from an accident? Is it something that only substances have?

Benson Mates wrote in his interesting paper, "Leibniz and possible worlds," that Leibniz was

> not content to take the trivial way out that just rereads or redescribes the sentence, 'David is the father of Solomon', for example, as ascribing the attribute 'father of Solomon' to David and the attribute 'having David as father' to Solomon; it is clear, to use some more recent terminology, that he

> would not be inclined to accept every open sentence with one free variable as expressing an attribute.[2]

But it is far from clear that Leibniz did not think that every open sentence with one free variable expresses an attribute. Leibniz's explanation of what an attribute is is not always consistent. But whatever their shortcomings, his explanations are generally more grammatical than metaphysical in nature:

> An attribute is the predicate in a universal affirmative proposition of which the subject is the name of a thing.[3]

Leibniz's definition of an accident is often equally grammatical and indistinguishable from his definition of attribute:

> An accident is an adjectival predicate of a substantival subject in an affirmative particular proposition only.[4]

or

> An accident is the predicate both in an affirmative particular and negative particular proposition with the same subject. For example, some man is learned and some man is not learned; therefore learned is an accident of man. If some *a* is *b* and some *a* is not *b*, then *b* is an accident of *a*.[5]

In the *New Essays* Leibniz does attempt on a few occasions to make a distinction between attributes and accidents or modifications in a non-grammatical way.[6] Here he seems to mean by attributes permanent properties and faculties or capacities of things. Thus the defining features of a species, or extension, solidity, as well as the capacity to perceive is said to be an attribute, while motion, shape, and perceptual states are said to be modifications, or accidents, of an individual. But often Leibniz is quite lax in his use of the word 'attribute' or 'accident' and uses them roughly in the sense of 'property.'[7] Other examples which he gives of attributes are being just, being merciful, being a multiple of 2. He objects to treating 'attribute' in too narrow a manner to mean only the essences or basic categories (e.g., extension and thought) as Spinoza did.[8]

In view of the fact that there have recently been several works which have attempted to show that individual accidents, together with individual substances, play a special role in Leibniz's ontology,[9] it is perhaps important to avoid the mistake of reading later Scholastic or Neo-Platonic metaphysics into him by pointing out how wide Leibniz's use of the word 'accident' was. He gives lists of *'accidentia mathematica,'* and has chapters on *'Accidens Oeconomicum'* and *'Accidens Politicum.'* Accidents can be ascribed by all sorts of predicates, and the things that have them can be abstract mental constructions, nations, or institutions, as well as physical things or monadic substances. What then is the common feature of accidents? They are modes or states of things, and thus cannot exist on their own, nor go in and out of things. We can identify accidents that are common to many things actual or possible, but this (universal) accident has existence only as an abstract mental entity, or *ens rationis*. The only accidents that actually exist are nothing more than states or modes of things. As he writes in many places, they are not to be treated as individual entities that exist in addition to things in which they inhere. "Accidents which are more than modifications," he writes, in his very mature age to Des Bosses, "are entirely superflous."[10] Modes should not be thought of as "self-subsistent beings which can fly in and out like pigeons housed in a pigeon-loft. It is unwittingly to turn them into substances."[11] It is important to realise that the impossibility of an accident's passing from one thing to another, and wandering in and out of substances has nothing to do with the 'individuality' of the accident as has often been claimed. It is not that an accident is like a passport that can belong only to one person and not be transferred to another person. An accident is not a detachable thing at all. It is the state or the modification of the person or the things itself.

These modifications, however, are essential characteristics of the individual *given* the external conditions. For whatever Leibniz thinks is the distinction between attribute on one hand and accident or modification on the other, it is clear that for him there are relational attributes and relational accidents. For example, there is an unpublished manuscript of 1703 where Leibniz talks of temporal and spatial order as "an attribute that is simultaneously in two subjects," to which Mugnai has drawn our attention.[12] And in §1 of the previous chapter we have seen that Leibniz talks of a relation as an accident that is in multiple subjects, and also describes the property of a line *L* of having a length which stands in a certain ratio to another line *M* as "that accident which philosophers call 'relation'." I have called them relational properties (which we would express by propositional functions that contain quantifiers ranging over individual objects) which correspond to the relation a thing has to something else. It is quite clear, as we will see in §4 of this chapter, that Leibniz considered the idea of such properties as constituting the individual concept of the thing.

But surely, it will be said, Leibniz believed that attributes of monads are more fundamental or real than the various relations monads have to one another. For what else could his theory of relations as *entia rationis* (ideal entities) mean? In order to answer these questions, let me disentangle four theses which have been linked with Leibniz's view on the ideality of relations, and examine the connection each has with the thesis that relations are reducible. I will then proceed to discuss the problem of causal relationships in Leibniz's philosophy, before coming back to the problem of individuals and their accidents.

2. *Relational properties presupposing non-relational properties*

The first thesis concerning relations and attributes which I discuss I shall call the presupposition thesis. It is Leibniz's claim that things cannot stand in a relation to each other without having non-relational properties. This is most clearly expressed in a fragment[13] where he says:

> The category of relations such as quantity and position do not constitute intrinsic [non-relational] denominations themselves, and what is more, they need a basis taken from the category of quality, or intrinsic denomination of accidents.
>
> [Quae ipsae per se nullam denominationem intrinsicam constituant adeoque esse relationes tantum quae indigeant fundamento sumto ex praedicamento qualitatis seu denominatione intrinsica accidentali.]

This argument reminds us of one with a similar form which Leibniz uses against Descartes' theory that the essence of matter is extension. Leibniz thinks that there is a conceptual inadequacy about such a theory. We must ask ourselves what it is that is extended: "Besides extension there must be a subject which is extended."[14] And Leibniz is right here, since it may be more the nature of the 'that' which is extended than the fact that it is extended which distinguishes matter. We can say, e.g., of a table that it is extended, that its surface is extended, that the colour has extension – but we would not want to say for this reason that there are three or more material substances equally extended. It is not merely the applicability of the property *extended* that defines matter for us. So long as we talk of extensions, we are identifying *something* which is extended. Likewise, he says, plurality, continuity, or coexistence involve things that are plural, continuous, or which coexist. Leibniz thought in a somewhat similar fashion that if we locate something we must "ask ourselves what it is that occupies the place."[15]

The presupposition thesis, then, is that things cannot stand in relation to each other without themselves having non-relational properties, or what he calls 'qualities' or 'intrinsic denomination of accidents'. If a and b are names of individuals and R expresses a relation, every time aRb is true, fa and ga have to be true also for some f and g where *f* and *g* are non-relational properties. To say that relations between things presuppose non-relational properties is definitely not to say that the former can be reduced to the latter. If someone points out that for a person to be able to divorce presupposes that the person is married, he is not saying that divorcing can be reduced to marrying. The claim that an *f* presupposes a *g* normally implies the difference between *f*'s and *g*'s. The presupposition theory however supports Leibniz's claim, quoted in Chapter 5 §3, that "there are no purely extrinsic denominations,"i.e., that there are no ways of denominating a thing by using a description that picks up only a purely relational property of the thing. In denoting a thing through its distinctive relational property to other things, we are presupposing, and thus implying the existence of, the non-relational properties of the thing we denote.

3. Non-relational individuating properties of substances

Leibniz sometimes seems to confuse the presupposition thesis with a somewhat stronger claim which one might call the thesis that individuation (what distinguishes one from another) is based on non-relational properties of things. This is the second thesis, which can be called the thesis of the existence of intrinsic individuating properties. He writes, for example, that

> it is always necessary that besides the difference of time and space there be an internal principle of distinction. . . . Thus although time and place (that is to say the relations they have to external things) serve us in distinguishing things which we do not easily distinguish by themselves, things are nevertheless distinguishable in themselves. The essence of identity and diversity consists, then, not in time and place, although it is true that the diversity of things is accompanied by that of time and place.[16]

It is not easy to make clear what Leibniz means by this claim. He is not merely stating the presupposition thesis – that if we claim that *A* and *B* are at different places at a given time, then we must be able to claim also that *A* and *B* have each a set of properties which do not carry reference to place and time. (For in this case, the set of non-relational properties which each has may be identical.) He is also saying that, although we may use relational properties such as location to tell *A* and *B* apart, the set of non-relational properties or some "internal principle of distinction" – which is not the stuff out of which *A* and *B* are made (as in Aristotle), but a characteristic of some kind which *A* and *B* have – must be adequate to distinguish *A* from *B*. He writes, for example, that

> it is not possible that two things should differ from each other only in place and time. But it is always necessary that some other internal distinguishing characteristic is there.[17]

What is the nature of this impossibility and this necessity? How could they be more than empirically established facts? For example, why couldn't mass-produced, quality controlled Ping-Pong balls have all their properties in common, and be numerically distinguished only by when and where they were produced and are destroyed?

In order to understand what is being claimed, it is important to realize that Leibniz never excluded the possibility of these internal distinguishing characteristics themselves being consequential upon or being related to, the spatial position that *A* and *B* have at a particular time, or founded in the truth of various temporal or coexisting relations holding between *A* or *B* and all other things in the universe, including the relations which hold between *A* and *B* themselves.

For example, Leibniz believed that the intrinsic feature of a mind is its successive states of awareness or perceptions and its desires, but he never claims that perceptions are not consequences of the mind standing to other things in the universe in a certain way. On the contrary for him the very nature of perception is that near-by things are perceived more distinctly and faraway things less distinctly. Then every characterization of a perceptual state of a thing would carry reference to relational facts of the thing.

Leibniz does not seem to be insisting, however, in these passages that each individual must have one essential non-relational property that individuates it and distinguishes it from all other things. He is saying that the set of non-relational properties of a thing must be enough to distinguish it from all others. And this theory, I would like to suggest, cannot begin to be defended as a metaphysical doctrine without the following supporting view.

4. Individual concepts and relational predicates

The doctrine of the existence of the set of non-relational properties that individuate things is equivalent, on my interpretation, to a third thesis of Leibniz's about relations, which I shall now discuss. It could be called the mirror thesis. According to Leibniz, every individual 'expresses' or mirrors the whole universe from its point of view.[18] So long as there is more than one individual in a given universe, truths about any individual which we may describe by monadic predicate expressions (such as the truth about the properties of the perceptions of an individual or the desires he has) are inseparable from the relational properties that are true of the individual, e.g., that it is closer to *A* than *B* and so on. Relational properties and non-relational properties are thus intrinsically bound up with one another. That is why, as I pointed out in the last chapter, Leibniz believed that there is no concept which is 'so detached,' i.e., which is about a property which involves one object in total isolation. Every concept must involve relations and lead us from the subject to other things with which the subject is related.

It is widely believed that, in the period in which he wrote the *Discourse on Metaphysics* and his correspondence with Arnauld, Leibniz was a firm believer in the reducibility of relations. But what exactly is meant by reducibility of relations? When Leibniz wrote in these works that the concept of an individual substance included all the predicates which are true of the individual, the predicates were taken explicitly or implicitly to carry reference to all the other things in the world to which the individual belongs. This means that the predicates include those which ascribe relational properties to the individual. As he wrote in a letter to Arnauld:

> I say that the concept of an individual substance involves all its changes and all its relations, even those which are commonly called extrinsic, that is to say which pertain to it only by virtue of the general interconnection of things, and in so far as it expresses the whole universe in its own way.[19]

Leibniz's often quoted claim that the concept of an individual substance is

> sufficient for the understanding of it and for the deduction of all the predicates of which the substance is or may become the subject[20]

should not be taken to mean that an individual concept corresponds to a set of non-relational attributes from which one can derive all predicates, including relational ones, that are true of the individual. It is rather that, for any true predicate, including relational ones,

> the content of the subject must include that of the predicate in such a way that if one understands perfectly the concept of the subject, he will know that the predicate appertains to it.[21]

In other words, all true relational predicates of an individual can be drawn out of the individual concept because they are already a part of it, not because one can derive them from a set of predicates expressing only the intrinsic properties of the individual that make up the concept. As Leibniz claims:

> That each singular substance expresses the whole universe in its own way, and that in its concept are included all of the experiences belonging to it together with all of their circumstances and the entire sequence of exterior events.[22]

In the language of contemporary logic, every propositional function sign with one free variable, which could express a true proposition when a name of an individual is put in the variable place, corresponds to a predicate of the individual. Some of the predicates which have logical forms like xRa or $(\exists y)xRy$ are grammatically monadic predicates but ascribe relational properties to the subject, as we have seen in the last chapter. This is why it is extremely difficult to say of a *proposition* (which we must recall again is a complex concept or thought, for Leibniz, not a sentence), whether it is a relational one or not. A proposition of the form Rab can be seen as obtained from giving an argument to x in Rxb or giving the argument a and b in Rxy. But whether we treat the proposition as having one subject or two subjects, we can at least agree that the property ascribed to either one or two of the subjects holds only if a relational fact obtains, and in that sense the proposition can be said to be relational.

5. *Reducibility of relations*

This mirror thesis then is quite different from Rescher's claim quoted in §2 of the last chapter that for Leibniz any relational property inheres in predications about the substances, implying both the existence and the reducibility of relational properties. (We will later try to make clearer what is a relational property, which we have already introduced into our discussions in §2 of the last chapter; but very intuitively it is a property that can be ascribed to an individual in virtue of the individual's standing in a certain relation to another existent.) In support of his claim, Rescher refers in a footnote to the following passage from Leibniz:

> Thus I hold, as regards relations, that paternity in David is one thing and filiation in Solomon another, but the relation common to both is a mere mental thing, of which the modifications of singulars are the foundation.[23]

But neither paternity nor filiation is a non-relational property in any straightforward sense. Rescher comments in parenthesis that Leibniz would have rejoiced over recent discoveries in the field of genetic coding.[24] But, even if a child's genes are entirely determined by those of his parents, the child's having that particular set of genes is not what we mean by ascribing 'filiation' to him. We mean that he was born of a certain woman who conceived him by a certain man – which are all relational properties. It is true that by ascribing paternity to David we do not identify any child whose father David is – we are saying that there is a person *X* such that David is the father of *X*. But in the sense in which the property ascribed to the subject holds if, and only if, the subject stands in a certain relation to another object, the property is a relational one. That is to say, although a predicate like "is a father" can be treated as a monadic predicate, it conceals a bound variable, and its sense depends on there being a two-place predicate: ". . . is a father of . . ."[25] A sentence containing such a two-place predicate is true only when the two expressions which fill the blank places designate two people who stand in a particular relation to each other.

In his *Philosophy of Leibniz,* which contains much scholarly research and a very helpful set of translations of passages on relations from a whole variety of Leibniz's texts as well as philosophical arguments, Benson Mates also defends the view that "There are no purely extrinsic denominations" means the reducibility of relations. I will briefly add a few words to explain why I think he has not made his case. We have already seen that some monadic predicates which conceal a bound variable clearly express relational properties. Reduction of sentences containing relational predicates into sentences containing only monadic predicates therefore does not necessarily mean that reduction of relational properties to non-relational properties has been carried out. If Leibniz did not believe that one can achieve a complete description of a substance without referring to its relational properties, it is not easy to envisage how such a reduction could be conceived. In addition it seems to me that the most natural way of interpreting the claim that there are purely extrinsic denominations is to take Leibniz to be distinguishing extrinsic and intrinsic denominations, and saying that one cannot have the former kind of denomination without involving the latter kind. This point would be lost if one can be reduced to the other. If I say, for example, that there are no purely Doric temples, I am implying that every temple that has Doric features has some features that are not Doric, but something else, e.g., Corinthian. I certainly would not be implying that Doric features can be reduced to other features, or that in reality there are only non-Doric features, and that we merely imagine them to have Doric features.

We have already seen in the last chapter that Leibniz claimed that when we characterize an object, even when we do not explicitly refer to its relational property, we do so covertly. That substances stand in various relations to each other in our universe is neither a fantasy nor a fiction but an ineradicable fact. The totality of the truths about a substance cannot omit the truths of all such facts about it. In his talk about *entia rationis,* what Leibniz is contrasting the relational properties with are not non-relational properties but ideal entities called relations.

In support of his reading of Leibniz, as asserting the reducibility of relations, Mates refers, in the first paragraph of his chapter "Relations and denominations," to a passage where Leibniz is said to claim that relations considered as accidents of multiple substances are not real but *ideae imaginariae.*[26] The passage cited in full by Mates at the end of the chapter says:

> It is no wonder that the number of all numbers, or that of all possibilities, all reflexions or all relations, are not distinctly understood, for they are *ideae imaginariae,* nor does anything correspond to them in reality; so if there is a relation between A and B and this relation is called C, and a new relation between A and C is considered, called D, and so on, ad infinitum, it is clear that we would not

say that all these relations are true and real ideas. For those things only are intelligible which can be produced, that is, which have been produced or are being produced. (Grua p. 266)

Leibniz is not saying here that all relations are imaginary. As someone who denied the idea of infinite whole as a totality, he is saying that the number of *all* numbers, or the number of *all* relations, is not distinctly understood, since the idea of all numbers, as well as the idea of all relations, is an imaginary idea. A particular relation *D* which relates *A* and *B* is perfectly producible and hence intelligible. (D being a relation may be *ens rationis* but not *ens imaginarium.*) But if we were to claim that there is now also a relation between A and D, and a relation between D and B, such relations do not correspond to any additional facts that had been produced. This means that we cannot produce the totality of all relations, since we can still think of a relation between this supposed totality and any of its constituent relation, and again the totality of the relations including the newly constructed one, and so on ad infinitum. Thus we do not understand what the totality of all relations could be. Leibniz writes in many works about the unclearness of the idea of totality of all numbers. It seems clear that what makes the idea of all relations imaginary, and not have anything corresponding to it in reality, is the infinite totality involved, not its being of relations.

Therefore, although Mates is right, both in his claim that Leibniz uses the word 'relation' to mean different things in different passages, and that he also often denies that it has *the same kind of* reality as individual substances, Mates has not shown that Leibniz denied all reality or objective existence to relations. Leibniz often compares truths or even eternal truths to relations, as they are all, according to him equally *entia rationis,* i.e., entities dependent on the mind. Yet it goes without saying that Leibniz believes in the reality of truths. It is true that Mates explains that for him the results of reductions need not be logically equivalent to the propositions reduced (as Russell, Broad, and Rescher believed) nor need the resulting propositions involve only truth-functional connectives and operators: he does not make clear what reduction would then amount to.

Some have recently suggested that one can give a 'supervenience reading' of the reducibility thesis as a "textually plausible interpretation of Leibniz's thesis about relations." Supervenience can hardly be called an interpretation of Leibniz's view, because as we can see from the passage from an unpublished manuscript quoted in footnote 3 of Chapter VI, which I will cite here again, it is the very word that Leibniz himself uses to explain the conceptual link of relations and the subjects related by them.

> Relation is an accident which is in multiple subjects; it is what results without any change made in the subjects but supervenes from them.

What did Leibniz mean by 'supervenience'? Did he mean what philosophers now understand by the word? We think that the concept of supervenience used by contemporary philosophers has its origin in Richard Hare's use of the word to discuss G. E. Moore's view of moral concepts. (The good and other ethical values are, according to Moore, intrinsic values of things that are neither natural properties nor subjective responses. They cannot be reduced to the natural properties of things but nevertheless supervene on them, in the sense that no change in the intrinsic values of acts or persons can come about without a change in the natural properties of the acts and persons.) There seems, however, to have been a quite long tradition of using *'supervenire'* to express a very similar concept. In the mediaeval Latin translation of Aristotle's *Nichomachean Ethics, 'supervenit'* is used to express such a concept. In book 10, Chapter 4, 1174B31, Aristotle wrote that pleasure perfects an activity not as a fixed disposition does, by being already present in the agent, but as a supervening perfection, like the bloom of vigour in youth. The word *'epigignómenon'* was translated *'superveniens,'* using a word that normally meant coming on top of, or in addition to. Now, presumably one can have pleasure without carrying out the particular activity in question. But can one have the same pleasure without carrying out the same activity? And how is it the other way around? Could one have carried out that very activity without having that pleasure? The same question must be raised about Leibniz's use of '*supervenit*'.

First we see from the quoted passage that Leibniz is not saying that a relational property of an individual thing supervenes on a non-relational property of the same individual. It is therefore not quite like the bloom of vigour that a person has which is said to supervene on his youth, or the pleasure that a person feels which is said to supervene on his carrying out an activity such as that of playing the violin. It is the relational property holding between several things that supervenes on facts about each of them. It supervenes on a truth about the multiple things if you think of them together. In another article, "On accidents," Leibniz seems to be again propounding a supervenient notion of relation and writes:

> Indeed since a relation results from a state of things, it never comes into being or is removed unless some change is made in its basis *[fundamento]*.

Although here he is not making very clear whether we have to think of a multiple of things together rather than of one thing, it seems that the basis on which the relation supervenes is the state of the related things, considered together. It is therefore not like a set of macroscopic properties of an individual supervening on a set of microscopic properties of the same individual. If paternity is "an accident called relation," i.e., a relational property, not only can it not be reduced to a mode or state (e.g., having the DNA structure) of a single individual who is the father, paternity does not supervene on such a mode or a state of an individual. It supervenes on the states of two separate individuals, the father and a child which we consider together, *and* as we have seen in §7 of the previous chapter, we see that the truth about a state of one entails the truth about a state of the other.

6. *Reification of relations*

This brings me to the fourth Leibnizian thesis about attributes and relations, which I will call the nominalist thesis. It is the thesis that our notion of relation is an abstraction from relational facts concerning things or the order and connection of things (just as our notion of colour is an abstraction from coloured things). Relations are abstract entities made by abstraction. The nominalist thesis is a thesis about the difference between relational facts or properties on the one hand and relations as entities created by reification on the other. It is *not* a thesis concerning the distinction between relational properties and non-relational ones.

Leibniz argues his case in some detail with reference to the notion of place. How do we refer to and individuate places? According to Leibniz:

> They consider that many things exist at once and observe in them a certain order of coexistence. . . . When it happens that one of the coexistent things changes its relation to a multitude of others which do not change their relation among themselves: and that one thing, newly come, acquires the same relation to others as the former had; we then say it is come into the place of the former.[27]

Thus the concept of place or a particular spatial position, and in general any concept of relation, is obtained by abstraction from consideration of things having certain relations to each other. When one refers to a relation, one is referring to an abstract entity – to what Leibniz calls *ens rationis*. By talking of these 'entities of reason' (ideal entities), one is not necessarily talking of fictitious objects like centaurs or abitrarily constructed objects, or imaginary objects like the number of all numbers.

> Although relations are of the understanding they are not groundless or unreal. For the divine understanding is the origin of things and even the reality of all things, simple substances expected, consists in the

fact that perception of phenomena is founded on simple substances.[28]

Leibniz even writes that he would prefer to call impossible fictitious objects (as distinct from proper ideal entities) *êtres de raison non raisonnante.* [29] But although relations are not fictitious, they are mental constructions all the same and can be given a contextual definition; sentences referring to them can be reduced to sentences in which individual constants only refer to substances.

What really exist as basic constituents of the world are individual substances for Leibniz. In the objective world we perceive, i.e., in the world of *phenomena bene fundata,* we identify and refer to corporeal substances; i.e., individual things that we learn to identify and re-identify in the spatial-temporal world. All other things we refer to when talking of the world, whether relations or qualities, are only entities made by our abstraction from the fact that things or the phenomena we perceive have these properties. According to Leibniz, the nominalists (following Ockham) have "deduced the rule that everything in the world can be explained without any reference to universals and real forms." Leibniz agrees that "nothing is truer than this opinion," and from very early on to the end of his career he did not change his position. "For concrete things are really things; abstractions are not things but modes of things. Modes are usually nothing but the relation of a thing to the understanding"[30] (1670) and again: "Every accident is a kind of abstraction; only substance is concrete"[31] (1712). Thus, when we refer to relations, as when, according to Leibniz, we refer to places or to ratios, we are referring to *entia rationis.* (He thought that 'numbers, unities, fractions' also depended on the mind for their existence and thus had "the nature of relations (1706)."[32] This holds of every relation, and not only of certain relations which have been arbitrarily determined by human thought.[33] For although Leibniz distinguished between relations which held between things because of the regularity of nature and relations which come about by convention or agreement, like that which holds between an army commander and his men, it is not this conventional feature which he is talking about when he repeatedly asserts that relations are beings of reason. He seems rather to be saying that, although we can quantify over or refer to relations, what we are referring to are not entities which are the basic constituents of the world in the manner that individual substances are.[34]

But as I have said before, in subscribing to this nominalist thesis, Leibniz is *not* casting any doubt on the reality or irreducibility of relational facts or relational properties in general. As I have mentioned in Chapter III, in one article Leibniz tries to list the most basic concepts from which all other concepts can be defined. Among these concepts, which are for him not further analysable and thus relatively the most basic, occur 'act on,' 'acted on,' 'successor,' 'prior,' 'posterior.'[35]

We have seen in the previous sections that propositions in which the subject is a relation can be reduced to a set of propositions in which relational predicates are ascribed to individuals. We now see that propositions in which relational predicates occur cannot always be reduced to propositions in which no such predicates occur. For, although relational properties are not things which exist over and above substances, they are real. Their reality consists in the modification of individual substances *and in the harmony or agreement between them.*

Before I leave the Nominalist Thesis, let me refer to the rather muddled passage in Leibniz's letter to Clarke,[36] which I briefly mentioned before and which is quoted by most who have ascribed the reductionist thesis to Leibniz.[37]

> The ratio or proportion between two lines *L* and *M* may be conceived in three different ways: as a ratio of the greater *L* to the lesser *M;* as a ratio of the lesser *M* to the greater *L;* and lastly as something abstracted from both, that is, as the ratio between *L* and *M,* without considering which is the antecedent, or which the consequent; which the subject,

> and which the object. . . . In the first way of considering them, *L* the greater, in the second, *M* the lesser, is the subject of that accident which philosophers call relation. But, which of them will be the subject in the third way of considering them? It cannot be said that both of them, *L* and *M*, are the subject of such an accident; for if so, we should have an accident in two subjects, with one leg in one, and the other in the other; which is contrary to the notion of accidents. Therefore, we must say, that this relation, in this third way of considering it, is indeed out of the subjects; but being neither a substance, nor an accident, it must be a mere ideal thing, the consideration of which is nevertheless useful.

Leibniz does not here make clear why there is something contradictory about accidents having two subjects. He himself often defines relations as accidents in multiple subjects, as we have just seen in the previous section. According to Leibniz, an accident is something real which none-the-less has no existence apart from the substance in which it inheres. But as the notion of 'inherence' is not a spatial one for Leibniz and since "*f* inheres in *a*" merely means that the concept of *f* is a part of the notion of the subject *a*,[38] there is no reason why an accident should not inhere in two subjects – that is, there is no reason why it should not concern two substances. (As a matter of fact, some of his theories implicitly presuppose the notion of many-place predicates.) But his main message is clear. He believes that there is no difficulty about ascribing the sort of "accident which philosophers called relation" or relational properties to individual subjects. We can say of *M*, for example, that it lies between *L* and something else, and so on. What is an ideal thing is a certain ratio which we find holding between *M* and *L* and which we consider as an abstract object *M/L* but which we might find holding between many other different lines or magnitudes. It is not the relational property which a particular line has which is ideal.

As Russell pointed out, and as Leibniz seems to have perceived in a confused way, there is of course a special difficulty about treating what is expressed by a propositional function with more than two free variables as an accident with two or more subjects. For if the relation is an asymmetrical one, then the direction of the relation becomes relevant. The order in which one considers the different subjects vis-à-vis the relation matters. And that is why relational propositions have special kinds of entailment which a logic based entirely on the analysis of propositions into a subject and a monadic predicate cannot cope with.

7. *Ideality of space and time*

Leibniz strongly denied the Newtonian concept of absolute space and time and tried, in his last years, to explain the philosophical basis of his contention in a series of letters to Clarke, a follower of Newton. It has often been maintained that, since Leibniz thought that space and time were nothing but the order and relation of things, his theory of the ideality of space and time implies his denial of the reality of relations.

But to deny that spatial and temporal positions exist in their own right, and to go on to deny an absolute space and time which are made up of a totality of such points, is *not,* we should insist, to deny the reality of spatial or temporal facts. Surely nobody thinks that Leibniz denied that events succeed one another, that processes have certain durations, or that the world we perceive is a spatial one in which things co-exist. Leibniz writes:

> . . . time is no more nor less an ideal thing *(ens rationis)* than space is. To co-exist and to pre-exist is something real; though these should not be, I confess, as real as substances or matter are, as is widely assumed.[39]

Russell criticised Leibniz because he believed that things being in certain places presuppose the existence per se of space; but this is exactly what Leibniz considered a conceptual confusion. As we have already seen in the previous section of this chapter, according to Leibniz we only individuate places as the points of reference for things which stand in a "certain order of coexistence." Leibniz proceeds:[40]

> And that which comprehends all these places is called space, which shows, that in order to have an idea of place and consequently of space, it is sufficient to consider these relations and the rules of the changes without needing to fancy any absolute reality outside the things whose situation we consider.

If we specify a spot on the mountain by the location of a tree, we pick out a position with its own identity by reference to the tree. The spot, in turn, is a particular point on the earth, of a certain latitude and longitude, so many feet from the summit, and so on. The earth, again, can be located relative to the sun. But the relation of, say, the sun to its place in so-called absolute space is not like that of the tree to the place on the mountain. We can specify the position of a moving body against a set of material bodies which provides the inertial frame, but we can never provide the criteria of identity of places and instants which are not relative to some framework. Thus, as Leibniz replies to Clarke, the hypothesis that God might have created the universe sooner, or that he could push the finite material universe, just as it is, in a straight line in an infinite universe, is "a chimerical supposition."[41]

Leibniz is not saying that it is an uncheckable hypothesis which it is a waste of time to make. Neither is he arguing about whether we could ever come to know such an act or not. He is saying that it is not properly speaking a hypothesis at all because we have failed to describe an action. If we have no criteria for distinguishing the state of affairs which existed before God was supposed to have acted, from the state of affairs which resulted after his action, then we have not specified any act. Thus by making such a hypothesis, a man "would say nothing that is intelligible. For there is no mark or difference whereby it would be *possible* to know that the world was created sooner."[42] It would be in Leibniz's words *"agendo nihil agere"* (acting without doing anything) because of the indiscernibility and therefore according to him, not a useless fiction, but an *'impossible'*[43] one.

According to Russell, Leibniz's claim that space is ideal and based on the relation of perceived objects conflicts with Leibniz's contention that each monad has, as it were, its own point of view. Russell seems to think that different points of view can only be explained in terms of monads being situated *in space* in different places. This is surely a hangover from the Newtonian picture of absolute space containing things in the universe. Russell thinks it follows that Leibniz must be implicitly assuming an objective space in which monads exist prior to the phenomenal and subjective space of each monad's perception. But is this so? That monads exist prior to phenomenal and ideal space, which is nothing but the relation of perceived objects, is true. It does not follow from this that one can say of monads that they exist *in* space. Leibniz's view was that one cannot raise questions about space unless one is talking about phenomenal objects, i.e., things that are individuated by perceptible properties. Whatever is in space is infinitely divisible.[44] Space is the order of coexistent phenomena.

It is easy to see the point of Leibniz's scepticism. Time and space have no quality of their own which enables one to distinguish one part from any other part, and yet it is claimed that they are infinitely immense and exist eternally. But if no part of time and space has any qualities of its own, what are *they* which exist eternally and which are infinitely immense? To say of things that they are 'in space' *is* to say that things which we perceive stand in a certain spatial relation to one another, and nothing more. Only in his later life when he talks of the mind as the dominant monad of a corporeal substance to des Bosses, can the monad be said to be where the body is. To think that a thing's being 'in space' is like being 'in the sea,' and that it implies the existence of an independent 'container' in which the thing finds itself, is to mistake the logical grammar of "is in space."

For Leibniz then, not only is it meaningless to assume, as Russell was to do, that things being in certain places presuppose the existence per se of space, but it is also contradictory to do so. The existence of space means nothing more than things being in certain places, and the possibility of their being in other places relative to each other. If space was another entity, one could ask of it, "Where is it?" Is it 'in space' as well? It does not follow, as Russell believed, that for Leibniz "the identity implied in speaking of the *same place* is an illusion."[45] It is no more of an illusion than the referrent of "the same place on Earth" which is a relative specification.

It is also important to remind ourselves that by denying the absolute reality of space and time, Leibniz was not propounding a subjectivist view of space and time, if by this one understands a view which claims that spatial and temporal relations are nothing but the relation of events as reflected in each person's mind. Objects of perception are, according to Leibniz, *phenomena bene fundata,* that is to say, phenomena which are objectively founded on the existence of individual substances. Leibniz clearly distinguished, as Kant was to do, between perceptions and the objects of perception. The order and relation of the objects of perception, which are objective, is distinct from the order of the perceptions, which is subjective. Leibniz writes in the *New Essays*[46] against Locke:

> A succession of perceptions arouses the idea of duration in us, but it does not make it. Our perceptions never have a succession sufficiently constant and regular to correspond to that of time, which is a continuum uniform and simple, like a straight line. Changes in our perceptions prompt us to think of time, and we measure it by uniform changes. But even if nothing in nature were uniform, time could still be determined.

As I have already mentioned, Leibniz strongly believed in the relativity of time and space, which distinguished his views from those that Kant was to hold later. But Leibniz never meant by this that the identity of time and space depends on each particular person's experience of ideas. Again, in the *New Essays* Leibniz refutes Philonous, the imaginary Locke who claims that the ideas of determinate length, such as an inch or a foot, are created in men's minds. Leibniz retorts that you cannot have such notions without a standard measure based on a physical object in the world which you assume not to change in size.[47]

> . . . it is impossible to have the idea of a precisely determined length. You can neither say nor understand by the mind what an inch or a foot is. And you can preserve the meaning of these terms only by real measures, which you suppose unchanging.

He goes on to give examples of what may be used as standards, such as the pyramids, pendulums of certain lengths, the revolution of the fixed stars.

It is clear, then, that by opposing the Newtonian concept of absolute time and space, Leibniz was never claiming that time and space were subjective in the sense of being illusory or personal. Neither was he merely making an epistemological or psychological claim about whether we can make correct judgments about space and time. His claim concerned what the criterion of identity of spatial or temporal position, distance, or duration is, and can only be.

It is quite wrong to think that Leibniz's notions about the ideality of space and time and the ideality of relations are entailed by Leibniz's subject-predicate logic. Russell writes that, if space is admitted to exist per se while the doctrine of substance is retained, then "there will be a relation between the substances and the spaces they occupy. But this relation will be *sui generis*. It will not be a relation of subject and predicate, since each term of the relation exists and may continue to exist though the relation be changed."[48] Russell claims here that it is only because Leibniz was a careful philosopher and carried through to the end the consequences of his subject-predicate logic that he was brought to deny the reality of relations in general, and of space and time in particular.

I find this view unconvincing. Leibniz did not deny that substances were connected to other substances in various ways which changed or that aggregates of substances stood in many altering relations to each other. He did not think that he had to deny this because of subject-predicate logic. The concept of an individual could include all the changing relations it had to every other object in the world throughout its existence. Similarly, *if* every spatio-temporal position were an individual in its own right, with discernible properties, then a concept for each spatio-temporal point would include all the changing relations it had to all things which at different times occupied it, approached it, or remained at a distance from it.

This is impossible because spatio-temporal points have no discernible features of their own, and are only *entia rationis* whose identity depends entirely on the relative position of things.

There are many more important philosophical issues concerning space and time raised by Leibniz. An interesting discussion of Leibnizian concepts of space and time and physics can be found in John Earman's "Was Leibniz a Relationalist?" (1979.) I have discussed only those related to his philosophy of logic and language.

8. Causal relations and the pre-established harmony

It is now important to consider Leibniz's view of what we normally consider to be causal properties of objects, since Leibniz is often believed to have been a metaphysician who denied causal interaction. His claim in the *Discourse of Metaphysics* that each substance "is like a world apart, independent of everything but God,"[49] and his claim that "monads have no windows" have led some to believe that Leibniz's vision of the world was unscientific – that is, a vision in which nothing causally affects or is affected by anything else. This is thought, moreover, to be linked to Leibniz's view about subject-predicate propositions. We have already seen that there is nothing in Leibniz's philosophy which implies that the complete truth about a substance is describable by predicates which carry no reference to other things. Far from denying what is commonly called causal relations, Leibniz asked, "Who would deny that a substance is modified by the effect of another substance, for example, when a body is thrown back by an opposing obstacle?"[50] He also asserted, "Nature must be explained mechanically and mathematically, provided one bears in mind that the principles of the laws of mechanics themselves do not derive from mere mathematical extension, but from metaphysical reasons."[51]

As is clear from many fragments, Leibniz's denial of the philosophical doctrine of causal interaction was raised first as a reaction against causal views about the mind-body problem. He writes that the popular philosophy of causal influence assumes "material particles which can pass from one of these substances to another" and it is *this* notion which he thinks must be abandoned[52] – for explaining the relation not only of the mind and body but of any two things. Things do affect each other, but not by further things going out of one and going into another. If *a* affects *b,* it is not as if there are windows in *a* and *b* through which further things *c* and *d* go in and out. (Such model would never provide an explanation, since we would always have to enquire further why *c* goes out of *a* and into *b* when *a* and *b* are in contact, which would involve a causal influence between *a* and *c* and *b* and so on ad infinitum.)

Leibniz's solution is the hypothesis of the pre-established harmony, i.e., that the nature of *a* and *b* is such that, following the laws of nature, the change in one does correspond to change in the other. This according to him "removes any notion of miracles from purely natural actions, and makes things run their course regulated in an intelligible manner; whereas the common system has recourse to absolutely inexplicable influences."[53] To say that every change in an object can be explained from its nature and natural laws of the world is *not* to say that things behave as if they were not connected to other things. Everything *is* like a mirror which reflects the whole universe. He describes the relation between himself and some other object which he affects as follows: "My earlier state of existence contains the ground for the existence of the later. And since, because of the connection of all things, the earlier state in me contains also the earlier state of the thing, it also contains the ground of the later state of the other thing."[54] What we normally call a causal relation is not a necessary link which exists above and apart from the things which stand in such a relation. On this point Leibniz's view partially resembles that which Hume was to put forward half a century later. What we call causation consists precisely in the regular correspondence between certain changes in things of kind – with certain changes, say, of kind – in other things. We cannot hope to observe necessary connections in nature apart from constant conjunctions. Hume and Leibniz, however, drew opposite conclusions from this.

Leibniz believed that the necessity of such laws of nature resided in the nature of each individual substance. For example, it is in the nature of every piece of iron that it will be drawn to a magnet. The constitution which makes the iron stick to the magnet is already in the iron. And thus if we know the laws of nature (in this case laws involving certain structures of ferrous metals and magnetic fields) we can *deduce* what will happen to the piece of iron in the vicinity of the magnet. That is why Leibniz believed in the Principle of Sufficient Reason, which he formulates as ". . . all truths – even the most contingent – have an *a priori* proof, or some reasons why they are truths rather than not. And this is just what is meant when it is commonly said that nothing happens without a cause, or that there is nothing without a reason."[55] It is evident that the contingent truths can be given an a priori proof *only* on the basis of accepting certain laws of nature (as already given by God). These are based for Leibniz on God's choice for the best, which we are not competent to calculate, even though we may understand the general principle involved in maximizing the number of essences realised. But what is logically important is that contingent truths can be given an a priori or deductive proof *once* we accept certain laws of nature.

These laws of nature determine how each individual thing behaves in various situations. Each individual thing is a thing of a certain kind, for example a particular metal or a particular shape. And all these facts determine the nature of the individual, including how it acts or reacts in correspondence with other objects, given any actual situation. But to say this is *not* to deny that what we *normally* call causal interaction takes place. One of the basic features of the universe for Leibniz was "this *connection*, or this adaptation of all created things to each and of each to all,"[56] or

> the fact that God has . . . created the soul or any other unity in such a way that everything arises in it from its own internal nature through a perfect spontaneity relative to itself, and yet with perfect conformity to external things.[57]

9. Logical possibility of solipsism

Side by side with this strong belief in the interconnection of multiple substances, we find a conflicting belief held by Leibniz in the logical possibility of there being only God and one created mind. In his letter to Arnauld, immediately after writing the passage quoted earlier about an individual concept including relational properties, Leibniz goes on to make the often quoted claim that every state of a monad follows from its own preceding state "as if there were nothing but God and itself in the world." In my view this is a strange inconsistency. It contradicts Leibniz's previous assertion and is incompatible with his basic position. For if the set of predicates which makes up the description of an individual concept includes relational predicates or somehow expresses relational properties, then these predicates would not be true of that individual in a universe in which there were nothing except that individual substance and God (and hence the set would not give the concept of the individual).

Even the perceptual states of an individual substance which succeed one another, the description of which might seem to be possible without reference to anything else, are not logically independent of the truths about the existence of other substances. To say of a substance that it perceives or mirrors or represents another object presupposes that the monad stands in a certain connection to the other object:

> One expresses another, in my use of the terms when there is a constant and regulated relation between what can be said of the one and of the other.[58]

Perception, intellectual knowledge, animal feeling are all, Leibniz says, species of expressions or representations. Therefore to say of a substance that it perceives the universe from its point of view is to say that there is a regulated relation between what can be said of that substance and what can be said of all the other objects in the universe.[59] Thus one would be ascribing a perceptual state to an individual monad falsely if there were nothing else in the universe for the monad to perceive. God may be able to make a monad believe falsely that it perceives what it does not, but even God cannot make the monad perceive or have *perceptual* states if there is nothing else in the universe. What the monad was doing would not, by definition, be perceiving.[60] "It is certainly true that the perceptions and expressions of all substances intercorrespond so that each one, following with care the established reasons or laws which it has observed, meet with others who have done this also."[61]

Leibniz, then, was in any case clearly being inconsistent when he wrote that the succeeding states of individual substances follow each other "as if there were nothing in the universe but God and itself." It is incompatible with *any* standard interpretation of his mirror thesis, and not merely with my interpretation. Indeed, as Leibniz goes on almost immediately to say in the letter to Arnauld, he wanted to maintain that this independence, as he calls it, of substances "does not lessen the interconnection (commerce) between the substances." So long as substances are individuated by their perceptual states, as Leibniz claims that they are, it is a logical truth that they are connected to each other in a definite way. This is the other side of the truth, rightly pointed out by Benson Mates, that in Leibniz's system an individual concept can be instantiated only in one world.[62] As Leibniz says "this mutual connection or accommodation of all created things to each other and of each to all the rest causes each simple substance to have relations which express all the others and consequently to be a perpetual living mirror of the universe."[63] This is what I earlier called the mirror thesis.

Leibniz's idea of the possibility of there being only God and oneself, which conflicts with the mirror thesis but which keeps on intervening in his discussions on monads, is not an alternative metaphysical position at which he arrived by weighing other logical possibilities. He claims to have got the idea from Saint Theresa of Avila,[64] and it seems to come rather from his mystical leanings in religion.

Understandably, Leibniz tried to give a plausible philosophical account of this idea as well. He says for example that a mind would continue to carry out the same kind of mental activity even if everything else apart from God and itself were to cease to exist "because it can contemplate [its] ideas of possible things."[65] This may be an argument for the way in which a mind can continue to be active but scarcely one for how a mind can continue to perceive. To contemplate ideas of possible things is to think how things could be otherwise, and is hardly a kind of perception.

Leibniz asserted against the occasionalists that, although men owe their origin to God, they do not need God's intervention in order to perceive material objects. Our mind is such that with its own power it perceives the world around it.[66] But to say that a mind perceives because of its own power and nature is not to say that perceiving is nothing but thinking. If the correspondence or connection with objects external to it were not an essential property of perception, many of Leibniz's most interesting theories about perception would become inconsistent.

For example, Leibniz claimed against Locke and the Cartesians that 'awareness' was not an essential feature of perception. We can have perceptions without being aware of the fact, and yet we can realise that they have left traces in our minds. Sounds that we hear but of which we take no notice when our mind is focused on something else, things we hear while we sleep, are examples. Leibniz believes that perceptions of which we are aware are only a subset of perceptions, and he calls the former 'apperceptions.'[67] But if perceptions were the kind of thing that a mind could have even if there were nothing in the universe apart from God and it, would any distinction between perception and apperception be possible? How could we have unconscious perceptions in a world in which there were no external objects? Could we perhaps unconsciously perceive our own sensations, desires, or thoughts? What is the difference between unconsciously perceiving one's own desires and merely having such desires without being aware that one has them? There are many difficulties involved in maintaining Leibniz's theory of unconscious perception in a solipsistic world.

It seems, therefore, that the notion of a plurality of substances co-existing with a certain interconnection and order amongst them is a central part of Leibniz's philosophy. Similarly, our basic concepts include relational ones, and we cannot exclude relational terms from "the alphabet of human thinking."

VIII. Hypothetical truths

All hypothetical propositions assert what would be or would not be, if some fact or its contrary were posited. (Letter to Foucher, 1675.)[1]

1. Conditional assertion of the consequent

Throughout his life Leibniz was interested in what he called hypothetical truths or truths that were expressed by conditional propositions. As his concern did not seem to be shared by his philosophical contemporaries (nor for that matter by many philosophers who wrote after him), he did not work out his thoughts as thoroughly as in areas where he was able to make long critical studies of the views of other philosophers (as for example, on essence, on definitions, on innate ideas, on the mind-body problem, on causal interaction) or where he entered into philosophical exchanges and debates with other important thinkers (as on matter, force, space and time, freedom and necessity, and as we have seen, on the infinitesimals). Nevertheless some of his thoughts on conditional propositions embody insights that were only rediscovered and articulated by twentieth-century thinkers such as Frank Ramsey[2] and von Wright.[3]

Truths whose realizations depend on the obtaining of specific premises were among the topics that exercised Leibniz's thoughts since very early on. His interest in this

This chapter was published in *Leibniz: Critical and Interpretative Essays* edited by Michael Hooker, copyright © 1982 by the University of Minnesota Press. It developed from a paper given in French, in a conference of the 200th anniversary of Leibniz, organized by the Leibniz Gesellschaft of Hannover, held in Chantilly near Paris. I profited from comments by Jonathan Bennett and Hugh Mellor in preparing the original paper. In writing this version I profited from discussions with David Wiggins and Hans Kamp.

subject was first aroused when he was a young law student. Many rights that people have under the law are not absolute rights but conditional rights. For example, a person has a right to the family estate if his father dies; a person has a right to change his name so long as it does not lead to misappropriation. A man's liabilities may be conditional also. An insurer may be liable to pay a certain amount if a building burns down. This liability is something objective, not a subjective belief. If anyone buys his business, it is worth that much less.

When Leibniz was nineteen, he wrote a baccalaureate dissertation called *De conditionibus* (On conditions). Leibniz explains that his aim is to clarify what is asserted by hypothetical propositions in law. He wrote two papers on the subject. He incorporated these into a more substantial paper *Specimina Juris (Samples of Law),* which he finished in 1669 when he was twenty-three.[4] In these papers, as we shall see later in more detail, his algorithmic talents are used to work out a numerical computation of the likelihood of the truth of the consequent of conditional propositions given in the form: "If one of the ships returns from Asia, I shall give you 100 (thalers)."

Because Leibniz was prompted to his investigation of the logic of conditionals by his interest in conditional rights, he was able to treat the subject in a fresh way. The stoic and the mediaeval logicians who discussed conditionals, such as Abelard and Peter of Spain, understood conditional statements as assertions of necessary connection between propositions.[5] Peter of Spain had written that all conditional truths were necessary. The necessity was assumed to come from the nature of the antecedent and consequent. In law, on the other hand, hardly ever does any logical or necessary relation of meaning exist between conditions and the rights they qualify. If we think of Leibniz's example given above, no one would be tempted to think that there is any logical relation, or meaning relation between the propositions "One of the ships returns from Asia" and "I give you 100 thalers." Thus Leibniz was able to see that what was in question was a particular kind of link between the truth of one proposition and the truth of another. He was also able to see the assertion of a conditional not as the assertion of the existence of the link, but as a conditional assertion of the consequent. The assertion *indicates* but does not itself assert the link.

Three years later Leibniz went to Paris where he was to remain for four years. (He wrote that he hardly knew mathematics when he arrived, and had read Euclid as one would read history. But he invented the differential calculus during his stay.) He was exposed to the theories of games of chance that were then being developed by Pascal, Huygens, and Bernouilli, and he became interested in determining the degree of probability of a conjecture relative to given data.[6] The problem was to estimate the degree of objective likelihood or probability of a conjecture, relative to a set of evidence and a body of beliefs. It is easy to see that this is a natural development of his attempt to work out the logic of hypothetical truths in law.

Leibniz also began to link his interest in hypothetical truths with his philosophical interest in the nature of things, and in essences. This is revealed most clearly in his letter to Foucher written in 1675, some passages of which we will examine later. In fact Leibniz's early interest in conditionals ties in with the central areas of his philosophical interest – the nature of things, essence, and modality, as well as with probability.

The view Leibniz expressed in his very early papers on conditionals were original and still seem so. The idea that the assertion of a conditional proposition is an expression of a conditional truth, or a conditional asserting of the consequent, is not only different from the view that the conditional expresses a special kind of link between two asserted propositions; it also diverges from what Frege claimed at the end of the nineteenth century, that when one asserts a conditional proposition, one is affirming *neither* the antecedent *nor* the consequent. For Frege, the status of the antecedent and the consequent of a conditional is the same so far as their illocutionary force is concerned.[7] Neither proposition occurs assertively.

Leibniz too believed that the antecedent and consequent have force only as constituents of the whole conditional. Each is a *"propositio partialis"* (non-independent proposition). For Leibniz, however, the illocutionary status of the antecedent and consequent are quite different. The antecedent, which he calls the condition *(conditio),* is not affirmed – it is dangling *(in modo non indicativo sed conjunctivo)* – whereas the consequent, which he calls the conditioned *(conditionatum),* is asserted *(in modo directo seu indicativo).* What is Leibniz's point here? Suppose I assert, "If the child will have no brothers, she will inherit the throne." Surely I am not asserting that the child will inherit the throne. So what is gained by saying that the proposition, "The child will inherit the throne" is given in a direct or indicative mode? Although I am not making an unqualified assertion of this fact, Leibniz holds that I am making a conditional assertion of it. I am asserting that the child will inherit the throne on the condition that she will have no brothers. This is a qualified assertion of the consequent. The role that the antecedent is playing is quite different. I am not asserting in any manner whatsoever, qualified or unqualified, that the child will have no brothers. This is even clearer when I assert, "If I can find absolutely no one else with any competence, I will employ you." Not only am I not asserting that I will not be able to find anyone with the competence, I insert this antecedent because I think it so likely that the opposite is true.

Just as a judge giving a suspended sentence can be described as giving a sentence in a certain qualified manner (i.e., on the condition of the convicted one's failing to behave in a certain manner during a specific period of time), so I can say of my previous assertion that I was asserting in a certain qualified manner that the child will inherit the throne. (I have been told by Professor Stig Kanger and Professor Ingmar Pörn that in Swedish and

Finnish the word for suspended sentence in law literally means 'conditional sentence'.) Leibniz also refers to the consequent as "the principal" *(Principale)* and to the antecedent as "the accessory" *(Accessorium)*.

A conditional proposition is not considered by Leibniz primarily as a complex proposition or a complex of propositions as contrasted with a simple proposition. He contrasted a conditional proposition with a pure proposition. In other words, it is a conditional assertion of the consequent, as opposed to a pure unqualified assertion of the consequent. We might say that we are committing ourselves to the consequent only if the antecedent obtains. As Leibniz writes to Foucher, "All hypothetical propositions assert what will be or will not be, given that some fact or its contrary holds."

Leibniz realizes that in making a conditional assertion of the consequent one is also indicating a certain specific connection between the truth of the antecedent and the consequent. Leibniz calls this a conditionality *(conditionalitas)*. It is a link *(junctura)*, which is as it were the form of the inference we make. The antecedent and consequent can be considered as the truths that are linked.

This link can be expressed either as an inference *(illatio)*, which is the move from the truth of the antecedent to the truth of the consequent, or as a suspension *(suspensio)*. Suspension (contrary to our philosophical expectation, as well as to the literary meaning) is not any suspending at all, but the move from the falsity of the consequent to the falsity of the antecedent. In fact it is *modus tollens*. (I had originally expected it to mean a move from the falsity of the antecedent to the suspension of the consequent. We will soon see that Leibniz's logic of conditionals does include such a rule, but what he says about *suspensio* cannot be read in this way.)

Leibniz somewhat misleadingly says at one point that the relationship of conditionality between antecedent and consequent is that of a necessary connection. It is clear from his examples that he is talking about the connection of their truth-values. That is to say, given the facts about the world and about our legal institutions, a necessary connection exists between the truth-value of the antecedent and of the consequent.

Three questions now arise about Leibniz's view on conditionals.

1. What happens when the antecedent is false (and when we do not know whether the consequent is false)?

2. If the chief point of treating an assertion of a conditional proposition as a conditional assertion of the consequent was to enable one to estimate the likelihood or the probability of the truth of the consequent, can one still talk of the truth of the conditional proposition itself?

3. If conditional propositions can be said to be true or false, where do their truth-values come from? Are there objective grounds for their truth-values?

Let us begin with 1. In considering what happens when the antecedent is false, we must examine (a) what happens in this case to the acceptability of the conditional itself, and (b) what happens to the truth of the consequent. (a) The falsity of an antecedent is, in general, compatible with the acceptability of the conditional. The conditional link does not depend on the obtaining in the world of the state of affairs expressed by the antecedent. The fourth theorem of Leibniz's *Specimina* is "An antecedent does not posit anything." The fact that a proposition occurs as an antecedent of a conditional does not entail its truth, or the truth of anything else, including that of the consequent. Thus the falsity of the antecedent does not by itself undermine the conditional link. Nor by itself does it render acceptable the conditional, as a false antecedent of a material implication would. The hypothetical truth "If the fleet returns from Asia, Titius will have 100 thalers" will not become false just because the fleet does not return. Neither will the conditional link be confirmed by the non-return of the ships. Thus the contingent falsity of an antecedent will never affect the truth or falsity of the hypothetical truth, or the acceptability or unacceptability of the conditional link. When the antecedent is an impossibility, or a contradictory proposition, the condition never obtains, and the conditional assertion of a truth becomes empty. Similarly the assertion of a right, conditional on the obtaining of an impossible situation, does not amount to any assertion of a right. In this case we can ignore the whole conditional. As Leibniz writes, "An impossible condition has no effect on rights." Nor need the antecedent be logically impossible but merely physically so. Thus if I say, "If your mother remarries, I will give you the house," when your mother is already dead, it is as if I have made no undertaking of any kind. If the antecedent is a logical impossibility, no state of affairs corresponds to it in any possible world (to use the formulation of his later years). So there could be no link between the proposition and any other proposition. In other words, if *p* corresponds to a logical impossibility, a conditional of the form "If *p* then *q*" does not say anything that could obtain. This relates to the seemingly controversial view that Leibniz expressed later when he wrote, "A non-being has no properties," a thesis which we will examine in Chapter IX §2. He meant that all propositions of the form, "If anything is *f* then it is *g*" are false if *f* is an impossibility (a *non-ens*). Suppose that in "If *a* is *f*, then *a* is *g*," *f* is an impossible property. Then the antecedent of this hypothetical is a logically impossible proposition that can have no link with any other proposition. In other words, it could not be the case that "*a* is *g*" is true only on the condition that "*a* is *f*" is true, if the latter is impossible. As Leibniz equates 'false' with 'not true,' this means it is false that "If *a* is *f*, then *a* is *g*."

(b) How is the truth-value of the consequent affected when the antecedent is false? As we have seen, if the antecedent is a logical impossibility, it is as if no conditional assertion has been made at all. So we need not even consider the consequent. If the antecedent is contingently false, that by itself does not affect the truth-value of the consequent. Suppose, for example, that the conditional truth "If the metal in the box is gold, it is malleable" is true, and that the conditional link holds. Even if it is also true that the metal in the box is not gold, and that the antecedent is therefore false, the consequent may still be true or false. The metal may be malleable tin, or it may be cast-iron.

When the antecedent is a logical impossibility, Leibniz assigns the numerical value 0 to the conditional. When the antecedent is a necessary truth, then it is as if one asserted the consequent unconditionally. So Leibniz gives the numerical value 1 to the conditional. (These numbers correspond to the degree of likelihood of the antecedent, which conditions the consequent and are used to 'weigh' the conditional.) When the antecedent is neither a logical impossibility nor a necessary truth, but a contingent proposition of which it is prima facie equiprobable that it be true or false, then the right expressed by the consequent is properly conditional, and Leibniz initially gives ½ as the value attached to the conditional right. We can often do better than that, however. The estimation of conditional rights comes from a complex assessment of the right expressed by the consequent and of the degree of probability of the realization of the antecedent, which leads to an assignment of a more complex logical structure to the conditional itself. In assessing the first two items, we often find that the consequent or the antecedent (or both) can be seen to be a disjunction or conjunction of further constituent propositions. This enables us to make a further logical analysis of the original conditional propositions. We often find that it is a disjunction or conjunction of conditionals, each having as antecedent or consequent one of the constituent propositions into which the antecedent and consequent of the original conditional was analyzed. Then the numerical value attached to the original conditional right may no longer be ½. It is calculated on the basis of the numerical value attached to the conditional right expressed by the constituent disjuncts or conjuncts. (The value we find is derived with the help of a kind of Boolean algebra, whose elements are n-tuples of 0 and 1 for some appropriate n. It would be the nth direct power of the two-element Boolean algebra. The simplest example would be when the condition or the antecedent p of the conditional "If p then q"

can be analyzed into a disjunction p_1 v p_2 . . . v p_n. Then the original conditional will be a conjunction of conditionals " 'If p_1 then *q*' and 'If p_2 then *q*' . . . 'If p_n then *q*'." Some of the conjuncts may be given the numerical value 0, in which case the whole conjunction will be given 0, but if not, then since the others may be given the value of 1 or ½, the numerical value of the conjunction as a whole can be calculated accordingly.) Thus Leibniz writes that the numerical value attached to the conditional right can turn out to be any rational number between 0 and 1.

Leibniz's calculus of the degree of conditionality of the consequent carried out in this early work is both too abstract and inadequate. We can nevertheless gauge his intentions.

We come now to the second question, 2. We see that when Leibniz gives a numerical value to a conditional right, the value that is derived from the measure of likelihood of the condition is meant to correspond to the degree in which the right expressed by the consequent is conditional. Similarly, when Leibniz talks of hypothetical truths, he is interested in establishing how the obtaining of the truths expressed by the consequent is dependent not only on the antecedents explicitly given but on other data or indications we have. Here we do not analyze the antecedent but weigh it in conjunction with other conditions. (He writes that reasons or indications should not be counted but weighed.[8]) The aim then is to assess the status of the consequent. Is this compatible with Leibniz's occasional talk of "the truths of hypothetical propositions"? It seems that for Leibniz the truth of a hypothetical proposition corresponds to the acceptability of the move from the truth of the antecedent to the truth of the consequent, or from the falsity of the consequent to the falsity of the antecedent; it is the truth of the consequent, given the antecedent. Thus when the conditional assertion of the consequent is justified, one can talk of the truth of the hypothetical proposition.

We are led to the third question, 3. What are the

grounds of the conditional truths, of the acceptability of these inferences? Leibniz writes that hypothetical truths depend on something objective, even if neither antecedent nor consequent is realized. (That is to say that whether the consequent is true on the supposition that the antecedent is true depends on things that are independent of us.) Often the acceptability of the inference depends on a promise or contract that people have made, as in the case of conditional rights, which we examined before. In many other cases, the acceptability of the inference, that is, the truth of conditionals, does not depend on contracts or man-made laws. It is an objective fact or something to be discovered.

A hypothetical truth does not correspond to an arbitrary fantasy. Nor do we make hypothetical truths by just defining the meaning of words. We cannot arbitrarily define 'gold' to *mean* "metal that dissolves only in aqua regia," and thus make analytically true the following hypothetical: "If this is made of gold, it will dissolve only in aqua regia." Leibniz says that these truths in no way depend on us. We do not make the truth up, we discover it. And as he points out to Foucher, the possibility, or necessity of these matters "is not a chimera that we create, since all that we do consists in recognizing it, in spite of ourselves and in a constant manner.[9] Why is this so? I think we can understand Leibniz's view in the following way. We do not assess hypothetical truths in isolation. To assess a hypothetical truth of the form "if p then q" is to assess whether q is true on the supposition that p is true. We have a body of knowledge and a set of beliefs and assumptions. The antecedent p together with all of these, will lead us to discover whether we are justified in asserting the consequent q. (There are, as we know, difficulties about counter-factual suppositions that Leibniz does not discuss here.)

On what then do the truths of hypothetical assertions depend? According to Leibniz, they depend on what is necessary, and what is possible or impossible in reality. "Necessity, possibility and impossibility make up [compose] what are called essences or the nature of things, as well as these truths which are usually called eternal truths."[10]

Two points of clarification must be made here.

First, it is clear that the modalities in question in this passage are not epistemic ones, but as Leibniz says, have to do with the nature of things. For example, when Leibniz writes in a later work about the possibility of a one-legged man (to point out the weakness of the definition of man as a featherless biped), he is not merely saying that he doesn't know whether there are one-legged men or not.[11] We do of course use the word "possible" for such epistemic purposes, as when I say, "It is possible that she will come wearing a red hat." But he was saying that, when a man loses his leg, he doesn't lose whatever it is that makes him human. Thus we can understand the possibility of a one-legged man whether we encounter one or not. The modality here has to do with whatever nature it is that men have that distinguishes them from other living things.

Second, although the modalities in question all have to do with the nature of things, Leibniz is not talking about one kind of necessity, possibility, impossibility. There are hypothetical propositions about logical and mathematical truths, about physical phenomena, or even about institutional or social arrangements. Correspondingly, the necessity or possibility on which the truth-value of these propositions depends may be logical or mathematical necessity, physical necessity, or even the connection that is consequential upon acceptance of certain institutions or arrangements that are based on natural possibilities. Leibniz mentions the nature of things involved in "arithmetic, geometry, propositions of metaphysics, or physics, and of morals."[12] It is interesting to note that Leibniz here says that the necessities, possibilities, and impossibilities make up what are called essences or natures on the one hand *and* also what are called eternal truths on the other. The nature of physical things is what *we express* in our attempts to formulate laws of nature. We formulate them as general hypothetical propositions, and commit ourselves to the truth of each of their instantiations.

Here we might be reminded of what Ramsey suggested 250 years later when he wrote that "variable hypotheticals are not judgments but rules of judging."[13] For Leibniz, no laws of nature existed apart from things and their properties. He thought that the foundation of the laws of nature was the conservation of energy, the property that all material things shared.[14]

The traditional dispute between realists and nominalists has been translated in recent times into a new idiom. There has been a lively realist-nominalist controversy concerning modalities. And sometimes the debate has been taken to turn on the question whether *de dicto necessity* depends on *de re* necessity or vice versa; this is to ask whether all notions of *de re* necessity derive *ex vi terminorum* or not. In the case of Leibniz, however, there is no room for so simple an opposition. He believes that things have natures or constitutional properties that make them behave in the way they do. But he also believes that we know these constitutional properties by acknowledging certain hypothetical truths. To grasp the nature of things *is,* for Leibniz, to acknowledge our commitment to these general hypothetical truths. In view of recent controversies, it is perhaps important to notice that there is nothing in Leibniz's letter to Foucher or elsewhere that implies that necessity or possibility is attached to a predicate. The claim he makes is only that the modality of hypothetical propositions are determined by and express *either* the nature of things *or* logical truths, *or* both. He proposes no property of necessarily being hot or necessarily being trilateral, as distinct from being hot or being trilateral. This is not of course to deny that it may be necessary that if something is a fire, then by the very nature of fire it is hot, or that is may be necessary that if something is a triangle, then by its very nature it is trilateral. It is rather the hypothetical proposition of the form "If *a* is *f,* then *a* is *g*" (rather than just any hypothetical of the form "If *p* then *q*") that is necessary, given how things are. As I have said, the necessity of such particular hypotheticals may be derived from a general hypothetical truth whose necessity is assumed. But again this necessity is the necessity of the truth of any instantiation of a propositional schema of the form "If *fx* then *gx*" and not of a predicate. In general, Leibniz uses 'necessity' only as a qualifier of truth or connection of ideas. Indeed, for Leibniz, propositions are made up of ideas, which he calls 'terms'. So necessity for Leibniz does derive *ex vi terminorum* (he considered himself a nominalist). However, just as a truth may be ascribed to a proposition, but is nevertheless a truth concerning the objects the proposition is about, so the necessity that is ascribed to a hypothetical proposition may concern the things the hypothetical proposition is about. It is *de re,* or about the nature of things.

Again it is important to remind ourselves that by the necessity of a proposition, Leibniz does not understand the analyticity of the sentence that expresses it. For Leibniz, a proposition "*S* is *f*" says that the instantiation of the concept *S* is an instantiation of concept *f*. (This is true if and only if the concept *f* is contained in the concept *S*. What is meant by "contained in" and *inesse* we have seen in Chapter VII §5. I have argued elsewhere on the topic in more detail.[15] I will not go into detail here. Very simply, the concept *S* contains the concept *f* just in case *S* is *f*.).

To say that the proposition that *S* is *f* is necessary is to say that its truth does not depend on the free decree of God, and his creation.[16] In other words, in all possible worlds an instantiation of the concept *S* also instantiates the concept *f*. Its contrary implies a contradiction. So its truth does not depend on facts about this world. This is not to say that the meaning of the expression '*f*' is part of the meaning of the expression '*S*,' or that the two meanings are identical. 'Triangle' does not mean 'trilateral', and the meaning of the latter is not part of the meaning of the former. Thus, "A triangle is trilateral" is not true in virtue of a synonymy, but because the nature of a triangle is such that in all possible worlds it will have three sides.

Similarly, to say that the proposition "*S* is *f*" is necessary, given the nature of things, is to say that in all possible worlds in which things are created, *S* is *f*. To assert the necessity of the proposition "If the cup is gold, it will dissolve in aqua regia" is not to assert that a part of the meaning of "is gold" is "dissolves in aqua regia." The proposition will be true in all possible worlds in which the laws of nature are the same, (i.e., where things of same structures interact in the same way), if dissolving in aqua regia follows from the very structural properties of the stuff we call 'gold' and 'aqua regia'.[17] But this does not mean that people have to know the structure of gold to be able to use the general word 'gold'. It need not be a part of the meaning of the word 'gold' that the stuff it designates dissolves in aqua regia. So the hypothetical sentence used above is not an analytic one. It is the hypothetical propositions then that can be necessary or contingently true. In other words, that which justifies the move from the truth of the antecedent to the truth of the consequent may be necessary or contingent. But the necessity comes from the nature of the things that the hypothetical propositions are about.

If the truth-value of hypothetical propositions does not depend on us, how do we discover it? The truth of hypotheticals that depend on the physical nature of things cannot be discovered in the same way as hypotheticals that depend only on logical and mathematical truths. As Leibniz says, if all of us think carefully, we all come to the same conclusion about the nature of circles. Whereas, the power of reasoning by itself never gets us all the way to truths that depend on the nature of gold. These truths depend on how things in this world interact with other things in this world, i.e., on regularities of nature or the pre-established harmony, regularities that we must observe to come to any knowledge about the nature of things.[18]

Later in the *New Essays* Leibniz disagreed with Locke, who had claimed in the *Essay* that the real essence or nature of things was unknowable. According to Leibniz, the conjectures we base on observation may often be mistaken, and we may come to realize this by making further observations; but there is no a priori reason why we should not come to know the structural property of a thing that makes it the kind of thing it is.[19]

It is true that in the letter to Foucher quoted earlier, Leibniz does not work out the distinction between hypothetical truths that depend on logic and mathematics and those that depend on physics, or on morals. (His later works show much more reflection on these matters.) But it is interesting that Leibniz does not, as is often said, assimilate hypotheticals about empirical matters to logical truths. If anything, the direction of assimilation is the other way around. Leibniz here says of *all* necessities that "although they are first in the order of nature, they are not the first in the order of our knowledge." That is to say that even hypothetical truths concerning mathematics, such as "If *a* is a triangle, its angles add up to 180°," are often discovered through the observation of particular drawings of triangles. By understanding that what we discover follows from the geometrical nature of lines and angles, we can see that they are necessary truths. To identify an object as a triangle is to identify an object whose angles add up to 180° in any possible world.

Now Leibniz thinks that we can discover necessary hypothetical truths of physics in the same way. We can observe that these truths seem to be constant and independent of us (this will be the case even if we take a phenomenalist view about the external world, as Foucher does), and we can then understand the nature of the objects that the propositions are about and give these hypothetical propositions determinate modalities. What we observe, Leibniz insists, is only concomitance or regularities. We can, however, grasp the necessity of the concomitance, by relating it to the nature of things and the laws of nature they embody. Leibniz therefore agrees with Foucher that we only observe regularities, and yet he tries to develop a theory that will escape Foucher's phenomenalism. The first step is to notice that although a hypothetical proposition "does not assert the existence of anything in the external world," its truth is "something independent of us and does not depend upon us."[20]

We can elucidate Leibniz's thought with an example from the *New Essays*. Think of propositions like "If it is gold, it resists nitric acid" or "If it is gold, it is denser than any other body." Both these hypotheticals were thought to be true in Leibniz's time. But Leibniz insists they are conjectures that we make on the basis of observation and induction, and could turn out to be false (as indeed one of them did). If a conjecture of this sort is true, it is true because of the structural property of gold (which Leibniz agreed with Locke that their contemporaries did not yet know).[21] That is to say that the structural property of gold, plus the relevant physical laws, would, if one knew it, enable us to demonstrate why gold has these other properties as well. For example, let a structural property of gold be that its atomic number is 79. If the number of electrons in the outermost shell determines the chemical reactions of atoms, we would see why gold, having this structural property, resists nitric acid and dissolves in aqua regia. Such structural properties are what Leibniz calls essence in the case of physical bodies that are aggregates.

It is important to realize that there may be hypothetical judgments, which we may be justified in asserting at a given time, given the evidence that we then have, but which are nevertheless false (as in the case of the hypothetical judgment that, if something is gold, it is denser than other metals). We may come to realize that it is false by acquiring further evidence. Thus the truth of hypothetical propositions does not depend on the *actual* state of knowledge in an individual, or even of the human community that has a store of common knowledge. Similarly in the case of conditional rights, the right a man has is dependent on constraints and conditions that actually exist and not merely on those that are believed to obtain. One can think analogously in the case of other hypothetical propositions. The truth of "If p then q" is the truth of q on the condition that p, and *not* on the condition that we believe that p or that we know that p.

It is of course *we* with our interests who assert conditional propositions. And it is only against the background of our knowledge of regularities in nature and of logical truths, that we can work out the truth-value of these conditionals that we assert. The assumptions and background knowledge presupposed depend on the context in which the hypothetical propositions are asserted. But hypothetical truths depend on the nature of things and not on our ideas or habits. Thus the truths may depend on facts about which we are still ignorant, or about which we are mistaken.

Let me summarize what I think is interesting in Leibniz's treatment of hypothetical truths:

1. By treating the assertion of conditional propositions as the conditional assertion of the consequent, Leibniz was not tempted to look for a logical relation or a meaning relation between the antecedent and consequent in isolation. He saw that what is in question is assessing the truth-value of the consequent conditionally upon the truth of the antecedent *and* the existing body of our knowledge, true beliefs, and institutional agreements.

2. He was able to treat conditionals with impossible antecedents in such a way as to be able to ignore them and thus avoid the paradox of strict implication.

3. He attempted, though in a not too successful way, to evolve a method of calculating the measure of conditionality of the consequent.[22]

4. Leibniz believed that there were objective grounds for the truth of conditionals, even in cases where as a matter of fact the antecedent does not obtain; he realized also that these truth grounds do not depend simply on how we choose to define the meaning of words. Some conditional truths are necessary, and this necessity also comes from the things outside us. Leibniz therefore committed himself to the view that necessary hypothetical truths were based either on eternal truths of reason or on the nature or essence of things, and that this was the explanation of why conditional statements could represent real discoveries or errors.

We must now examine what Leibniz thought about modality in a more general way.

IX. Necessity and contingency

> But this possibility, impossibility or necessity . . . is not a chimera which we create. Since all that we do consists in recognising them, in spite of ourselves and in a constant manner. So of all the things that actually are, the possibility or impossibility of being is itself the first. But this possibility and necessity form or compose what are called the essences or nature. (Letter to Foucher, c. 1676.)[1]

1. The Praedicatum inest subjecto *thesis and the distinction between necessary and contingent truths*

We have seen how Leibniz attempted to understand the logical form and the special features of hypothetical propositions throughout his life. We will now examine how his theory of hypotheticals link with his understanding of modal notions.

In the *Theodicy* written comparatively late in his life and the only philosophical book which Leibniz published in his lifetime (apart from the early logical work *Dissertatio de Arte Combinatoria*), the question of modality is dealt with in considerable detail.[2] Philosophers are familiar with the way in which he attempts to make clear the nature of the possible and the necessary by introducing the notion of possible worlds and of the actual world, which is only one of infinitely many possible worlds. In this chapter, we will examine the various strands of argument which Leibniz gives concerning the distinction between necessary and contingent truths, and to see how it squares with the other logical doctrines of Leibniz which we have examined, such as those of concept-identity and of truth in general.

As I mentioned in the Introduction, it was one of Couturat's main contentions that for Leibniz all true propositions are analytic. Russell also expounded the slightly weaker thesis that for Leibniz all subject-predicate propositions are analytic. Because the works of these two philosophers were so important in enabling people to re-assess the value of Leibniz's philosophy of logic, their views were accepted and have now set the standard for interpreting Leibniz. The doctrine of the analyticity of all true propositions has naturally led people to wonder how the distinction between necessary truths and contingent truths which Leibniz was so eager to make could be maintained. I hope to show that one can coherently describe the distinction between necessary and contingent truths in Leibniz's philosophy.

R. Kauppi has rightly said that Leibniz's system of logic is not intensional in the sense specified by C. I. Lewis, because in Leibniz's logic the modal properties of propositional functions and theorems are not symbolized and made explicit.[3] However, as we shall see, Leibniz was very much concerned about the modalities of propositions.

In Chapter III we saw that, according to Leibniz, when a subject-predicate proposition is true, the predicate is said to be 'included' in the subject (where subject and predicate are both understood as concepts), and that this means that whatever falls under the concept of subject satisfies the concept of the predicate. This is always the case whether the proposition expresses a contingent truth or a necessary truth:

> My idea of a true proposition is such that every predicate, necessary or contingent, past, present or future, is included in the idea of the subject.[4]

Thus, in asserting that in all true subject-predicate propositions the predicate is included in the subject, Leibniz certainly did not mean to imply that all subject-predicate propositions were necessary. He explains that the required link between subject and predicate exists only *a parte rei* (from the side of the thing).[5] This is obviously contrasted with a link which exists *a parte dicti* (from the side of what is said), or *ex termini* (due to [general] conceptual links). A predicate that is true *a parte rei* is always in some manner contained in the nature of the subject. Nevertheless, it includes "all that pertains to it only by virtue of the general connections of things." Elsewhere he writes that the link between a predicate ascribing such a property and the subject cannot be demonstrated through the concept of the subject itself alone but with the addition of the concept of time which involves the total series of things and God's free will. It is misleading, to say the least, to assume that "the predicate in the subject" thesis says or implies that all truths are analytic. Unfortunately, since Russell and Couturat, this has become a standard charge against Leibniz.

To add to the confusion, Leibniz himself used the expression 'analytic' and 'synthetic' in connection with the method of organisation of knowledge, but in a quite different sense from that of Kant. At one point Leibniz uses the word 'analytic' in the *New Essays* in connection with 'practical' to refer to the technical methods used to dissect a problem in order to bring about a given goal, in contrast to 'synthetic' which is used in connection with 'theoretical' and means something like systematic.[6] It seems better, therefore, not to use 'analytic' and 'synthetic' at all, with their post-Kantian associations, to characterize Leibniz's theories. It was no part of Leibniz's views, for example, that if a predicate is included in the concept of the subject, one can eventually see that this is so. If the subject is an infinitely complex concept – i.e., the concept of an individual object of which infinitely many predicates are true – then it follows that one would *not* always automatically know of any given predicate whether it is included in the subject or not. The only exception is the predicate which expresses the species to which the subject belongs. Leibniz believes that, since identifying individuals already involves picking them out as an individual of a certain kind, one does not get from individuals to species by abstraction.[7] For example, we do not obtain the concept 'human being' by abstraction from observing what is common to John, Mary, Peter. We pick out John, Mary, or Peter as a human being already. The species is implicitly given when the individual is given. This means that, if the predicate of a proposition expresses the species to which the subject belongs, one should be able to see that the proposition is true. But this is an exception. In general, the 'predicate-in-subject' definition of truth does not make all propositions either analytic or uninformative. As Rescher has argued, the a priori proof that exists in principle for contingent truths concern the calculi of the best world that God created, not about any direct logical connection between subject and predicate.

The difference between the views of Leibniz and Kant on necessity is often pointed out by mentioning that Leibniz considered mathematical truths to be true by definition whereas Kant decided they were synthetic though a priori. However, even the theories of Leibniz and Kant on the nature of mathematical propositions are not as different from one another as is customarily thought. Remember that the main reason why for Kant mathematical judgments like 7 + 5 = 12 were synthetic was that "we must go beyond the conceptions and have recourse to an intuition which corresponds to one of the two – our five fingers, for example – and add the units contained in the intuition to the conception of seven."[8] Leibniz also believed that mathematical truths needed to be expressed by signs or diagrams, and that these would be a conventional expression of what might ultimately be expressed by strokes or fingers, which shows our way of collecting units into an aggregate. This would hardly have made mathematical truths synthetic for Leibniz. For him the necessity of thinking in terms of strokes or perceivable signs or of counting in time, did not make the mathematical propositions any *less* of an identity. What he regarded as crucial was that the concepts of five, seven, and sum made an a priori proof of the above proposition possible.

So let us forget Kantian classification and simply begin by asking whether Leibniz's definition of truth for subject-predicate propositions is compatible with the distinction between necessary and contingent truths which he makes in the *Theodicy* and elsewhere, and which he believed was so important. Leibniz himself was troubled by this problem. As he wrote:

> There is something which has perplexed me for a long time. I did not understand how the predicate could be in the subject, without the proposition thereby becoming necessary. . . . But the knowledge of geometrical things and especially that of infinite analysis showed me light, so that I came to understand what it is for concepts to be resolvable in infinity.[9]

We will examine later in § 6 whether the analogy of infinitesimal analysis is at all helpful in making the distinction between necessary and contingent truths. We will look first at some other explanations which Leibniz gives of the distinction. The main one is that "truths of reason are necessary . . . and their opposite is impossible."[10] This is closely linked with his thesis that a contingent truth is true in the actual world (and *not* in all possible worlds) whereas truths are true in all possible worlds. A possible world is a world God could have created. As he only created the actual world which is our world, all other possible worlds exist only as ideas. In other words, they are conceivable worlds. Truths of reason hold in every conceivable world, and hence are necessary.

Why are truths of fact contingent? Is it true as Russell claimed that no subject-predicate proposition could really be contingent for Leibniz? Leibniz gives as an example of a contingent truth the truth that Caesar crossed the Rubicon.[11] That this is true implies that the concept "crossed the Rubicon" is included in the concept of Caesar. How then can the opposite, i.e., the proposition "Caesar did not cross the Rubicon," be possible? For, as we have seen, if the concept of Caesar includes all the predicates that are true of him and nothing else, "Caesar did not cross the Rubicon" could never have been true. Hence it might seem that it is not possible for Caesar not to have crossed the Rubicon.

Doesn't everything that an individual does, as well as what he encounters, turn out to be necessary to his individual concept? Leibniz attempts a reply in *Discourse of Metaphysics* §13:

> To answer it squarely, I say that there are two kinds of connections or sequence. One is absolutely necessary, for its contrary implies a contradiction, and this deductive connection occurs in eternal truths like those of geometry. The other is necessary only *ex hypothesi,* and by accident, so to speak, and this connection is contingent in itself when its contrary implies no contradiction. A connection of this kind is not based on pure ideas and on the simple understanding of God but also on his free decrees and on the sequence of events in the universe. (G., *Phil.* 4., p. 437, Loemker, p. 310.)

Leibniz is suggesting that, the world being as it was, Caesar encountered other people at certain times. Things were brewing in Rome when he was in Gaul, and Caesar freely chose to cross the Rubicon and return. The world could have been very different and a person with all the past and character of Caesar may have encountered different situations in Gaul or things could have been otherwise in Rome. And Caesar may have decided to act differently. God could have created any of these possible worlds rather than our world. These worlds were all ideas in God's mind, and the problem whether there could be the same individuals in more than one possible world has no factual answer. The Roman general in this world that was created, who freely crossed the Rubicon, is Caesar. He could have chosen not to cross the Rubicon but he did cross it. What Leibniz meant therefore by saying that the opposite of "Caesar crossed the Rubicon" is possible, is that such a world could have been created, namely, there could have been – in a different world – a person like Caesar who does not cross the Rubicon, and experiences its attendant consequences. He is not Caesar, that particular historical person in this world. So, strictly speaking, it is not the case that "Caesar did not cross the Rubicon" could be true. But it is possible for there to be another complex concept which contains almost all the predicates of Caesar, but which contains "did not cross the Rubicon" *instead of* "crossed the Rubicon." That is a consistent concept which characterizes an individual in a different possible world which God could have created.

It might be thought that the whole point of introducing talk about possible worlds is to think about worlds in which what true counter-factuals say about individuals in the actual world does actually happen. For example, if we think that the counter-factual "Had Caesar not crossed the Rubicon, Pompey would have defeated him" is true, then we can think of a possible world in which Caesar did not cross the Rubicon and was defeated by Pompey. As Kripke wrote in his important and influential article "Naming and necessity" it may seem pointless if we do not think of the same individuals as occurring in different possible worlds.

Now Leibniz would *not* deny that talk about truths in different possible worlds is another expression of what is necessary and what is possible in our world. He would not deny either that when we wonder what would have happened had Caesar crossed the Rubicon, we are thinking about Caesar and our world. But he thought that when we describe possible worlds which fit our counter-factual claims, we are not describing the historical Caesar himself, even though we do use the proper name 'Caesar'. We use 'Caesar' here to express an individual concept in which we then go on to make certain alterations by eliminating a predicate and replacing it by its contradictory. Thus although we *are* indeed thinking of a possible world, describing in terms of a counter-factual in which reference is made to an individual in *this* world, the possible world so described does not contain Julius Caesar himself. It is a world in which a similar Roman general stays in Gaul. In the *Theodicy* Leibniz talks of showing worlds in which Sextus has futures different from the one he is to have in this world:

> These worlds are all there, namely in thought. I will show you where one can find, not exactly the same Sextus whom you have seen (this is not possible, he carries always within himself what he will be), but beings resembling Sextus who will have all that you already know of the real Sextus, but not all which, without our perceiving it, is already within him, nor consequently all that will happen to the real Sextus.[12]

The possible worlds shown do not contain the real Sextus. Yet they show what is contingently true of the real Sextus by exhibiting that God could equally have made a world in which Sextus did not have the particular things happening to him – or, more accurately, worlds in which people who had everything in common with the real Sextus up to a certain period of his life had divergent lives afterwards because of what they freely chose to do.

If we allow that there could be propositions which are neither true nor false of a certain world if the subject-concept is not instantiated in the world, and if we take necessary truth as being expressed by propositions which are not false in any world, rather than true in all worlds, then every true proposition in which the subject expresses an individual concept would be necessary. Some men may not be liable to sin in another world, but a Caesar who did not cross the Rubicon, or a weak Zeus, does not exist in any world. Leibniz could not think in this way since he believed in the principle of bivalence. On the contrary, he regarded propositions like "Caesar crossed the Rubicon" as being contingent because God could have made a world in which that was not the case. (What the content of such a belief comes to is the subject of our investigation in this.)

A general proposition of the type "*f* is *g*" is contingent for Leibniz if God could have made worlds in which this does not hold; that is, not everything which is *f* is *g* in other possible worlds, even if it is in ours. Difficulty arises in describing what God could have done in creating a world which shows that Caesar need not have crossed the Rubicon. We cannot say, Leibniz believes, that there are instantiations of the individual concept 'Caesar' in other worlds which did not cross the Rubicon. What God could have done is to instantiate another individual concept which we can partially specify by replacing "crossed the Rubicon" by its contrary in the individual concept of our Caesar, with various consequent changes. The corresponding proposition that is true in other worlds would be about an individual sharing many properties with Caesar. It is a technical metalogical problem whether we should treat this conceptualised individual as Caesar or not. Thus there are contingent singular propositions as well as contingent general propositions within Leibniz's framework.

2. *Existential import*

What then is the status of propositions like "Pegasus flies"? Some recent logicians have suggested that for Leibniz any sentence which has a name that does not denote an individual in this world as subject is false.[13] This is not true unless the sentence is taken as expressing an existential proposition, i.e., a proposition which ranges only over actual things. Such a reading seems to be quite contrary to the basic attitude which prompted Leibniz to choose an intensional rather than extensional interpretation of truth-conditions, which we saw in Chapter III. As you will recall, he explained that he preferred to consider universal concepts, and their combinations, since they do not depend on the existence of individuals.

It is important to realise that Leibniz believed that all singular propositions could also be treated as universal propositions, which in turn can be treated as hypotheticals.[14] According to Leibniz, the singular proposition "The apostle Saint Peter denied his Master" states that whoever was Saint Peter the Apostle denied his Master, just as the universal proposition "The square is a rectangle" states that whatever is a square is a rectangle. We can take these hypotheticals, however, to range over entities in all possible worlds or only over entities in this world. In the former case, even when there is no individual corresponding to the definite description in this world, as in "The fourteenth disciple denied Christ," the proposition will not become trivially true (as it would, were it to be taken as an existential hypothetical, because of the falsity of the antecedent).

As we have seen in Chapter III, Leibniz thought that neither universal nor particular categorical propositions carried existential import. Singular propositions in which the subject-concept is expressed by a definite description carry no more existential import than does a universal proposition, a point which will be discussed later in §4.

In later mediaeval logic, it appears that both universal and particular affirmative propositions were at various times taken to carry existential import. Leibniz nevertheless took the opposite view. He noticed that a universal affirmative proposition was traditionally supposed to carry no existential import whereas a particular affirmative proposition was supposed to do so. According to this traditional view, an argument such as "every laugher is a human being therefore some human being is a laugher" would be invalid, since "the former is true even if nothing laughs, whereas the latter is not true unless someone actually laughs." However, Leibniz says that "a difficulty of this kind does not occur if you remain within the limit of possibles. Then even if no laugher exists, 'Some human being is a laugher' is not true, for laugher is taken for a species of human being not for an actual laugher'."[15] It is unlikely, therefore, that Leibniz was simply confused about *conversio per accidens,* i.e., the inference from "All *A* is *B*" to "Some *B* is *A*," as some have said, or was unaware of the difficulties involved.[16] Similarly, in Leibniz's logic one can move from "All *A* is *B* to "Some *A* is *B*."

The fact that in Leibniz's logic "All *A* is *B*" entails "Some *A* is *B*" helps us understand a controversial thesis asserted by him that a non-entity has no attributes. *Non entis nulla esse attributa* or *Nihili nullas esse proprietate* – there are no attributes of a non-entity (Couturat *OFI,* pp. 252, 356). Leibniz claims that this follows from the definition of 'non-entity', namely the definition that if *N* is not *A*, *N* is not *B*, *N* is not *C*, etc., then *N* is a non-entity. Leibniz also says of non-entity that it is a mere privation.[17] We have seen that by a 'non-entity' Leibniz does not usually mean something like Pegasus, an entity which could exist in another world but which does not exist in this world. Talk of non-entity often occurs when he is expressing an essential proposition and uses 'non-ens' to mean a being which could not exist in any world, like the greatest number, or a man who is a stone. He writes for example that "If *A* is *B*-not-*B* then *A* is a non-entity,"[18] and that "An impossible concept is a non-entity."[19]

But if a non-entity *A* is *B*-not-*B*, then it would at least seem to have the attribute *B* and the attribute not-*B*, since ex hypothesi *A* is *B* and *A* is not-*B*. Leibniz's solution is that if a subject-concept *A* appears to contain some concept *B* and its negation not-*B*, we *stipulate* that *A* contains no concept and has no attribute. This is because *A* is not a proper concept. It is a concept which is inconsistent and hence can have no instantiation.

We can see why Leibniz would have to say this. For suppose we did not stipulate that a non-entity has no attribute; that is, suppose we allowed that for some attribute *C*, *N* is *C*, where *N* is a non-entity. We have already seen that in Leibniz's logic "All *N* is *C*" entails "Some *N* is *C*." The latter is equivalent to "Some possible instance of *N* is *C*," which entails that there are some possible instances of *N*. This contradicts our hypothesis that *N* is a non-entity, or that *N* is a contradictory concept which cannot be instantiated in any possible world.[20]

It is important to remind ourselves of the fact which we examined in Chapter III that Leibniz (like the Frege of the *Begriffsschrift*, like Russell, and unlike Frege in *Über Sinn und Bedeutung* or Strawson)[21] wanted to maintain bivalence, i.e., the principle that every proposition is either true or false. Thus propositions which have contradictory concepts as subjects are all false, and existential propositions (propositions asserted under the assumption that one is talking about things in this world) which have subjects which are not instantiated in this world are false rather than without truth-value. In the *General Enquiries,* Leibniz makes a logical analysis of particular affirmative, particular negative, universal affirmative, and universal negative propositions and explains how none of them carries existential import. Their truth does not depend on the subject-concept being instantiated in this world. Nevertheless, he writes:

> . . . it remains that every proposition which lacks a *constantia subjecti,* i.e. a real term, is false. In the case of existential propositions this is far removed from the way we speak; but this is of no concern, since I am seeking appropriate signs, and I do not intend to apply generally accepted names to these.[22]

By a proposition lacking *constantia subjecti,* late mediaeval logicians meant a proposition which is asserted without the assumption that the subject-concept is instantiated. Mates suggested in his "Leibniz and possible worlds" that it is a proposition which has as subject a name which does not denote anything in this world. But the assumption of the *constantia subjecti* of a proposition is not always an assumption that the subject-concept is instantiated in *this* world. The assumption might be that the subject is instantiated in some possible world. In the passage quoted above, Leibniz is talking about both kinds of cases.

Nor does the question of *constantia subjecti* always involve propositions expressed by sentences with singular terms. In the *New Essays,* Leibniz writes of the problem of *constantia subjecti* disputed by the scholastics. According to him it is the problem how a proposition about a certain subject can have real truth (value) if this subject does not exist.[23] His answer is that truth (or falsity) lies in the connection of ideas. Leibniz illustrates his point by the proposition "The angles of a three-sided figure are equal to two right-angles." Why do we not need to assume that there are trilaterals when we assert this proposition? His answer is that even if (in some world) a three-sided figure does not exist, the proposition is true, for it is only conditional and "says, in case the subject ever exists, it will be found such."

Leibniz is not saying (as some modern logicians would) that the propositions will be trivially true in a world in which there are no three-sided figures, since the antecedent of the conditional is false. He is saying that the claim is about three-sided figures in any possible world. There cannot be a possible world in which there are three-sided figures whose angles do not add up to two right-angles. In contrast to such propositions, one which has a contradictory concept as subject could not have an instantiation in any possible world; that is, we cannot presuppose that something corresponding to the contradictory subject exists. It lacks *constantia subjecti*. Thus such a proposition will always be treated as false.

3. Essential propositions and existential propositions

As we have already seen, Leibniz distinguished essential and existential propositions, but not in the way that would coincide with Russell's division of Leibnizian propositions into subject-predicate ones that were all analytic, and existential ones which were synthetic because they assert the existence of an entity in this world. In the fragment that Mates refers to, Leibniz writes clearly that to say *AB* is a thing, or *AB* exists, could mean either possible existence (i.e., *AB* exists in some possible world) or actual existence (i.e., *AB* exists in this world), depending on whether the proposition is 'essential' or 'existential'. An existential proposition does not necessarily assert existence. An existential proposition is contingent, and the examples given are "Every man is liable to sin" and "A man liable to sin exists or is an actual being." Presumably, the first is true of all men in the actual world because of original sin, and it could be otherwise in a different world.[24] A man not liable to sin, then, has no actual existence, and so in the context of this existential proposition alone can one say that a man not liable to sin is a non-entity, or is not an (actual) thing.

Every predication about a man not liable to sin is false. For example the proposition "A man not liable to sin feels no temptation" is false. This is the kind of consequence which Leibniz thinks is contrary to ordinary usage.

We are now a bit clearer about the distinction Leibniz makes between 'essential propositions' and 'existential propositions'. He does not symbolize the difference between the two, but assumes that we distinguish between them by seeing in which of two ways the truth conditions of a given proposition are to be understood. Propositions of the former type are about possibles, propositions of the latter type about actuals. Thus in an essential proposition like that of the trilateral having three angles one is making a claim about trilaterals in any possible world. In modern logical terminology, the quantifiers are assumed to range over entities in every possible world. In an existential proposition like that which we usually make by asserting "Every man is liable to sin" or "A man liable to sin exists," we are talking only about the actual world (as he says that "it is manifestly a contingent proposition"). Thus the quantifiers are assumed to range only over entities in this world.

The reason why many people have believed that particular affirmative propositions carry existential import in Leibniz's logic may be because Leibniz writes that the particular affirmative proposition "Some *A* is *B*" is the same proposition as "*AB* exists."[25] We must, however, remember Leibniz's comment that 'exist' here means "it can be conceived," "it can be understood," and that the existence ascribed is "possible or actual depending on whether the proposition is essential or existential."[26] If "*A* is *B*" is an essential proposition, "*AB* exists" merely means that in some possible world *AB* exists. The proposition "*A* is not *B*" can be similarly converted to "*AB* does not exist" or "*AB* is not a thing." But again "not exists" or "is not a thing" can be taken in the sense of an actual thing or possible thing (and not only the former, as Mates assumes). Thus if "No *A* is *B*" is an essential proposition, then "*AB* is not a thing" or "*AB* does not exist" means "In no possible world is there something which is A and B." In other words, it says that *AB* is a contradictory concept, which cannot be instantiated in any world. Although Leibniz himself has no symbolism to indicate the difference between what he calls essential propositions and existential propositions, the former correspond to what is expressed by a necessity operator such as in the formula $\Box(x)\ (fx \rightarrow gx)$.

If a sentence of the form "No *A* is *B*" is taken to express an existential proposition, then we should understand it as saying that in this actual world there is no *A* which is a *B*, or that *AB* does not exist in this world.

Whether the proposition "No *A* is *B*" is existential or essential, the proposition "No *A* is *B*," which can be expressed as "*AB* is not a thing," is also, Leibniz believes, expressible (if we use the '$\Box$' sign to express "it is necessary that") as "$AB = \Box \neg$ AB." That is to say, wherever "No *A* is *B*" is true, we should artificially stipulate that *AB* is not identical with *AB*. Thus a round square is not a round square, and in the case of existential propositions we get odd results such as that a man not liable to sin is not a man not liable to sin, which is, as Leibniz says "far removed from the way we speak." Recall however that for Leibniz categorical propositions and hypothetical propositions had the same logical form. "*A* is *B*" is identical with the proposition "If anything is *A* it is *B*." Moreover, as we have already seen, the hypothetical "If anything is *A* it is *B*" does not have the truth-condition of a material implication. The hypothetical does not become true by the falsity of the antecedent. Rather, its truth-condition is that there is an *A* in some possible world, and that in every world if anything is an *A* it is a *B*. Recall also that "$A = B$" means for Leibniz that "*A* is *B* and *B* is *A*." And we know from what Leibniz says that "$\neg A = B$" should be read as "It is not the case that: *A* is *B* and *B* is *A*" rather than as "*A* is not-*B* and *B* is not-*A*."

This means that "$AB = \Box \neg AB$," which seems at first sight so counter-intuitive, says that "it is not the case that, in some possible world, there is an *AB*, and in every world if anything is an *AB* it is an *AB*." Since ex hypothesi nothing is *AB*, the first conjunct is false, and "$AB = \Box \neg AB$" is true.

Matters are even more complex with sentences which can be taken as expressing either essential propositions or existential propositions such as "A man not liable to sin is a man liable to sin." If this is taken as expressing an essential proposition, it is true. If it is taken as expressing an existential proposition, it will become false, because in this world there are no men who are not liable to sin, and hence a man not liable to sin is a non-entity in this world. Leibniz has some reservations about this consequence and writes, "But if someone prefers signs to be used in such a way that $AB = AB$, whether *AB* is a thing or not, and that in the case in which *AB* is not a thing, *B* and not-*B* can coincide – namely *per impossibile* – I do not object."[27] If this rule is adopted, the proposition "A round square is a round square" will be true rather than false, and also "A man not liable to sin is a man not liable to sin," even taken as expressing an existential proposition, will be true. But then, as Leibniz says, P and $\neg$ P will have the same truth-value, which would have disastrous consequences.

The difficulty of Leibniz's distinction between essential and existential propositions is that he has no way of expressing the distinction *inside* his symbolism, say as operators on propositions. As he has no quantifiers, he can hardly be expected to have two kinds of quantifiers, as some contemporary logicians do, one for the possibles and one for the actuals. He seems to take the distinction to be a matter of *presuppositions* made on the occasion of stating a proposition, about the domain of entities which are in consideration. This means that one and the same proposition can have different entailment relations depending on whether it is taken as an essential proposition or as an existential proposition. Thus, unless one strengthens the object language so that one can express in it what is presupposed, e.g., by having names to refer to different possible worlds, one can derive inconsistencies.

4. *Proper names and definite descriptions*

We are now clearer about the status of propositions like "Zeus is strong," which, according to Mates, is false in Leibniz's logic, because 'Zeus' is a name which does not denote. (It is difficult to be sure what Leibniz's explicit beliefs were, since, when he talks about a proposition in which the subject is a non-entity, he does not give examples of this kind. Leibniz's example of a non-entity is a man who is a stone, or a man who is not an animal.)[28]

There are, however, two possible answers to this, and the second is the one which must be ascribed to Leibniz. According to the first view 'Zeus' is treated as expressing an individual concept which is instantiated in a possible world but not in ours. By claiming that "Zeus is strong" we assert that, in the world in which the concept 'Zeus' is instantiated, he is strong. "Zeus is strong" then becomes a true proposition, and, for the reason given in §1, it would seem to be a contingent or existential proposition. That is to say, if the concept 'Zeus' could be treated as an individual concept, a point which will be queried later, then "Zeus is strong" is contingent only in the way in which "Caesar crossed the Rubicon" is contingent for Leibniz. For if a person did not cross the Rubicon, he is not the historical Caesar and so "Caesar did not cross the Rubicon," could not be true in any possible world. Similarly, if a person were not strong, he would not be *the* mythical Zeus, and so in no possible world could Zeus not have been strong. Yet, just as it is possible for a man to have existed in a possible world who had all the properties of Caesar except those related to his crossing the Rubicon – a man very like Caesar but not he – it is logically possible for a god to have existed who was like Zeus except that he was not strong – and thus in this sense, the "contrary is possible" and the proposition "Zeus is strong" is contingent.

Leibniz, however, seemed to take a different, alternative view: namely, that we have the means only to treat individuals in this world as properly individuated entities and have corresponding individual concepts, and that 'Pegasus' or 'Zeus' express only a general concept. Then "Zeus is strong" will be a true essential proposition.

As others have claimed that 'Pegasus' or 'Zeus' express individual concepts, I must explain in detail why I do not take this to be the case. First, it is important to remember that concepts are logical entities which do not depend on the owner. In contrast to this having a concept and understanding a concept are abilities or dispositions which are properties of the agent who is a thinker. God's understanding of a concept is obviously different from our inadequate and partial understanding of the concept. We often have, as Leibniz says, clear but confused, or non-distinct ideas of things. We may have a clear idea of Julius Caesar – we can distinguish him from other people. Yet we know very little of his properties, even some very important ones. We know none of his genetic properties – we do not know what his blood type was, for example. The individual concept of Caesar however includes all predicates of him – whether we know them or not. There is no God's concept of Caesar and our concept of Caesar.

As Leibniz says, it is the nature of individual substances (that is to say, individuals in the actual world) to have complete individual concepts – corresponding to the particular 'haecceitas' (thisness) of the individual. We cannot, however, get at the 'haecceitas' of things which exist in other possible worlds. We cannot point to them, for example. We try to reach them through the description of the features that they have. But any description we give can be satisfied by different things in different worlds. For example, if we think by 'Pegasus' the winged horse on which Bellerophon rode, there are indefinitely many ways of filling in the details of other properties, each corresponding to a creature in a different possible world. Thus 'Pegasus' does not name an individual in one possible world. According to Leibniz, the concept of an individual substance is such that "from it a reason can be given for *all* the predicates of the subject to which this concept can be attributed."[29] The concept of Alexander the Great is a full individual concept even if we do not know the full details of all that is true of Alexander, since we know *whom* it is of and hence that every predicate that is true of him is a component of the concept, and that nothing else is. The concept of Pegasus is not fully determined in this sense. Leibniz often writes that an abstraction does not have a complete concept. We could treat all names of fictitious beings like Pegasus as definite descriptions (obviously *not* to be analysed in the Russellian manner but to be treated as complex singular terms) which may be instantiated in multiple different possible worlds by slightly different fictitious beings.

Obviously there are infinitely many individual concepts that are not instantiated in our world and only instantiated in different possible worlds. Each individual concept is instantiated in only one possible world. But we cannot individuate one possible individual or one possible world if it is not an actual one. Thus we cannot use a proper name to designate *an* individual in one possible world.

Even when we use a proper name that designates a particular individual in this world, the moment we use it to introduce a counter-factual situation, it ceases, according to Leibniz, to designate one individual. It corresponds to indefinitely many possible individuals in indefinitely many possible worlds. The proper name then functions like a description. In a reply to Arnauld, who accused him of talking of several possible Adams, Leibniz replies that he is in agreement with Arnauld that one cannot conceive of several possible Adams. But he explains, when he spoke of several Adams (each of whom behaved differently in the Garden of Eden), what he did was the following:[30]

> But when I speak of several Adams, I do not take Adam for a determined individual but for some person conceived under a general understanding (sub

> ratione generalitatis), under circumstances which *seem to us* to determine Adam to be an individual but which *do not truly do so sufficiently;* as for instance, when we mean by Adam the first man, whom God puts in a pleasure garden, which he leaves through sin, and from whose side God made a woman. But all this does not sufficiently determine him, and so there might be several other disjunctively possible Adams, or several individuals whom these conditions fit. This is true no matter what finite number of predicates incapable of determining all the rest one takes.

We are made to realize that, in Leibniz's logic, proper names which stand for individuals in this world and express individual concepts instantiated in only one world play a role quite different from definite descriptions or seeming names, which actually mean general description that may be instantiated by different objects in different worlds. Any general description has two readings. For example, let it be that "the first man" is instantiated by Adam in the actual world. But in a different possible world, where the history is quite different, the definite description will pick out a quite different individual. Thus, as in the case of universal propositions, the same sentence with the same definite description can be asserted to make either an essential proposition or an existential proposition. In the latter case, the proposition will say that the object which happens to instantiate the definite description in this world has a certain property, whereas the former says that in every possible world the object which instantiates the description in that world has a certain property in the world.

In contrast to this 'Adam' used as a name in the Old Testament denotes a particular individual in this world and expresses an individual concept which cannot be instantiated in any other possible world. (This means that, in Leibniz's system, unlike Frege's or Quine's, proper names and definite descriptions cannot be assimilated to one another apart from the counterfactual contexts mentioned above where proper names are used to stand for general descriptions.)[31] Although Leibniz sometimes wrote as if, in his logic, he assimilated all singular propositions to universal propositions, there is a fundamental difference in his system between a proper name which expresses an individual concept corresponding to an infinite list of predicates and other general terms or descriptions (which do not contain a proper name as part). Strictly speaking, we can use proper names to express individual concepts of things only when they name things in this world. We cannot use names from God's point of view. All expressions we use have rules of their use. We cannot use a name to express an individual concept in God's mind if we do not know *which* individual concept it is. Names like 'Pegasus' cannot express a 'complete' individual concept consisting of infinitely many predicates and can only be treated as a shorthand for definite descriptions of finite length.

As we saw, if a definite or complex general term expresses a contradictory concept which cannot be instantiated in any possible world, then for Leibniz the proposition expressed by a sentence in which it occurs becomes always false. Thus "The round square = the round square" and "The round square is round" are both false.

On the other hand we can assert true propositions about things which we know do not exist in this world, or about things of which we do not know whether they exist in this world or not. We can not do this, however, through the use of a name that expresses a complete individual concept of them.

5. *Existence as predicate*

Leibniz believed, as we have seen, that to be (*esse*) or to exist (*existere*) could mean either possible existence or actual existence, depending on the presupposition. Possible existence of an individual *X* meant for Leibniz that the concept of *X* was a possible one. It may not be compossible with the other concepts instantiated in our world, but it is possible for it to be instantiated in some world. To assert possible existence, then, means nothing more than to make a claim about a concept, i.e., that it is a concept an instantiation of which is a constituent of some possible world. Possible worlds also, Leibniz writes, are only ideal, and have existence in the mind of God.[32]

What about actual existence? Surely, we would like to say, actual existence cannot be a feature of certain concepts. Of course, if something does actually exist, it follows, as Leibniz says, that the concept of that individual is compossible with other concepts instantiated in this world. Thus actual existence entails some truth about the features of certain concepts, but it can surely not be identical with it.

Leibniz was somewhat confused with his difficulty, as he was attempting to work out a logic using a symbolism which had no quantifiers, and no apparatus to express second-order concepts. He did not, it seems, arrive at the kind of distinction Kant was to make a century later in his attack on the ontological argument. Leibniz rightly says that the question "What is an existent?" will be raised since an existent is a being or a 'possible' and something else as well. "We understand 'existent' or the actual as something added to possibility or essence."[33] At this point, however, he attempts to resolve the question by saying that "an existent is that which is compatible with the greatest number of things, i.e., the most possible entity." Is Leibniz aware here that he is referring to what he believes to be a contingent truth of our universe, or is he suggesting that actual existence amounts to *nothing more* than a feature of an individual concept – namely, that the individual concept is one which can be instantiated together with the greatest number of other individual concepts?

If his view is the latter, then, as Russell has said[34] it is untenable. For if existence is a possible of a certain kind, and if a possible exists only as an idea in God's mind (i.e., a possible instantiation of an individual concept), then an existent will end up by being a special kind of possible – the most compossible one – which exists as an object of thought in God's mind.

In another fragment, Leibniz says that "nothing in the concept of existence is explicable except that it goes into the perfect series of things."[35] If 'things' (*res*) here means actual existents, the explanation is circular, and if it means possibles, then we are again making existence to be explained only as a feature of concepts. It is obvious that Leibniz believed that there was a complete difference between the actual world of existent things and possible worlds which exist only as ideas. The efforts he made to explain the difference, however, were far from satisfactory.[36] This is probably because the existence of the actual world was never separable in his mind from God's creation. The feature of possible worlds, or concepts, which could enable God to choose to instantiate one rather than the other, was easily confused with what it is that God does when he does instantiate them. In other words, there is a confusion between the definition of the kinds of possibles that would be made actual and the definition of what it is to be an actual existent.

6. *Concepts resolvable at infinity*

Let us now return to the claim with which we began the chapter. Leibniz says that in a true proposition the predicate is contained in the subject, and yet he believes that this does not make all propositions necessary because in a contingent proposition the inclusion of the predicate in the subject is only "resolvable at infinity."

Think of various propositions with 'man' as the subject. In order to follow the method of *Ars Combinatoria* given in Chapter III, and to proceed to "find all the predicates" of 'man', we have to know something about the concept 'man', so as to be able more or less to fix its extension. One cannot look for further predicates of 'man' without at least knowing that a man is an animal and not a stone or a plant, or that man is a kind of being that has language, and so on. Therefore for Leibniz

"Man is an animal" is an essential proposition. 'Man' may be a complex concept. But if we know the use of the concept 'man' and recognize that, in any possible world, if a thing were not an animal it could not be a man, this gives us what we need for the a priori proof of the proposition.[37]

In contrast, think of the proposition "All men are sinners." Let us take it as expressing a contingent, or existential, proposition in the sense argued for in the two previous sections. The proposition then is understood as saying that all men in our world are sinners. The predicate "being a sinner" is contained in the concept 'man', *so long as we think only of men in our world,* i.e., "is a sinner" is a predicate true of all men – in this world. (They would have original sin for Leibniz.)

Why is this provable by infinite analysis? As Leibniz says, it is only by non-deductive a posteriori means that *we* know contingent truths such as this one (if we know it at all).[38] We have no a priori proof that all men are sinners which gives us the answer in a finite number of steps. But from this we can conclude that it is resolvable at infinity, i.e., that there is a proof for this proposition available to an infinite mind which involves infinitely many steps (say, like a proof employing a Ω rule) only if we already know that all contingent propositions can be proved. Leibniz believed that his discovery of differential calculus, which involves "resolution at infinity," would provide a counterexample to Aristotle's and his own previous conviction that proofs cannot have infinitely many steps. He thinks for example that we must understand clearly that we *can rigorously* prove that ½ + ¼ + ⅛ . . . = 1, although the number of terms of the series is not finite. But to give a proof of a truth involving infinitely many terms is surely not to give a proof which itself has 'infinitely' many steps.

Let us make clearer what Leibniz means by "resolvable at infinity" in mathematics. We have already seen in Chapter V that Leibniz denied that there are infinite numbers or an infinite quantity in the sense in which there are finite numbers or quantities. Leibniz writes that "despite my Infinitesimal Calculus I admit no true infinite number, though I confess that the multitude of things surpasses every finite number, or rather every number."[39] Thus in saying that the number of terms in the series on the left side of the equation $\frac{1}{2} + \frac{1}{4} + \frac{1}{8} \ldots = 1$ is 'infinite', he does not mean that there is a given number of its terms which is an infinite number. (Leibniz even attempted a proof to show that the notion of an infinite number is inconsistent. The proof will not be considered valid today as he begins by assuming that anyone who believes in an infinite number believes it to be the greatest number, an assumption which is not warranted.) We should heed his claim that 'Infinity' is a manner of speech.:

> When we speak of the infinite itself having made a leap to the end [of a series], or when we speak of the infinitely small, we are using a convenience of expression or a mental abbreviation. We speak truths only loosely, and these are made rigorous by explanation.[40]

It was the fact that the assumption of inexhaustibly many units of terms in the series is compatible with a rigorous proof involving only finite steps that for Leibniz threw light on the nature of contingent truths. In the proposition "All men are sinners," the predicate "is a sinner" is not necessarily involved in our understanding of the concept of man and need play no part in fixing its extension. We can know quite clearly what kind of entities we are talking about and yet may still have to find out whether each of them is a sinner or not. A proper understanding of the fact involves reference to the rest of the universe. To understand why this universe was created requires an infinite analysis of the concepts which God alone can carry out. Leibniz believes that God can do this, not because He sees the end of the analysis, there being no such end, but because He knows the principle which combines the concepts to be analyzed (i.e., the principle of perfection). It is like our using mathematical induction to give a finite proof of a truth concerning an infinite totality.

Leibniz supports his analogy with two kinds of arguments. They are independent of each other, but I believe that both are unconvincing. The first is the argument which says that, in order to understand any contingent fact, we need knowledge of all parts of the infinite universe and the infinitely complex relation of the fact to everything else.[41] What we understand by an infinity of things in the universe is very similar to what Leibniz believes we understand by 'infinitely many' terms of an inexhaustible series for an irrational number. "Properly speaking, it is true that there are always more of them than can be assigned. But there is no infinite number or line or any other infinite quantity, if these are understood as true wholes, as it is easy to prove."[42] However, since every existent is related to infinitely many other objects in *this* sense, an adequate proof of any contingent fact about an existent presupposes an unending list of reasons referring to the inexhaustible number of objects in turn. The example he offers is the way in which we need knowledge of all the moving planets to prove the contingently true proposition "The sun shines now." What is in question here is the non-finite process required to prove the links in what he elsewhere calls hypothetical necessity, i.e., that a particular event happens necessarily given the initial state of our universe and its laws of nature. God alone knows why this happens "since he sees everything which is in the series,"[43] which involves an infinite series. Again, this is not because God sees the last term of the series, since there is no such term, but because he understands how any term of the series comes about. Leibniz seems thus to be suggesting that the a priori proof which God alone could give is like our proving, e.g., that $1/2 + 1/4 + 1/8 \ldots = 1$. God understands the general principles which generate the infinite series of events in the universe in the same way that one may grasp a rule which generates a convergent series of infinitely many terms.

This argument would hold even if God had no choice in the universe he created, so long as the universe he did create consisted of infinite substances, and so long as the principle of sufficient reason operated in it. Nothing is random in the world. Every event and state has a reason why it is thus rather than otherwise. In an infinite universe the reasons become infinite too, and so we cannot give a proof in a finite number of steps. God knows the principle by which one reason is related to another and can give the proof despite its involving infinitely many steps. This first argument depends on the assumption that the universe is 'infinite' – that our world consists of infinitely many substances – as well as the principle of sufficient reason.

The second argument concerns not the 'infinitely many' connections which a particular fact in the universe has to other objects in it, and our laws of nature, but the explanation of the existence of our universe itself, with its constituents and laws of nature. Contingent truths, Leibniz claims, do not have a priori proofs, because they depend on how our universe is, which originates in God's will. However, God does not exercise his will at random. He freely but unfailingly acts on the *principle of what is best*.[44] In creating the world that he did create, God thought of infinitely many possible worlds and chose to actualize the best of them all. (As Rescher quite rightly says,[45] this Principle of What is Best, which God follows, has to be invoked to understand why one world was created rather than another. Once we agree with it, we will see that it gives a reason for the creation of this universe, which is demanded by the general principle of sufficient reason. But the Principle of the Best cannot itself be a consequence of the principle of sufficient reason as Couturat maintained. The most we could say in defence of Couturat is that if it is agreed that God's nature is benevolent, then, since the principle of sufficient reason demands that God has a reason for his actions, his nature will make him act on the Principle of the Best.)

The Principle of the Best, however, expresses the particular way in which Leibniz understands what is to count as the best possible world. Perfection is nothing, he claims, but the quantity of essence.[46] Thus each possible world is defined by a set of compossible concepts (i.e., a set of concepts which can be instantiated together), and the best world is the one in which the greatest variety of things exists in the most elegant simple manner. One can thus in principle carry out a calculus to determine the best of the infinite possible worlds. "A certain divine mathematics or metaphysics is exercised in the actual origination of things."[47] This means that the reason why God chose to create our universe rather than another can be given a proof, although it is a calculus involving infinitely many possible objects.

The second argument does gives us logical grounds for the proof of a contingent truth being "resolvable at infinity." But it relies on the Principle of the Best, which claims that God always freely chooses to realize the best, supplemented by a more specific and esoteric claim about what a better world is. As we have seen in the preceding section, what it gives is at most the criterion governing God's choice in his creation, and thus, unless one accepts Leibniz's idea of God's creation, it does not give us the logic of proof of the truths about created things, nor does it show us the nature of contingent truths.

Neither of the two arguments shows that the relation between contingent truths and their proofs is at all like infinite analysis in calculus, as Leibniz claims. In the latter, notions like limit, or irrational numbers, can be given a clear definition, and their existence can be proved by logical means. What it does show us is that there can be rigorous finite proofs for conclusions involving infinite series.

We are made to conclude that Leibniz's modal concepts have their logical basis in his notion of possible worlds. I must disagree with Kauppi who, in her interesting monograph, writes that Leibniz's definition of a necessary truth as one whose negation involves a contradiction does not *presuppose* the notion of possible worlds or assume the existence of possible worlds.[48] According to Kauppi a necessary truth would only be true in all possible worlds *were we to conceive of* such entities. However, as I have argued, the definition of a contingent truth as one whose negation is also possible cannot be given *any sense* without invoking the notion of other possible worlds in which there exist things very similar, but not identical, to the ones in this world. The denial of a contingent truth like "Augustus was emperor of Rome" can superficially be shown to contain a contradiction in a finite number of steps, depending on the knowledge one has of the individual concept of Augustus. The belief that such demonstrations do not amount to a proof of the logical impossibility of the negated proposition involves us, according to Leibniz, in thought about possible worlds.

In other words, if Leibniz is to hold the *praedicatum inest subjecto* thesis of truth in general and still maintain the difference between necessary truth and contingent truth, then he has to have recourse to other possible worlds. But this is nothing but a picturesque way of expressing the truth-values that we assign to various hypothetical propositions, including counter-factual ones.

Leibniz realized that we cannot arbitrarily assign truth-values to hypotheticals. We do not deduce their truth-values from some higher principles; but, as he so perceptively says, we find ourselves deciding the truth or falsity of hypotheticals "in a constant manner." What makes us assign such truth-values to hypothetical propositions is our understanding of the concepts we use. Our concepts are what they are by virtue of our using language (or other systems of signs) to refer to individuals and say things about them, as well as by virtue of our understanding what could be true if certain facts which do obtain had not been obtained. It is the denotation of individual names and the extension of predicates, or rather our gradual understanding of the nature of their denotation and extension, which give us our concepts (individual concepts and general concepts alike), and not vice versa. Thus the relations of concepts, Leibniz insists, are explained through truths of propositions.

7. *Concluding Remarks*

We have by no means covered all of the potentially interesting and thought provoking problems in Leibniz's philosophy of logic and language. Yet after our investigation into fields as different as Leibniz's treatment of our language of sensible qualities, his newly invented language of infinitesimals, the language and logic of relations, and the language of modality, we can discern three very important features of Leibniz's philosophy of logic and language. These give Leibniz's thought a very modern twist, despite his constant invocation of God and metaphysical principles and his deep respect for Plato, Aristotle, and some mediaeval thinkers.

The first and foremost feature is his insight that ideas must be discussed in the context of propositions: his insistence on identifying ideas expressed by words through how they contribute to the truth-conditions of the propositions in which they occur. This approach, which we examined in Chapter II as the *salva veritate* principle, is used in his analysis of words like 'heat' and colour words, his analysis of the language of infinitesimals, and his rewriting of sentences expressing certain relational facts. The very principle that enabled him to develop a realist view of secondary qualities and what one might call a referential theory of the meaning of words expressing sensory qualities enabled him to propose a rigorous language of infinitesimals while insisting that we can refer only to finite numbers and finite quantities.

The second important feature of his thought is the belief in objective necessary truths about possibles that coexists with what one might call his ontological actualism: in other words, the belief that only the actual world exists and that possibles exist only as ideas. Ideas are not to be taken as actual entities existing in this or any other world. This brings Leibniz closest to being what we now call a conceptualist. He was a Platonist in epistemology and an Aristotelian in his ontology. Leibniz invokes both his conceptual objectivism and actualism in his attempt to distinguish contingent truths from necessary truths, which was one of his central concerns. Whether Leibniz succeeded in giving a coherent logical characterization of this distinction without resorting to theistic intuitions is, as we saw, a difficult question, especially in the case of singular propositions. The contingency of singular propositions meant that counterfactual suppositions about actual individuals made sense; and yet, Leibniz insisted, actual individuals only exist in this world and in no other possible worlds. We have tried to make sense of Leibniz's position. Whatever we may think of the details of Leibniz's claims about possible worlds there is no doubt that Leibniz's approach has had a deep influence on modal logicians in this century since C. I. Lewis, and has enabled us to think about modality in a much more precise way.

The third important feature in Leibniz's philosophy of logic and language is what might be called his interest in *de re* ideas. This, I believe, reveals itself in the importance he attaches to clear but non-distinct ideas, and in his notion of a complete individual concept. Moreover, his claim that in all true propositions the predicate concept is included in the subject concept is impossible to grasp without understanding how *de re* concepts function.

As I indicated in Chapter II, the favourite example used by Leibniz of concept identity is that of a triangle and that of a trilateral. The idea of a triangle is the same as the idea of a trilateral, even if 'triangle' does not mean the same as 'trilateral'. It is the idea *of* the same geometrical shape. The word 'triangle' and 'trilateral' *refer* to the same geometrical shape in all possible worlds. We also saw, in Chapter IV § 2, that according to Leibniz a secondary quality is identical with a primary quality. When we have a clear but confused idea of the sensible quality, we call it a secondary quality, and when we have a distinct idea of the same sensible quality we grasp it is as a primary quality. In § 1 of this chapter, we quoted Leibniz explaining that when he says that in a true subject-predicate proposition the predicate is included in the subject, the required link between subject and predicate exists only *a parte rei*. Only by grasping what the subject concept is a concept of, can we see that the predicate belongs to it, i.e., see that the object falls under the predicate concept. We have also seen that for Leibniz a proper name which is used to designate an actual person expresses a complete individual concept, whereas when one talks of possible Adams or possible Sextuses, the names 'Adam' and 'Sextus' do not designate particular individuals and hence do not express complete individual concepts. We are shifting the use of the names to express general ideas. This is why I have suggested that we can only designate an individual in this world, and any reference to a possible individual refers to an indefinite number of possible individuals in different possible worlds, each satisfying a definite description given explicitly or implicitly by the shifting use of proper names in counterfactual contexts. Truths that can be established *a parte rei* on one hand and only *a parte dicti* on the other, are grasped in very different ways. I agree with Leibniz on this, but even those who disagree with him cannot deny the importance of the cluster of theories that he generated through his *de re* notion of ideas.

Insights that are most original in the thoughts of a genius like Leibniz are often imperfect, expressed in various tentative ways. Sometimes, as we have seen, the way they are expressed leads to unexpected difficulties. It is important to develop a feel for what was original in Leibniz and to understand what Leibniz was aiming at even if he did so imperfectly. It is not very fruitful to use the well-developed logical techniques of today not merely to show the difficulties in Leibniz's formulation of a problem, but to discredit the whole of Leibniz's enterprise in that area. Leibniz would obviously have been happy to clarify and make rigorous the various formulations of his ideas, which often come from unedited manuscripts, letters, or loose notes he kept for himself. Indeed, the three features of Leibniz's philosophy of logic and language mentioned above have to be assessed in the context of yet another general characteristic of Leibniz's thought. This is his obsession with proofs, algorithmic methods, and the establishment of particular truths, combined with his continuing interest in what is not exhausted in the finite and in the mechanical. If the two types of mentality which have had the greatest popular appeal in the twentieth century are those of positivism and Hegelianism, both, in opposite ways, are very remote from the spirit of Leibniz. According to Hao Wang, Kurt Gödel believed that of all the philosophers Spinoza was the best man and Leibniz the most intelligent. And perhaps there is something in Leibniz that would appeal to the best in the twentieth-century mind: the openness that leads beyond accepted solutions, an interest in seeing any problem in a wider setting, supported by a concern for methodological rigour and technical competence.

Notes

Chapter I

1 Memorandum to the Duke of Würtenberg, § 50, 1668–9, *Akademie,* 4th series, vol. 1, p. 108: ". . . so ist auch eine ganz der vorigen wiederwärtige Maxim nöthig, dass nehmlich die gelehrten und studirenden, soviel möglich bey conversation, bey Leuten, und in der Welt sein sollen."

2 Letter to Huygens, 20/30 February 1691, G. *Math.* 2, p. 85: "N'y a-t-il personne à present qui médite en philosophie sur la médicine? Feu Mr. Crane y estait propre, mais messieurs les Cartesians sont trop prevenus de leur hypothèses. J'aime mieux un Leeuwenhoek qui me dit ce qu'il voit, qu'un Cartesian qui me dit ce qu'il pense. Il est pourtant nécessaire de joindre le raisonnement aux observations."

3 Political memorandum, 1697, "Ermahnung an die Teutschen" (Advice to Germans), *Klopp,* Vol. 6, p. 188.

4 Letter to Edmond Mariotte, July 1676, *Akademie,* 2nd series, vol. 1, p. 269.

5 "Spongia Exprobationum seu quod nullum doctrinae genus sit contemnendum," in D. Mahnke, "Leibniz als Gegner der Gelehrteneinseitigkeit," *Wissenschaftliche Beilage zum Jahresbericht des königlichen Gymnasiums* (Stade, 1912), pp. 94–100.

6 G. *Phil.* 7, pp. 172–173; *Wiener,* p. 45.

7 The episode must have struck Jonathan Swift quite differently. In *Gulliver's Travels* he describes Balnibarbi, a country ruined by the projects of Academicians. In particular he describes a mill made on the advice of an Academician based on speculative hydraulic principles. After a hundred men have been employed for two years, the work fails, and the mill is left in ruins.

8 Letter to Landgraf Ernst of Hesse Rheinfels, 4/14 August 1683, in C. von Rommeld, ed., *Leibniz und Landgraf Ernst von Hessen-Rheinfels,* Vol. 1. (Frankfurt 1847), English translation in P. Riley, ed., *The Political Writings of Leibnitz,* p. 187.

9 "Ursachen warum Cannstadt füglich zur Hauptstatt des Herzogsthums Würtenberg zu machen," § 47, *Akademie,* 4th Series, Vol. 1, p. 107, cited in R. W. Meyer, *Leibniz und die europäische Ordnungskrise* (Hamburg, 1948), translated as *Leibniz and the Seventeenth-Century Revolution,* by J. P. Stern, p. 97.

10 Letter to Thomas Burnett, c. 1700–1, G. *Phil.* 3, p. 277. Translation in P. Riley, ed., *Political Writings of Leibniz,* p. 193.

11 *Über der Wille in der Natur,* 1836, Preface to 2d edition, 1854.

12 *Logische Untersuchungen,* vol. 1, chapter 10, § 60.

13 In a letter to Des Billettes (G. *Phil.* 7, p. 451) he writes: "Mon système dont vous estes curieux, Monsieur, de sçavoir des nouvelles, n'est pas un corps complet de Philosophie, et je n'y prétends nullement de rendre raison de tout ce que d'autres ont prétendu d'expliquer." (My system about which you are curious to learn, sir, is not a complete system of philosophy, I do not purport to justify at all what others have purported to explain.)

14 Louis Couturat, *La Logique Leibniz d'après des documents inédits* (Paris, 1901). Although writers such as Ruth Saw have objected to Russell's and Couturat's basing Leibniz's philosophy on logical principles, Leibniz writes: "J'ay reconnu que la vraye Métaphysique n'est guères different de la vraye Logique, c'est-à-dire, de l'art d'inventer en general." (I realised that true metaphysics is no different from real logic, namely from the art of discovery in general.) Letter to Duchess Sophie, G. *Phil.* 4, p. 292. Quoted in L. Couturat, "Sur la métaphysique de Leibniz," *Revue de métaphysique et de morale,* 1902, p. 14.

15 R. Carnap, *Meaning and Necessity,* pp. 9–10; S. Kripke, "Semantic analysis of modal logic," *Zeitschrift für mathematische Logic und Grundlagen der Mathematik* 9, 1963; "A note on quantification and modalities" *Theoria* 23.195 J. Hintikka, *Models for Modalities* (Dordrecht, 1969); D. Lewis, "Counterpart theory and quantified modal logic," *Journal of Philosophy* 65, 1968.

16 H. Reichenbach, "Die Bewegungslehre bei Newton, Leibniz und Huyghens," *Kantstudien* 29, 1924, pp. 416–38. English translation, "The theory of motion according to Newton, Leibniz and Huyghens," in M. Reichenbach and R. Cohen, eds., *H. Reichenbach Selected Writings, 1909–1953* (Dordrecht and Boston, 1978).

17 For details of this, see Jonathan Cohen, "On the project of a universal character," *Mind,* 53, 1954.

18 In his 1986 book *The Philosophy of Leibniz,* Mates's view on non-ens is much more complex, and I am in agreement with much of what he says there.

19 I have defended a non-reductionist interpretation of Leibniz's view of relational properties as far as spatial and temporal predicates were concerned in a paper published in Japan in 1967. A defence of a general non-reductionist interpretation of Leibniz's doctrine on relations can be found in the interesting paper by J. Hintikka in *Ajatus,* 1969. (G. Parkinson also casts doubt on reductionist interpretation in his book, but does not give positive arguments in support of any view which would replace it.)

Chapter II

1 Letter to Placcius, 16 November 1686, *Dutens* 6, part 1, p. 32: "Quanquam enim mihi non alia ibi videatur opus esse demonstratione quam quae pendet ex mutue aequipollentium substitutione."

2 Couturat, *OFI,* p. 259.

3 Michael Dummett, *Frege: Philosophy of Language,* 2d ed. London, 1981, p. 195.

4 G. Frege, *Foundations of Arithmetic,* p. 76.

5 B. Mates, *Elementary Logic,* p. 215.

6 For example, W. V. O. Quine, *Word and Object,* p. 116.

7 Hector Neri Castañeda has contended that this passage shows that the *salva veritate* principle gives a criterion of coincidence of terms and not of their identity. He agrees that terms are concepts. Nevertheless in his interpretation 'coincidence' means 'coextension', and hence non-identical concepts can be coincident. There are, however, too many formulations of the *salva veritate* principle in which the words 'same' or 'identical' alone are used to warrant such an interpretation, and also many passages, as in the one cited above, where Leibniz writes 'coincidence or identity', suggesting that he is using the two words to express the same concept.

8 As noted by Parkinson, *LRLM,* p. 6, and by B. Mates, *The Philosophy of Leibniz,* pp. 47–51.

9 P. Geach, *Reference and Generality,* p. 22.

10 Parkinson is therefore misleading when he translates a passage of Leibniz as "All terms are understood to refer to concrete things alone" (Parkinson, *LLP,* p. 47), which suggests again that terms are words which are used to refer to things. But in Leibniz's original text there is no mention of referring. It merely says that all terms are understood to be about concrete things (*de concretis*), Couturat, *OFI,* p. 356. Here again Leibniz is thinking of concepts, and though he uses words like substantives, he should be taken as meaning concepts expressed by substantive expressions. Otherwise one cannot make any sense of his claim that the term 'big' is the same as 'a big one' because obviously they are not the same words.

11 B. Mates, *The Philosophy of Leibniz,* p. 125.

12 'Dialogus', August 1677, G. *Phil.* 7, pp. 190–3, "Dialogue on the connection between things and words," *Loemker,* pp. 182–5.

13 Frege, Letter to Linke, 24 August 1919, *Philosophical and Mathematical Correspondence,* p. 98, and Notes for Darmstädter, July 1919, *Posthumous Writings,* pp. 255–6.

14 Frege, Notes for Darmstädter, July 1919, *Posthumous Writings,* p. 253.

15 B. Mates, *Philosophy of Leibniz,* p. 126.

16 "*Generales Inquisitiones de Analysi Notionum et Veritatem,*" 1686, Couturat, *OFI,* p. 362: "Nam respectus illi [Terminus] per propositiones sive veritates explicantur."

17 Although the very same concept is expressed by expressions that are not formally identical in the two occurrences, this will not make them different concepts that are contingently coincident, as Castañeda has suggested.

18 *NE*, Book 4, Chapter 7, § 12.

19 The expression '*materiale*' which I interpret as 'opaque' must refer to the mediaeval logicians' talk of "*suppositio materialis,*" where a word was used to refer to the word itself: "Est igitur suppositio quaedam materialis, quaedam formalis. Et dicitur materialis quando ipsa dictio supponit vel pro ipsa voce absolute vel pro ipsa dictione composita ex voce et significantione, ut si dicamus 'Homo est disyllabum', 'Homo est nomen'." (William of Shyrewood *Intro-*

ductiones, p. 75). However, it is not the particular word which in Leibniz's Latin text is the word '*triangulum,*' which, "by its nature" leads us to the truth that it has 180 degrees. The same nature would be true of what is expressed by the English word 'triangle' or the German word '*Dreiecke*'. Just as in "*Homo est nomen*" the truth survives translation.

20 "Über Sinn und Bedeutung," *Zeitschrift für Philosophie und philosophische Kritik* (1892), 100. English translation, "On sense and reference," in P. T. Geach and M. Black, eds., *Translations from the Philosophical Writings of Gottlob Frege.* (Oxford, 1952).

21 *Dialogus,* 1677, G. *Phil.* 7, pp. 190–4; *Wiener,* pp. 9–10.

22 As F. Feldman queries in, Review of Ishiguro's *Leibniz's Philosophy of Logic and Language, International Philosophical Quarterly,* June 1974, p. 247.

23 B. Mates, *The Philosophy of Leibnitz,* p. 127.

24 *NE,* Book 4, Chapter 2, § 1, p. 363, and Book 4, Chapter 7 § 4, p. 408. Thus we cannot read these passages as proving that the concept of triangle and the concept of trilateral are different as some have done.

25 *NE,* Book 2, Chapter 22, § 2. Also Book 3, Chapter 5, § 12 and Book 4, Chapter 8, § 5.

26 "Quid Sit Idea," 1676, G. *Phil.* 7, p. 263; *Wiener,* p. 281.

27 Ibid.

28 Ibid.

29 Ibid.

30 *NE* Book 3, Chapter 4, § 17.

31 Ibid. Book 2, Chapter 1, § 1.

32 "Der Gedanke," in *Beiträge zur Philosophie des deutschen Idealismus,* I (1918), translated by A. and M. Quinton, in *Mind,* 65, 1956. Also in *Philosophical Logic,* 67, p. 17, edited by P. F. Strawson.

33 Couturat, *OFI,* p. 363; Parkinson, *LLP,* p. 54.

34 Couturat, *OFI,* p. 360. Parkinson, *LLP,* p. 51.

35 Such second-order properties are introduced by Richard Montague as semantic counterparts of singular terms in the paper "The proper treatment of quantification in ordinary English." Richmond Thomason, ed., *Selected Works* 1976.

36 Parkinson, *LLP,* p. 58

37 See Fred Feldman, *International Philosophical Journal,* June 1974, p. 246, as well as Benson Mates.

38 Bodemann *LH* IV, viii, 61 r.

39 "Elements of calculus," 1679, § 10. Couturat, *OFI,* pp. 49–57. *Loemker,* p. 237.
40 Ibid., § 12 *Loemker,* pp. 237–8.
41 *NE,* Book 4, Chapter 2, § 1; *Akademie,* 6th Series, Vol. 6, p. 363.
42 Ibid. Book 4, Chapter 7, § 4, p. 408.
43 Husserl's point, made in his *Philosophie der Arithmetik* seems to have been based also on his assumption that the *salva veritate* principle was for Leibniz a definition of identity of things. Such a principle would, for Husserl, presuppose our ability to intuit individual things (prior to grasping various properties of them) and thus cannot be a definition of how individual things are to be identified.
44 G. Frege, Review of E. G. Husserl, *Philosophie der Arithmetik,* Vol. I in *Zeitschrift für Philosophie und philosophische Kritik,* (1894) pp. 313–32; and in P. Geach and M. Block, eds. and trans., *Translations from the Philosophical Writings of Gottlob Frege,* (Oxford, 1952), p. 80; reprinted in *Kleine Schriften*. I. Angelelli, ed., (Darmstadt, 1967).
45 In rewriting this chapter I profited from the criticism and queries raised by many philosophers who had reviewed the first edition or who have since written on the problems discussed in it, in their works, and I thank them very much. I must specially mention those of Benson Mates, Fred Feldman, Hector Neri Castañeda, Peter Remnant and Hans Burkhardt to whom I have tried to reply. I was also helped by comments of Richard Spensor-Smith, Robert Tragessar, and David Wiggins.

Chapter III

1 Letter to Tschirnhaus, May 1678, *Akademie,* 2nd series, vol. 1, p. 411.
2 "Dialogue on the connection between things and words," 1677, G. *Phil.* 7, p. 192; *Wiener,* p. 9.
3 *Dissertatio de Arte Combinatoria,* 1666, G. *Phil.* 6, pp. 27–102. This is an expanded version of a dissertation presented to the University of Leipzig; it was reprinted twice in Leibniz's lifetime, without Leibniz's knowledge.
4 Letter to Oldenburg, 2 August 1676, *G. Math.* 1, pp. 121: "Ea vero nihil differt ab Analysi illa suprema, ad cujus intima, quantum judicare possum, Cartesius non pervenit. Est enim ad eam constituedam opus Alphabeto Cogitationum humanarum. Et ad Inventionem ejus Alphabeti, opus

est Analysi Axiomatum."(Indeed this is not different from that supreme analysis, to the secret of which, as far as can be judged, Descartes did not succeed in attaining. This is because for this analysis to be constituted the alphabet of human cognition is necessary and for the discovery of the alphabet, the analysis of axioms is necessary.)

5 *Préface à la science générale,* Couturat, *OFI,* p. 153; *Wiener,* p. 16: "D'autant qu'il n'y aura point d'equivocations ny amphibolies; et que tout ce qu'on y dira intelligiblement, sera dit a propos."

6 "*Generales Inquisitiones de Analysi Notionum et Veritatum,*" 1686, Couturat, *OFI,* p. 377; Parkinson *LLP,* p. 66: "Si ut spero possim ‹concipere omnes propositiones instar terminorum, et› Hypotheticas [concipere] instar categoricarum et universaliter tractare omnes, miram ea res in mea characteristica et analysi notionum promittit facilitatem, eritque inventum maximi momenti."

7 *Elements of a Calculus,* 1679, Parkinson, *LLP,* p. 20; Couturat, *OFI,* p. 53.

8 Michael Dummett, review of Rescher's "Leibniz's interpretation of his logical calculi," *Journal of Symbolic Logic* 21, 1956.

9 We will see in Chapter VII that depending on whether the proposition is an essential one or a contingent one, "Some *f* is *g*" should be understood either as "If in any world there were *f*s, then some of them would be *g*s" or "If in this world there are *f*s, then some of them are *g*s."

10 See G. *Phil.* 7, pp. 211–217; Parkinson, *LLP,* p. 115.

11 "De Affectibus," 1674; Grua, 2, p. 537: "Propositio *A est B* hoc significat: si quid est *A,* id est *B*. Est *B* id est conceptus eius involvit conceptum *B*."

12 N. Rescher, "Leibniz's interpretation of his logical calculi," *Journal of Symbolic Logic* 19, 1954. Rescher says that this is an interpretation which Leibniz actually gives. I do not know where Leibniz explicitly says that his inclusion relation of concepts can be interpreted as inclusion relation of properties. As Leibniz has written so much, I assume that it is in parts that I have not come across.

13 Professor Remnant has commented on these remarks, which were already in my first edition (*Canadian Journal of Philosophy,* March 1975), and writes that like Michael Dummett, I have overlooked the possibility of attributing the disparateness of 'gold' and 'silver' to the fact that on analysis one of them is found to contain a property logically inconsistent with some property of the other. This interpretation of 'disparateness' is quite different from that of Rescher, since the property of silver could contain a property "logically inconsistent" with some property of gold, without the "set of properties" of each being disjoint. More importantly, it does not seem to me at all clear that every pair of non-overlapping concepts must involve "logically inconsistent" properties. A pair of properties that would be incompatible, were they to be possessed by one and the same thing, may perfectly be compatible were different things to have them. It is therefore unclear what are "logically inconsistent" properties. Are any properties of an apple inconsistent with some properties of the number 3? Yet, the concept of an apple and that of the number 3 are obviously disparate.

14 G. *Phil.* 7, p. 208; Parkinson, *LLP,* p. 112.

15 Again Peter Remnant has expressed dissatisfaction with this reading, since he rightly remarks that for Leibniz "some *f* is *g*" means something which is both *f* and *g* is possible, which he (wrongly, I believe) thinks is not equivalent to "if there were some *f,* some of them would be *g.*" If this last proposition is taken as ranging over possibles, surely it is equivalent to the preceding proposition?

16 "*Generales Inquisitiones*" Couturat, *OFI,* p. 377; Parkinson, *LLP,* p. 66.

17 "*Introductio ad Encyclopaediam Arcanam*" Couturat, *OFI,* p. 514: "Non videtur satis in potestate humana esse Analysis conceptuum, ut scilicet possimus pervenire ad notiones primitivas, seu ad ea quae per se concipiuntur; sed magis in potestate humana est analysis veritatum, multas enim veritates possumus absolute demonstrare et reducere ad veritates primitivas indemonstrabiles; itaque huic potissimum incumbamus." (It is not clear whether it is sufficiently in human power to analyse concepts and whether we can arrive at primitive concepts, namely to those concepts which can be conceived by itself; however it is more in human power to analyse truths, and we can demonstrate absolutely many truths and reduce them to indemonstrable primitive truths. Thus we depend on these above all.)

18 Couturat, *OFI,* pp. 220–1. It is interesting to notice how Leibniz's reasoning here is similar to that which Wittgenstein was to make for the independence of elementary propositions in the *Tractatus.*

19 "Dissertatio De Arte Combinatoria," § 65, *Akademie,* 6th series, Vol. 1, p. 195; Parkinson, *LLP,* p. 4.

20 *Discours de métaphysique,* § 23, G. *Phil.* 4; *Loemker,* p. 318.

21 Letter to Foucher, 1687, G. *Phil.* 1, p. 392: "Cependant il ne faut pas s'imaginer que nous puissions tousjours pousser l'analyse à bout jusqu'aux premiers possibles, aussi ne l'est-il pas nécessaire pour la science." (However one should not think that we can always carry out the analysis until the end when we reach primary possibles. Nor is it necessary for science to do so.)

22 "Projet d'un art d'inventer," 1686, Couturat, *OFI,* p. 176; *Wiener,* p. 51.

23 *Principia Mathematica,* vol. I, part I, p. 161: "It is unnecessary in practice to know what objects belong to the lowest type, or even whether the lowest type of variable occurring in a given context is that of individuals or some other. For in practice only the relative types of variables are relevant; thus the lowest type occurring in a given context may be called that of individuals so far as that context is concerned. Accordingly the above account of individuals is not essential to the truth of what follows. All that is essential is the way in which other types are generated from individuals, however the type of individuals may be constituted."

24 Letter to Landgraf Ernst von Hessen-Rheinfels, 29 Dec. 1684, Rommel, ed., *Leibniz und Landgraf Ernst von Hessen-Rheinfels,* Vol. 2, p. 61. Frankfurt am Main 1847.

25 Letter to Bernouilli, 23 August 1696, G. *Math.* 3, p. 321: "Unum addo multum apud me interesse inter haec duo; in dubium vocare propositionem et demonstrationem ejus expectere. . . ." (Let me add one thing, of many that interest me. It is one thing to doubt a proposition, another thing to expect a proof of it. . . .)

26 For example Fred Feldman in a review of the first edition of this book in *International Philosophical Quarterly,* June 1974, p. 246–9, has written that since "Miss Ishiguro nowhere mentions any restrictions on what is to count as a paraphrase," the following difficulty would ensue: "Suppose someone should claim that 'x is an entity' expresses a simple concept. We can point out that this is logically equivalent to 'x is a thinking entity or x is a non thinking entity'. . . . So no word expresses a simple concept." These are indeed logically equivalent phrases but not, I believe, paraphrases, or 'definition' in Leibniz's sense.

Professor Feldman is wrong in suggesting that I think that all of what I call simple words – i.e. words whose meaning is not determined by the meaning of its parts – express simple concepts. Obviously some simple words express very complex concepts. (I was merely suggesting that in the case of simple words, whether they express simple concepts or complex concepts, synonymity and concept identity may come together.)

27 *Termini Simpliciores,* 1680–84: *Grua* 2, p. 542.

28 Yost, *Leibniz's Philosophical Analysis,* p. 181.

29 Letter to the Duchess Sophie, *c.* 1680, G. *Phil.* 4, p. 296.

30 "L'Art d'inventer," Maxime no. 5 bis, G. *Phil.* 7, p, 83–4: "Il est tres difficile de venir à bout de l'analyse de choses, mais il n'est pas si difficile d'achever l'analyse des vérités dont on a besoin. Parce que l'analyse d'une vérité est achevée quand on en a trouvé la demonstration, et il n'est pas tousjours nécessaire d'achever l'analyse du sujet ou predicat pour trouver la demonstration de la proposition."

31 "An vero unquam ab hominibus perfecta institui possit analysis notionum, sive an ad prima possibilia, ac notiones irresolubiles, sive (quod eodem redit) ipsa absoluta Attributa DEI, nempe causas primas, atque ultimam rerum rationem, cogitationes suas reducere possint, nunc quidem definire non ausim." Meditationes de Cognitione, 1684, *G. Phil.* 4, p. 425.

32 "General Inquiries about the Analysis of Concepts and Truths," 1686. Parkinson, *LLP,* p. 76; Couturat, *OFI,* p. 387.

33 *Russell,* p. 17.

34 "De Veritatibus Primis," G. *Phil.* 7, p. 195.

35 *NE,* Book 3, chapter 1, § 4, p. 276.

36 Ibid., Book 2, chapter 8, § 2, p. 129.

37 *G. Phil.* 4, p. 357: "Veritatum rationis prima est principium contradictionis vel quod eodem redit identicorum." (The first of the truths of reason is the principle of contradiction or, what comes to the same thing, that of identity.)

38 *NE,* Book 4, chapter 2, § 1, p. 363.

39 G. *Phil.* 7, p. 185.

40 See Parkinson, *LRLM,* p. 60.

41 "A negative proposition is 'A does not contain B' or 'It is false that A is B'." Couturat, *OFI,* p. 368; Parkinson, *LLP,* p. 58.

42 "Falsum in genere definio quod non est verum" in "De Analysi Notionum et Veritatum," Couturat, *OFI,* p. 371; Parkinson, *LLP,* p. 61.
43 *NE,* Book 4, chapter 2, § 1, p. 362.
44 Untitled manuscript on philosophical proofs, G. *Phil.* 7, p. 299.
45 Parkinson, *LLP,* p. 5; G. *Phil.* 4, p. 69.

Chapter IV

1 *NE,* Book 4, Chapter 2, § 14. *Akademie* 6th series, Vol. 6, 1962, p. 374.
2 The thoughts expressed in the first part of this chapter were first formed as a reply in a question raised by Paul Fischler in a graduate seminar given at Cornell University in 1969.
3 *NE,* Book 2, Chapter 29, § 4, p. 255. Also see Book 4, Chapter 17, § 13, p. 487.
4 Ibid.
5 Letter to Queen Sophie Charlotte of Prussia, 1702, G. *Phil.* 6, p. 492; *Wiener,* p. 355.
6 Ibid.
7 Ibid.
8 *NE,* Book 2, Chapter 2, § 1, p. 120.
9 Ibid., Book 3, Chapter 4, § 16, p. 299.
10 Ibid., Book 2, Chapter 8, § 21, p. 132.
11 "An introduction on the value and method of natural science," 1682–4, *Loemker,* p. 285 [Bodemann *LH*, XXXVII, iv, 1–6].
12 *NE,* Book 4, Chapter 6, § 8 and § 11, p. 405.
13 Ibid., Book 3, Chapter 11, § 24, p. 354.
14 Ibid., Book 2, Chapter 8, § 13; Book 4, Chapter 6, § 7, pp. 131, 403.
15 Ibid., Book 2, Chapter 8, § 10, p. 130.
16 E.g., G. Paul, "Lenin's theory of knowledge," in Margaret Macdonald, ed., *Philosophy and Analysis.* Oxford, 1954.
17 *NE,* Book 3, Chapter 2, § 3, p. 287.
18 *Preface to an Edition of Nizolius,* 1670, *Loemker,* p. 126: G. *Phil.* 4, p. 147.
19 *NE,* Book 3, Chapter 3, § 14, pp. 292–293.
20 Ibid., Book 3, Chapter 6, § 32, p. 323.
21 "A paper on some logical difficulties," Parkinson, *LLP,* p. 116; G. *Phil.* 7, p. 212.

22 David Lewis, "How to define theoretical terms," *Journal of Philosophy,* 67, 1970. I also profited from conversation with David Lewis in London in 1971 at the time I was writing this chapter in the first edition.

23 Ibid., p. 437.

24 Letter to Foucher, 1676, G. *Phil.* 1, p. 370; *Loemker*, p. 152.

25 Letter to Coste, 10 December 1707, G. *Phil.* 3, pp. 400–401; *Wiener,* p. 480.

26 Rudolf Carnap, "Meaning and synonymy in natural languages," *Philosophical Studies* 6, no. 3 (April 1955).

27 "De ipsa Natura sive de Vi insita Actionibusque Creaturarum," § 4, *Acta Eruditorum,* September 1698, *Loemker,* p. 499; *Wiener,* p. 140; G. *Phil.* 4, pp. 505–506.

Chapter V

1 See for example Philip Kitcher, *The Nature of Mathematical Knowledge,* chapter 10.

2 Letter to Foucher, 1692–1693?: G. *Phil.* 1, p. 416: "Je suis tellement pour l'infini actuel, qu'au lieu d'admettre que la nature l'abhorre, comme l'on dit vulgairement, je tiens qu'elle l'affecte partout. Ainsi je crois qu'il n'y a aucune partie de la matière qui ne soit, je ne dis pas divisible, mais actuellement divisée, et par consequent, la moindre particelle doit estre considérée comme un monde plein d'une infinité de créatures differentes." (I am so much for the actual infinity, that instead of admitting that Nature abhors it, as is commonly said, I maintain that infinity affects Nature everywhere. Thus I believe that there is no part of matter which is not, I would say, merely divisible, but actually divided, and consequently the smallest particle should be regarded as a world full of an infinity of different creatures.) Notice that Leibniz does not say that every parcel of matter is infinitely divided, but merely that it is divided, and the fact of such finite membership indefinitely descending makes it actually not finite. The model is that of a hereditary finite set. But this seems to be what Leibniz understands by his 'actual infinity'. For example in *NE,* Book 2, Chapter 17, § 1, he writes, "It is perfectly correct to say that there is an infinity of things, i.e. that there are always more of them than one can specify."

3 *NE,* Book 2, Chapter 17, § 8: "It [the absurdity of an actual idea of the infinite number] is not because we cannot have an idea of the infinite, but because an infinite cannot be a true whole." Also see reply to Nieuwentijt, circa 1685, *The Early Mathematical Manuscripts of Leibniz,* edited by J. M. Child (Open Court, 1920) p. 150: "Thus by infinitely great and infinitely small, we understand something indefinitely great, or something indefinitely small, so that each conducts itself as a sort of class, and not as the last thing of a class." Also *NE*, Book 2, Chapter 17, § 1: "But it is easy to demonstrate that there is no infinite number, nor any infinite line or any quantity if these be taken as genuine wholes."

4 Letter to Jean Bernouilli, 21 February 1699, G. *Math.* 3, p. 575; *Loemker,* p. 514: "I concede the infinite plurality of terms, but this plurality itself does not constitute a number as a single whole."(Concedo multitudinem infinitam, sed haec multitudo non facit numerum seu unum totum.)

5 H. J. M. Bos, "Newton, Leibniz and the Leibnizian Tradition," in I. Grattan-Guinness, ed., *From the Calculus to Set Theory,* (London, 1980), p. 70.

6 "Inquisitiones Generales," Couturat, *OFI,* p. 362; English translation "*General Enquiries,*" translated by O'Briant, p. 35.

7 "Responsio ad nonnullas difficultates ad Dr. Bernard Niewentijt circa methodum differentialem seu infinitesimalem motas," G. *Math.* 5, p. 322.

8 Letter to Jean Bernouilli, November 1698, G. *Math.* 3, p. 551; *Loemker*, p. 511.

9 Letter to Jean Bernouilli, 21 February 1699, G. *Math.* 3, p. 575; *Loemker,* p. 514.

10 Letter to des Bosses, 3 March 1706, G. *Phil.* 2, p. 305.

11 John Earman, "Infinities, infinitesimals and indivisibles: the Leibnizian labyrinth," *Studia Leibnitiana,* Band 7/2, 1975.

12 Letter to Varignon, 2 February 1702, G. *Math.* 4, p. 91; *Loemker,* pp. 542–543.

13 Letter to de L'Hospital, 14/21 June 1695, G. *Math.* 1, p. 288.

14 "Justification du Calcul des infinitésimals par celuy de l'-Algèbre ordinaire," 1702. G. *Math.* 4, p. 106; *Loemker,* p. 546.

15 Letter to Varignon, 20 June 1702, G. *Math.* 4, p. 110.

16 Letter to Varignon, 2 Feb. 1702, G. *Math.* 4, p. 92; *Loemker*, p. 543.

17 Letter to Pierre Bayle, circa 1698, to serve as a reply to the response of R. P. D. Malebranche, G. *Phil.* 3, p. 52.

18 C. H. Edwards, *Historical Development of the Calculus,* Berlin, 1982, p. 310.

19 Letter to Varignon, 2 February 1702, G. *Math.* 4, pp. 93–94; *Loemker,* p. 544.

20 Ibid. G. *Math.* 4, p. 93; *Loemker*, pp. 543–544.

21 "Differentials, higher-order differentials and derivatives in the Leibnizien calculus," *Archive of the History of the Exact Sciences*, vol. 17, no. 1, 1974.

22 John Earman, footnote 11.

23 Reply to Nieuwentijt, footnote 3, p. 147.

24 C. Boyer, *History of Calculus,* New York, 1959, p. 217. This in turn is a reprint of *The Concepts of the Calculus,* 1939.

25 Gotlob Frege, *Grundgesetze der Arithmetik,* Vol. 2, Chapter 1, § 97.

26 Bertrand Russell, *Principia Mathematica,* Chapter 3.

27 David Hilbert, "Uber die Unendlichkeit," *Mathematische Annalen,* Berlin, Band 95, 1926. English translation "On Infinity," in *Philosophy of Mathematics,* 2d ed., H. Putnam and P. Benacerraf, Cambridge, 1983, p. 197.

28 Bertrand Russell, *Principles of Mathematics,* London, 1903, Chapter 39.

Chapter VI

1 *Akademie,* 6th Series, Vol. 6, p. 228.

2 *Russell,* p. 9.

3 Bodemann, *LH* cat. no. 7, p. 74. Also quoted in *Kauppi,* p. 40: "Relatio est accidens quod in pluribus subjectis est-que resultans tantum seu nulla mutatione facta ab iis supervenit, si plura simul cogitantur, est, concogitabilitas." (Relation is an accident which is in multiple subjects; it is what results without any change made in the subjects but supervenes from them; it is the thinkability of objects together when we think of multiple things simultaneously.)

4 "Elementa Calculi," 1679, Couturat, *OFI*, p. 49: "By propositions I understand categorical propositions if I do not specify otherwise. Categorical propositions are the basis of other propositions and modal, hypothetical, and disjunctive propositions all presuppose categorical propositions." From Leibniz's other writings it seems that in the case of hypothetical propositions it is more correct to say that they are logically equivalent to categorical propositions.

5 *Russell,* p. 12.

6 See Bertrand Russell, *Introduction to Mathematical Philosophy,* London, 1919, p. 157.

7 Couturat *OFI*, p. 240; Parkinson, *LLP,* p. 36.

8 Leibniz's fifth letter to Clark, § 47, G. *Phil.* 7, p. 400.

9 As Leibniz uses 'subject' and 'predicate' to mean concepts, I will use the phrase 'predicate expression' here when I talk about a predicate as a linguistic entity.

10 John Locke, *Essay Concerning Human Understanding,* Book 2, Chapter 25, § 10.

11 *Russell,* p. 14.

12 N. *Rescher,* p. 75.

13 *NE,* Book 2, Chapter 25, § 5, p. 227. (See also Letter to de Volder, April 1702, G. *Phil.* 2, p. 240.)

14 Ibid.

15 See Norman Kretzmann, "History of semantics," in Paul Edwards, ed., *Encyclopedia of Philosophy,* New York, 1967, Vol. 7, p. 365.

16 *NE,* Book 2, Chapter 25, § 10, p. 228.

17 Ibid.

18 "Principles of nature and grace founded in reason" G. *Phil.* 6, p. 590; *Wiener*, p. 523.

19 *NE,* Book 2, chapter 22, § 10, p. 215.

20 Michael Dummett, "Truth," proceedings of the Aristotelian Society 19 (1958–9).

21 *NE,* Book 2, Chapter 1, § 19, p. 118.

22 Ibid., Book 2, Chapter 20, § 6, p. 165.

23 Ibid.

24 "Initia Rerum Mathematicarum Metaphysica," 1715, G. *Math.* 7, pp. 18–19; *Loemker*, p. 666; *Wiener,* p. 203.

25 E. Kant, "Concerning the ultimate foundations of the differentiations of regions of space," in *Selected Pre-Critical Writings,* pp. 36–42.

26 "Initia Rerum Mathematicarum Metaphysica," G. *Math.* 7, p. 19; *Loemker,* p. 667; *Wiener,* p. 204.

27 *Logica Hamburgensis,* 1638, edited with annotations as *Joachim Jungii Logicae Hamburgensis additamenta* by W. Risse (Göttingen, 1977). See also J. Ashworth, "Joachim Jungius and the Logic of Relations," *Archiv für Geschichte der Philosophie,* Vol. 49, 1967.

28 *NE,* Book 4, Chapter 17, § 4, p. 479.

29 "A Specimen of demonstrated inference from the direct to the oblique" sent by Leibniz to Vagetius, January 1687, *Dutens* 6, I, pp. 38–9; Parkinson *LLP* p. 88.

30 Couturat, *OFI,* p. 355.

31 Ibid. p. 244; Parkinson, *LLP,* p. 13.

32 Ibid. p. 287, Parkinson *LLP,* p. 14. Peter Geach, who has worked over this problem for a long time, helped me clarify the logical role of '*eo ipso*'.

33 As Jaakko Hintikka rightly says, "Paris loves someone" is of the form "(∃ x)aRx" and this can be seen as ascribing the monadic predicate "(∃x)− −Rx" to *a*. But as we have seen before, the same proposition can be thought to be obtained by giving arguments to different predicates, and it is not easy to decide whether it can be said to be relational or non-relational. I would prefer to call the proposition "(∃x) aRx" relational because it contains the predicate ". . . R_" which is originally a two place predicate, and hence the truth of the proposition involves the obtaining of some relational fact. It might be thought that any subject-predicate proposition of the form *fa* then trivially becomes relational, since the sentence "*fa*" is logically equivalent to various sentences with relational predicates, for example to "(∃x)((Rxa→fa) & Rxa)." It is indeed difficult to try to capture the intention of a past philosopher in a quantificational language which he himself did not have, without making it possible to generate example by technical manipulation that clearly go against the original intention. The suggestion given at the beginning of the chapter was, however, not that a proposition is relational if it can be expressed by some sentence or set of sentences containing a relational predicate. The suggestion was to consider it relational if it can be expressed only by such sentences after logical analysis.

34 Thus it might be thought that 'love' is an intensional verb in Chisholm's sense, since the existence of the object of love does not affect the truth-value of propositions of the form "*a* loves *b*." For example, one may say truly that Saint Francis of Assisi loved God, although one may strongly doubt whether God exists or not. If this is so, it may be asserted that ". . . loves God" just ascribes a particular state, or a disposition to a person which does not involve the truth of any relation holding between the subject and any other object. I myself think it is by no means clear whether the verb "x loves y" exhibits this feature of intensional verbs.

35 Leibniz attempted to rewrite sentences with nouns in the genitive case, adverbs, and token reflexive words. See Couturat, *OFI* p. 244; Parkinson *LLP*, p. 12.

Chapter VII

1 Letter to Arnauld, 14 July 1686. G. *Phil.* 2, p. 56; *Loemker,* p. 337: ". . . je dis que la notion de la substance individuelle enferme tous ses evenemens et toutes ses denominations, même celles qu'on appelle vulgairement extrinseques (c'est-a-dire qui ne luy appartiennent qu'en vertu de la connexion generale des choses)."

2 Benson Mates, "Leibniz and possible worlds," in Rootselaar and Staal, eds., *Logic Methodology and Philosophy of Science,* III (Amsterdam, 1956).

3 "A Specimen of the Universal Calculus," 1679–86?, Couturat, *OFI,* p. 241; Parkinson, *LLP,* p. 38.

4 Addenda to "A Specimen of the Universal Calculus," G. *Phil.* 7, p. 227; Parkinson *LLP,* p. 46.

5 Ibid., G. *Phil.* 7, p. 226; *Loemker*, p. 246; Parkinson *LLP,* p. 45. As the first line of the quoted original text is a puzzling one which has been translated correctly by Loemker, and this contradicts the lines that immediately follow as well as the other definition of accident in the same article, it has been assumed by Parkinson that Leibniz made a slip of the pen and wrote 'subjectum' instead of 'praedicatum.' I follow Parkinson, assuming that the sentence should have been: "Accidens est praedicatum pariter in propositione particulari affirmative et negative ejusdem subjecti."

6 E.g., in the Preface, p. 63, in Book 2, Chapter 22, § 1, p. 213, and in Book 3, Chapter 6, § 38, p. 325.

7 See, e.g., G. *Phil.* 4, p. 364.

8 Letter to de Volder, 20 June 1703, G. *Phil.* 2, p. 249; *Loemker,* p. 528.

9 K. Clatterbaugh, "Leibniz's doctrine of individual accidents," *Studia Leibnitiana,* Sonderheft 4 (1973); I. Angelelli, "On individual relations," *Studia Leibnitiana Supplementa* 21 (1980), H. Burkhardt, *Logik und Semiotik in der Philosophie von Leibniz.*

10 E.g., Letter to Des Bosses, 20 Sept. 1712; *Loemker*, p. 606; G. *Phil.* 2, pp. 457–8.

11 *NE,* Book 4, Chapter 3, § 6, p. 379.

12 Bodemann *LH,* iv,7c,Bl.76v. cited in Massimo Mugnai, "On Leibniz's theory of relations" *Studia Leibnitiana,* Sonderheft 15, 1988, p. 150.

13 Couturat, *OFI* p. 9.

14 Letter to the editor of *Journal des Savans,* June 1691, G. *Phil.* 4, p. 467.

15 Letter to J. Ch. Schulenburg, 17 May 1698, *G. Math.* 7, p. 242.

16 *NE,* Book 2, Chapter 27, § 1, p. 230.

17 Couturat, *OFI,* p. 8.

18 *Discourse on Metaphysics* §§ 14, 26, 33; G. *Phil.* 4, pp. 439, 451, 458; *Loemker,* pp. 311, 320, 324; *Monadology* § 62, G. *Phil.* 6, p. 617.

19 Letter to Arnauld 14 July 1686, G. *Phil.* 2, p. 56, *Loemker,* p. 337.

20 *Discourse on Metaphysics* § 8, *Loemker,* p. 307.

21 Ibid.

22 Ibid. § 9, *Loemker,* p. 308. It is true, as Fabrizio Mondadori and others have pointed out, that there is one passage in a letter to Arnauld where Leibniz concedes that an individual concept could consist of a set of basic predicates from which other predicates can be deduced. But elsewhere, Leibniz repeatedly writes that an individual is distinguished (from species or accidents) by its having a complete individual concept that includes *every* predicate that is true of it or "*everything* that can be said of that substance" (my italics).

23 Letter to des Bosses, 21 April 1714, G. *Phil.* 2, p. 486. *Loemker,* p. 609.

24 *Rescher,* p. 75.

25 In Russell's language of the *Principia Mathematica,* it is indeed obtained from the function "x is the father of y" by turning one of the variables of the function into an apparent (i.e. bound) variable.

26 Benson Mates, *The Philosophy of Leibniz,* p. 209. Mates cites a passage from Leibniz's article "De Mente," Grua, p. 266.

27 *The Leibniz-Clarke Correspondence,* fifth letter, § 47, G. *Phil.* 7, p. 400. English translation by H. Alexander (Manchester, 1956).

28 *NE,* Book 2, Chapter 12, § 5, p. 145.

29 *Theodicy* § 26, G. *Phil.* 6, p. 432.

30 *De Stylo Nizolii,* G. *Phil.* 4, p. 147; *Loemker,* p. 128.

31 Letter to Des Bosses, 20 September 1712, G. *Phil.* 2, p. 458, *Loemker,* p. 605.

32 Letter to Des Bosses, 11 March, 1706, G. *Phil.* 2, p. 304.

33 Gottfried Martin suggests this in *Liebniz's Logic and Metaphysics,* § 30.

34 There is a passage in the *Theodicy,* § 32, where Leibniz writes that there is a real distinction between substance and its modifications or accidents. But it is clear that Leibniz is not claiming here that modifications or accidents are entities which have independent existence. He is warning against the kind of mistake which, e.g., Russell was to make when he wrote that according to Leibniz a substance was the sum of its predicates. Leibniz's doctrine is that if a set of predicates is true of a substance, the set defines it. The substance is never identical with the sum of accidents; it *has* the accidents. Accidents or universals cannot exist on their own as particular entities – not even as a collection. A set of universals would not be an entity. It would at most be a complex universal under which particulars may fall.

35 *Grua* 2, p. 542. See Hidé Ishiguro, "Leibniz's denial of the reality of space and time," *Annals of the Japan Association for Philosophy of Science,* vol. 3, no. 2 (March 1967).

36 Fifth letter to Clarke, § 47.

37 E.g., Russell, Rescher, Parkinson.

38 I was not clear in expressing this point in the first edition. The critical remark made of it by Dr. Hans Burkhardt in his *Logik and Semiotik in der Philosophie von Leibniz,* p. 406, made me realise it and correct the expression of my thought.

39 Letter to De Volder, 23 June 1699, G. *Phil.* 2, p. 183. *Loemker,* p. 519.

40 Fifth letter to Clarke, § 47.

41 Ibid., § 55.

42 Ibid., § 55.

43 Ibid., § 29. He goes on to distinguish this unintelligible hypothesis from a possible one in which other states and events precede the events with which our world began.

44 Mates traces the subtle relation of the phenomenal, the monadic, and position in *The Philosophy of Leibniz*, Chapter XIII, p. 232, fn. 24.

45 *Russell,* p. 121.

46 *NE*, Book 2, chapter 14, § 16, p. 152.

47 *NE*, Book 2, chapter 13, § 4, p. 147.

48 *Russell,* p. 118.

49 *Discourse on Metaphysics,* § 14, *Loemker,* p. 312.

50 Letter to de Volder, 6 July 1701, G. *Phil.* 2, p. 226; *Loemker,* p. 524.

51 Letter to Arnauld, July 1686, G. *Phil.* 2, p. 58, *Loemker,* p. 338.

52 "Second éclaircissement du système de la communication des substances." *Histoire des ouvrages des savans,* February 1696, G. *Phil.* 4, p. 499, *Loemker,* p. 460; *Wiener,* p. 118. See also "Postscriptum eines Briefes an Basnage de Beauval," Hannover, 3–13 January 1696, G. *Phil.* 4, pp. 498–9.

53 "Considération sur le principe de vie et sur les natures plastiques," *Histoire des ouvrages des savans,* May 1705, G. *Phil.* 6, p. 541; *Loemker,* p. 587; *Wiener,* p. 192.

54 *Initia Rerum Mathemeticarum Metaphysica,* G. *Math.* 7, p. 18; *Loemker* p. 666; *Wiener,* p. 201.

55 Untitled manuscript, G. *Phil.* 7, p. 301.

56 *Monadology,* § 56, G. *Phil.* 6, p. 616; *Loemker,* p. 648.

57 "Système nouveau de la nature et de la communication des substances," *Journal des savans,* June 1695, G. *Phil.* 4, p. 484; *Loemker,* p. 457; *Wiener,* p. 114.

58 Letter to Arnauld, September 1687, G. *Phil.* 2, p. 112; *Loemker,* p. 339.

59 I realize that difficulties can arise again, since the verb "to say . . . of *x*" can be taken again as an intensional verb in Chisholm's sense, and hence might not entail "(∃*x*) a says f of *x*." But as Leibniz's theory of representation is so closely connected with his theory of the Pre-established Harmony, I would like to take it extensionally.

60 Montgomery Furth has written ("Monadology," *Philosophical Review,* 76, no. 2 [April 1967], p. 172) that " . . . the world of a monad is, in a phrase of Miss Anscombe's, an 'intensional' object of the monad's conscious or unconscious awareness. Hence for a monad there is no incompatibility between (on the one hand) its being to that monad as if things were thus and so, and (on the other) things not being thus and so – perhaps, for that matter, nothing else existing at all." But what is it "for it to be to a monad as if it were perceiving that things were thus" if it never had perceived? It seems to me that the expression "the world of a monad" is already misleading. The question is not one of the identity of the successive states of a monad which one may correctly or incorrectly characterize. It is the question of what is involved in the characterization of such states and the truth-conditions of predications of the states. As we have seen, Leibniz likens individual substances to mirrors which reflect the world. It might be said that one can produce the same image on a mirror by reflecting a real tree and, say, a clever two-dimensional picture of a tree; thus the 'state' of the mirror is the same in the two cases although its relational properties are different. As I have said already, Leibniz thought that, if the relational properties of a monad were different, its states would in consequence be different as well. But even if one were to dispute this as a matter of empirical fact, it still remains true that for a *mirror* to have an image there must be something other than itself which it reflects. It is not by accident that Leibniz uses the analogy with mirrors.

61 *Discourse on Metaphysics,* § 14, *Loemker,* p. 312.

62 "Leibniz and Possible Worlds" in Rootselaar and Staal, eds., *Logic, Methodology and Philosophy of Science.*

63 *Monadology,* § 56, G. *Phil.* 6, p. 616; *Loemker*, p. 648.

64 I was informed of this by Dr. John Hostler, who also told me of Leibniz's letter to Morell in which it is revealed, and of an article by J. Baruzi in *Revue Philosophique de la France et de L'Etranger,* 1946, pp. 391–409, in which it is discussed.

65 "Quia contemplatura esset Deum et seipsam et ideas rerum possibilium," *Notes sur Bellarmin,* 1680; *Grua* 1, p. 299. Also pointed out to me by John Hostler.

66 Letter to Hansch, "De enthusiasmo Platonico," 1707, *Dutens* 2, Chapter 224; *Loemker,* p. 593.

67 *NE,* Preface, pp. 53–5.

Chapter VIII

1 Letter to Foucher, 1675, G. *Phil.* 1, p. 370; *Loemker*, p. 152. See A. Robinet, *Malebranche et Leibniz.* Paris, 1955.

2 Frank Ramsey, "Truth and Probability," in *Foundation of Mathematics,* (London, 1926).

3 Georg. H. von Wright, "On Conditionals" in *Logical Studies* (London, 1959).

4 G. W. Leibniz, *Akademie,* 6th Series, Volume 1, pp. 367.

5 See William and Martha Kneale, *The Development of Logic* (Oxford, 1962), pp. 137, 235.

6 See Ian Hacking, "The Leibniz-Carnap Program for Inductive Logic," *Journal of Philosophy* 68, 1971, pp. 597–610.

7 I am using the expression 'illocutionary force' in the sense of John Austin. See *How to Do Things with Words* (Oxford, 1962).

8 Letter to Gabriel Wagner, 1696. "*Rationes non esse numerandas sed ponderandas,* Man muss die Anzeigungen nicht zählen sondern wägen." G. *Phil.* 7, p. 521; *Loemker*, p. 467.

9 Letter to Foucher 1675, G. *Phil.* 1, p. 369; *Loemker*, p. 152.

10 Ibid.

11 *NE,* Book 3, Chapter 10, § 18, p. 345.

12 Letter to Foucher, 1675.

13 Ramsey, p. 241.

14 See, e.g., "De Ipsa Natura," G. *Phil.* 4, p. 505; *Loemker* p. 499.

15 See my "Contingent truths and possible world," in *Leibniz: Metaphysics and Philosophy of Science* (Oxford, 1981).

16 *Discourse on Metaphysics,* § 13, 1686, G. *Phil.* 4, p. 437; *Loemker,* p. 310.

17 *NE,* Book 3, Chapter 3, § 18; Book 4, Chapter 6, § 8, pp. 294, 405.

18 "Specimen Dynamicum," G. *Math.* 6, pp. 241; *Wiener,* p. 130: "For not all truths pertaining to the physical world can be obtained from merely logical and geometrical axioms, but we must introduce other axioms about cause and effect, activity and passivity, and take account of the order of things."

19 *NE,* Book 3, Chapter 3, § 15, p. 293.

20 Letter to Foucher, 1675.

21 *NE,* Book 3, Chapter 6, § 13, and Book 3, Chapter 11, § 24, pp. 309, 354.

22 See Heinrich Schepers, "Leibniz' Disputationen 'De Conditionibus' Ansätse zu einer juristischen Aussagenlogik," *Studia Leibnitiana,* Sonderdrück, Acten des 2 Internationalen Leibniz-Kongress, Wiesbaden, 1975. As is clear, I disagree with several of Professor Schepers' interpretations of the formal calculi which he develops in this interesting paper.

Chapter IX

1 Letter to S. Foucher, c. 1675. G. *Phil.* 1, p. 370; *Loemker,* p. 152: "Car toutes les propositions hypothétiques assurent ce qui seroit ou ne seroit pas quelque chose ou son

contraire estant posé, et par consequent que la supposition en même temps de deux choses s'accordent ou qu'une chose est possible ou impossible, necessaire ou indifferente, et cette possibilité, impossibilité ou necessité . . . n'est pas une chimère que nous fassions puisque nous ne faisons que la reconnoistre et malgrez nous et d'une manière constante."

2 He wrote it in the years leading to 1710, G. *Phil.* 6.

3 *Kauppi,* p. 243.

4 "Identity in individuals and true propositions," in "Remarques sur la lettre de M Arnauld touchent ma proposition que la notion individuelle de chaque personne enferme une fois pour toutes ce que lui arrivera à jamais," May 1686, G. *Phil.* 2, p. 46.

5 Letter to Arnauld, 14 July 1686, G. *Phil.* 2, p. 57; *Loemker,* p. 337.

6 *NE,* Book 4, Chapter 21, § 5, p. 524.

7 *NE,* Book 3, Chapter 3, § 6, pp. 289–290.

8 Kant, *Critique of Pure Reason,* Introduction, p. v.

9 Couturat, *OFI,* p. 18; see also "On Freedom" (De Libertate), ca. 1679, *Nouvelle lettres et opuseules inédits de Leibniz* edited by Foucher de Careil, p. 180. *Loemker,* p. 264.

10 *Monadology,* § 33.

11 "Discourse on Metaphysic," 1686, § 13, G. *Phil* 4, p. 440; *Loemker,* p. 310.

12 *Essais de Théodicée,* § 414, G. *Phil.* 6, p. 363. Fabrizio Mondadori and Margaret Wilson pointed out a mistranslation I made in the first edition.

13 For example, L. Couturat in *La Logique de Leibniz.*

14 *NE,* Book 4, Chapter 17, § 8, p. 486.

15 G. *Phil.* 7, p. 211; Parkinson, *LLP,* p. 115.

16 This is claimed by Couturat, and also suggested by M. Dummett in his review of Rescher's "Leibniz's interpretation of his logical calculi,"

17 Couturat, *OFI,* p. 356; Parkinson, *LLP,* p. 47.

18 Couturat, *OFI,* pp. 259, 261.

19 Ibid., p. 368.

20 This argument was suggested to me by Bas van Fraassen.

21 In the case of Strawson, he does not talk of propositions but of sentences and statements, and his claim is that not all uses of indicative sentences succeed in making statements, and that statements are what are true or false. Whether sentences that are used but fail to make statements can be said to express thoughts and are thus propositions is a difficult question.

22 Couturat, *OFI,* p. 393; Parkinson, *LLP,* p. 82.

23 *NE,* Book 4, Chapter 11, § 14. Jenny Ashforth has informed me that in late mediaeval logic '*constantia subjecti*' was taken in two different senses. One meant that it was presupposed by the context that the subject was not empty—i.e., the concept was instantiated. The second meant that it was presupposed by the context that the universe of discourse (e.g., at the second premiss of a syllogism) was restricted, and kept unchanged.

24 This means, as Peter Geach has pointed out to me, that Leibniz who was a Christian was either oblivious of the fact that Christ was a man, or believed that Christ was liable to sin.

25 "Generales Inquisitiones," § 148, Couturat, *OFI,* p. 392; Parkinson, *LLP,* p. 81.

26 On certain difficulties about this, see Lambert and van Fraasen, "Meaning relations, possible object and possible worlds," in Lambert, ed., *Philosophical Problems in Logic.*

27 "Generales Inquisitiones," § 153, Couturat, *OFI,* p. 393; Parkinson, *LLP,* p. 82.

28 "A Paper on Some Logical Difficulties," G. *Phil.* 7, p. 211; Parkinson, *LLP,* p. 116.

29 Couturat, *OFI,* p. 403.

30 Letter to Arnauld, 14 July 1686, G. *Phil.* 2, p. 53; *Loemker,* p. 335.

31 Remarks on a correspondence with Arnauld, 13 May 1686, G. *Phil.* 2, p. 42.

32 Letter to Bourguet, December 1714, G. *Phil,* 3, p. 572.

33 Couturat, *OFI,* pp. 375–6.

34 *Russell,* Preface, pp. vi–vii.

35 Couturat, *OFI,* p. 9. ". . . nihil aliud sit explicabile in existentia, quam perfectissimam seriem rerum ingredi . . ."

36 Ian Hacking points to a similar confusion in Leibniz's notion of 'possible' in his probability theory. 'Possible' is at the same time a property of a concept which is not contradictory (which permits of no degrees) and also something of which there are degrees such that one event is said to be more possible than another. "The Leibniz-Carnap problem in inductive logic," *Journal of Philosophy,* November 1971.

37 Couturat, *OFI,* p. 272.

38 Ibid., p. 18.
39 G. *Phil.* 6, p. 629.
40 G. *Math.* 5, p. 389: "Cum vero saltu ad ultimatum facto ipsum infinitum aut infinite parvum dicimus, commoditate expressionis seu breviloquio mentali inservimus, sed non nisi toleranter vera loquimur, quae explicatione rigidantur."
41 Couturat, *OFI,* pp. 18, 19.
42 *NE,* Book 2, chapter 17, § 1.
43 "De Libertate," (around 1679) in Foucher de Careil, ed., *Nouvelles lettres et opuscules inédits de Leibniz,* p. 178–85; *Loemker,* p. 266.
44 "De Rerum Originatione Radicali," 1697, G. *Phil.* 7, p. 305; *Wiener,* p. 350.
45 *Rescher*, p. 33.
46 "De Rerum Originatione Radicali," 1697, G. *Phil.* 7, p. 303–4; *Wiener,* p. 347.
47 Ibid.
48 *Kauppi,* p. 247.

Bibliography

Works by Leibniz

Leibniz, G. W.: Sämtliche Schriften und Briefe. Edited by Deutschen Akademie der Wissenschaften. Darmstadt, 1923, Leipzig, 1938, Berlin, 1950; cited as *Akademie,* followed by series, volume, and page.

Die philosophische Schriften von G. W. Leibniz, i–vii. Edited by C. I. Gerhardt. Berlin, 1875–90; reprinted by G. Olms, Hildescheim, 1965; cited as G. *Phil.,* followed by volume and page.

Die mathematische Schriften von G. W. Leibniz, i–vii. Edited by C. I. Gerhardt. Halle, 1849–63, reprinted by G. Olms, Hildesheim, 1971; cited as G. *Math.* followed by volume and page.

G. W. Leibniz: Textes inédits, I and II. Edited by G. Grua. Paris, 1948; reprinted by Garland, New York, 1986; cited as *Grua,* followed by volume and page.

Die Leibniz-Handschriften der königlichen öffentlichen Bibliotek zu Hannover. Edited by Bodemann. Hanover, 1895; reprinted by G. Olms, Hildesheim, 1966; cited as Bodemann *LH,* followed by catalogue number and page.

Opuscules et fragments inédits de Leibniz. Edited by Louis Couturat. Paris, 1903; reprinted by G. Olms, Hildescheim, 1961; cited as Couturat *OFI.*

Leibnitii Opera Philosophica quae extant latina gallica germanica omnia. Edited by J. E. Erdmann. Berlin, 1840; cited as *Erdmann.*

Die Werke von Leibniz, Ie Reihe, *Historische, politische, und staatswissenschaftliche Schriften,* 11 vols. Edited by O. Klopp. Hannover, 1864–84; cited as *Klopp.*

G. W. Leibnitii Opera Omnia, 6 vols. Edited by L. Dutens. Geneva, 1768; cited as *Dutens.*

Nouvelles lettres et opuscules inédits de Leibniz. Edited by Foucher de Careil. Paris, 1857; reprinted by G. Olms, Hildesheim, 1971.

Leibnizens nachgelassene Schriften, physikalischen, mechanischen und technischen Inhalts. Edited by E. Gerland. Leipzig, 1906.

Opuscula Philosophica Selecta. Edited by P. Schrecker. Paris, 1959.

Leibniz: Philosophical Papers and Letters, 2d ed. Translated by L. E. Loemker. Dordrecht, 1969; cited as *Loemker.*

Leibniz: Selections. Translated by P. P. Wiener. New York, 1951; cited as *Wiener.*

Leibniz: Philosophical Writing. Edited and translated by Morris and G. H. R. Parkinson. London, 1973.

Leibniz: Logical Papers: A Selection. Translated by G. H. R. Parkinson. Oxford, 1966; cited as Parkinson *LLP.*

New Essays on Human Understanding. Translated by Peter Remnant and Jonathan Bennett. Cambridge, England, 1981; cited as *NE,* followed by book, chapter, and section. (The pagination of this edition corresponds to the pagination in the *Akademie* edition, 6th series, Vol. 6.)

The Leibniz-Clark Correspondence. Translated by H. G. Alexander. Manchester, 1956.

Theodicy. Translated by E. M. Huggard. London, 1952.

Discourse on Metaphysics. Translated by P. Lucas and L. Grant. Manchester, 1952.

Political Writings of Leibniz. Edited and translated by P. Riley. Cambridge, England, 1972.

The Early Mathematical Manuscripts of Leibniz. Edited by J. M. Child. New York, 1920.

Works on Leibniz

Adams, R. "Leibniz's Theory of Contingency," in M. Hooker, ed., *Leibniz: Critical and Interpretive Essays.* Minneapolis, 1982.

Angelelli, I. "On Identity and Interchangeability in Leibniz and Frege," *Notre Dame Journal of Formal Logic,* 8, 1967.

Baruzi, J. "Du Discours de Métaphysique à la Théodicée," *Revue Philosophique de la France et de l'Etranger,* 136, 1946, pp. 391–409.

Belaval, Y. *Leibniz: Critique de Descartes.* Paris, 1960.

"Le Probleme de l'erreur chez Leibniz," *Zeitschrift für philosphische Forschung,* Bd. 20, H. 3 and 4 (Zum Gedenken an den 250 Todestag von Leibniz).

"Sur la Lange Universelle de Leibniz," in *Langue et Langages de Leibniz à Encyclopédie*. Paris, 1977.

"Sur le simple et le composé" in *Etudes Leibniziennes, De Leibniz à Hegel*. Paris, 1976.

Bos, H. J. M. "Differentials, Higher-Order Differentials and Derivatives in the Leibnizian Calculus," *Archive of the History of the Exact Sciences,* Vol. 17, No. 1. 1974.

"Newton, Leibniz and the Leibnizian Tradition," in I. Grattan-Guinness, ed., *From the Calculus to Set Theory*. London, 1980.

Boyer, C. B. *The History of the Calculus and its Conceptual Development*. New York, 1959. (This is a reprint of *The Concepts of the Calculus,* 1939.)

Broad, C. *Leibniz: An Introduction*. London, 1975.

Burkhardt, H. *Logik und Semiotik in der Philosophie von Leibniz*. München, 1980.

Cassirer, E. *Leibniz' System in seinen wissenschaftlichen Grundlagen*. Marburg, 1902.

Castañeda, H. N. "Leibniz's concepts and their coincidence salva veritate," *Noûs,* 8, 4, 1974.

Couturat, L. *La Logique de Leibniz d'après des documents inédits*. Paris, 1901.

"Sur la Métaphysique de Leibniz" in *Revue de Métaphysique et de Morale,* 10 Jan. 1902.

"Sur les rapports de la logique et de la métaphysique de Leibniz," *Bulletin de la Société Française de Philosophie,* 2, 1902.

Curley, E. "Did Leibniz state 'Leibniz's Law'," *The Philosophical Review,* 80, 1971.

"The Root of Contingency" in H. Frankfurt, ed. *Leibniz*. Garden City, 1972.

Dascal, M. "About the Idea of a Generative Grammar in Leibniz," *Studia Leibnitiana* 3, 1971.

Dummett, M. *Frege: Philosophy of Language*. London, 1973, 2d ed., 1981.

Review of N. Rescher's "Leibniz's interpretation of his Logical Calculi," *Journal of Symbolic Logic,* 21, 1956.

Dürr, K. "Die mathematische Logik von Leibniz," *Studia Philosophica*. Basel, 1947.

Earman, J. "Was Leibniz a Relationalist?" *Midwest Studies in Philosophy* 4. Minneapolis, 1979.

"Who's afraid of absolute space?" *Australasian Journal of Philosophy,* 48, 1970.

"Infinites, infinitesimals and indivisibles: The Leibnizian Labyrinth," *Studia Leibnitiana,* 2, 1975.

Edwards, C. H. *Historical Development of the Calculus*. Berlin, 1982.

Feldman, F. "Leibniz and Leibniz's law," *Philosophical Review*, 74, 1970.

"Review of Ishiguro's Leibniz's Philosophy of Logic and Language," *International Philosophical Quarterly*, June 1974.

Fischer, K. *Leibniz: Leben, Werke und Lehre*. Heidelberg, 1920.

Frankfurt, H. G., ed. *Leibniz: A Collection of Critical Essays*. Garden City, 1972.

Friedmann, G. *Leibniz et Spinoza*. Paris, 1946.

Furth, M. "Monadology," *Philosophical Review*, 76, No. 2, April 1967.

Hartmann, N. *Leibniz als Metaphysiker*. Berlin, 1946.

Heinekamp, A. "Natürliche Sprache und Allgemeine Charakteristik bei Leibniz," *Studia Leibnitiana*, Supplementa 15.

Hintikka, J. "Leibniz on Plenitude, Relations and the Reign of Law," *Ajatus*. Helsinki, 1969. Reprinted in H.G. Frankfurt, Garden City, 1972.

Hooker, M. ed. *Leibniz: Critical and Interpretative Essays*. Minnesota, 1982.

Hostler J. *Leibniz's Moral Philosophy*. London, 1975.

Ikeda, Y. *Leibniz Tetsugaku no Shinkaishaku* (A New Interpretation of Leibniz's Philosophy). Tokyo, 1975.

Ishiguro, H. "Leibniz's Denial of the Reality of Space and Time," *Annals of the Japan Association for Philosophy of Science*. Vol. 3, No. 2, March 1967.

"Les vérités hypothétiques," *Studia Leibnitiana*, Supplementa 8, Tome 2, 1978.

"Preestablished Harmony versus Constant Conjunction," British Academy, 1979. Printed also in *Proceedings of the British Academy* 1987–88, and in A. Kenny, ed., *Rationalism, Empiricism and Idealism*. Oxford, 1986.

"Substance and Individual Notions," *Philosophy of Nicholas Rescher*. Dordrecht, 1979.

"Contingent Truths and Possible Worlds," *Midwest Studies in Philosophy*. Vol. 4, Minnesota, 1979. Revised version in Roger Woolhouse, ed., *Leibniz: Metaphysics and Philosophy of Science*. Oxford, 1981.

"Leibniz on Hypothetical Truths" in M. Hooker, Minneapolis, 1982.

"La notion dite confuse de l'infinitésimal chez Leibniz," *Studia Leibnitiana, Supplementa* 15. Wiesbaden, 1988.

Jourdain, P. E. B. "The Logical Works of Leibniz," *Monist*, 26, 1916.

Kalinowski, G. "Logique juridique de Leibniz. Conception et contenu," *Studia Leibnitiana* 9, 2. 1977.

"Leibniz et les sémantiques des mondes possibles," in *Leibniz, Werk und Wirkung*. Hannover, 1983.

(with J. L. Gardies) "Un Logicien déontique avant la lettre: Gottfried Wilhelm Leibniz," in *Archiv für Rechts und Socialphilosophie,* 60, 1, 1974.

Kauppi, R. *Uber die Leibnizsche Logik, mit besondere Besüchsichtung der Intension und Extension,* Supplementary Volume, *Acta Philosophica Fennica*. Helsinki, 1960; cited as *Kauppi*.

Kneale, William and Martha. *The Development of Logic*. Oxford, 1962.

Krüger, L. *Rationalismus und Entwurf einer Universellen Logik bei Leibniz*. Frankfurt, 1969.

Kulstad, M. "Leibniz's Concept of Expression," *Studia Leibnitiana* 9, 1977.

"A Closer Look at Leibniz's Alleged Reduction of Relations," *Southern Journal of Philosophy,* 18, 1980.

Loemker, L. *Struggle for Synthesis: The 17th century background of Leibniz's Synthesis of Order and Freedom*. Cambridge, 1972.

Mahnke, D. "Leibniz als Gegner der gelehrten Einseitigkeit" *Wissenschaftliche Beilage zu Jahrsbericht des königlichen Gymnasiums zu Stade*. Stade, 1912.

"Leibnizens Synthese von Universalmathematik und Individualmetaphysik," *Jahrbuch für Philosophie und phänomenologische Forschung,* VII.

"Leibniz als Begründer der symbolischen Mathematik," Isis, 9, 1927.

Martin, G. *Leibniz: Logic and Metaphysik,* 2d ed. Köln, 1967. English translation, *Leibniz' Logic and Metaphysics*. Translated by K. Northcott and P. G. Lucas. Manchester, 1964.

Mates, B. "Leibniz on Possible Worlds," *Logic, Methodology and Philosophy of Science,* III. Edited Rootselaar & Staal. Amsterdam 1963.

"Individuals and Modality in the Philosophy of Leibniz," *Studia Leibnitiana* 4, 1972.

The Philosophy of Leibniz: Metaphysics and Language. New York and Oxford, 1986.

Meyer, R. W. *Leibniz und die europäische Ordnungskrise*. Hamburg, 1948. English translation *Leibnitz and the Seventeenth* Century Revolution. Translated by J. P. Stern. Cambridge, 1952.

Mondadori, F. "Reference, Essentialism and Modality in Leibniz's Metaphysics," *Studia Leibnitiana* 5, 1973.

"Leibniz and the Doctrine of Inter-world Identity," *Studia Leibnitiana* 7, 1975.

Mugnai, M. *Astrazione et Realità Saggio su Leibniz.* Milano, 1976.

"Bemerkungen zu Leibniz' Theorie der Relationen," *Studia Leibnitiana* 10, 1978.

Nagai, H. *Leibniz Kenkyu: Kagakutetsugakuteki Kosatsu* (Study in Leibniz: an Investigation as Philosophy of Science). Tokyo, 1954.

Parkinson, G. H. R. *Logic and Reality in Leibniz's Metaphysics.* Oxford, 1965; cited as Parkinson *LRLM.*

Patzig, G, "Leibniz, Frege und die sogenannte 'lingua characteristica universalis,' " *Studia Leibnitiana, Supplementa* 3, 1969.

Poser, H. *Zur Theorie der Modalbegriffe bei G. W. Leibniz.* Wiesbaden, 1969.

"Signum, notio und idea: Elemente der Leibnizschen Zeichentheorie," *Zeitschriftt für Semiotik,* 1, 1979.

Rescher, N. "Contingency in the Philosophy of Leibniz," *Philosophical Review,* 61, 1952.

"Leibniz's Interpretation of his Logical Calculi," *Journal of Symbolic Logic, 19, 1954.*

The philosophy of Leibniz, Englewood Cliffs, 1967; cited as *Rescher.*

Leibniz: An Introduction to His Philosophy. Totowa, 1979.

Robinet, A. *Malebranche et Leibniz.* Paris, 1955.

Russell, B. *A Critical Exposition of the Philosophy of Leibniz.* London, 1900; cited as *Russell.*

"Recent Work on the Philosophy of Leibniz," *Mind* 12, 1903. Reprinted in H. Frankfurt, ed., *Leibniz.* Garden City, 1972.

Schepers, H. "Begriffsanalyse und Kategorialsynthese von Logik und Metaphysik bei Leibniz," *Studia Leibnitiana, Supplementa* 3, 1969.

"Leibniz' Disputationen 'De Conditionibus': Ansätze zu einer juristischen Aussagenlogik," *Studia Leibnitiana, Supplementa* 15, 1975.

Schmidt, F. "Leibnizens rationale Grammatik," *Zeitschrift für philosophische Forschung,* 9, 1955.

"Zeichen, Wort und Wahrheit bei Leibniz," *Studia Leibnitiana, Supplementa* 2, 1969.

Schrecker, P. "Leibniz et le principe du tiers exclu," *Actes du Congres International de Philosophie Scientifique, fasc Vi*I. Paris, 1936.

"Leibniz and the Art of Inventing Algorithm," *Journal of the History of Ideas,* Jan. 1947.

Sleigh, R. "Leibniz on Individual Substances," *Journal of Philosophy* 72, 1975.

Wilson, M. "Leibniz and Materialism" *Canadian Journal of Philosophy,* Vol. 3, No. 4, 1974.

"Confused Ideas" in M. Kulstad, ed. *Essays on the Philosophy of Leibniz.* Houston, 1977.

Yamamoto, M. *Leibniz Tetsugaku Kenkyu* (Study in Leibniz's Philosophy). Tokyo, 1953.

Yost, R. *Leibniz and Philosophical Analysis.* Berkeley and Los Angeles, 1954.

General Works

Anselm. *De Grammatico* in *Opera Omnia.* Edited by F. S. Schmidt. Edinburgh, 1946.

Aristotle. *Categories.* Translated by J. Ackrill. Oxford, 1963.

Ashworth, J. "Joachim Jungius and the Logic of Relations," *Archiv für Geschichte der Philosophie,* Vol. 49, No. 1, 1967.

Austin, J. *How to do things with words.* Oxford, 1962.

Carnap, R. *Meaning and Necessity.* Chicago, 1947.

"Meaning and Synonymy in Natural Languages," *Philosophical Studies,* Vol. 6. No. 3, April 1955.

Church, A. "Existential Import of Categorical Propositions" in *Logic, Methodology and Philosophy of Science* (Proceedings of 1964 Congress). Amsterdam, 1965.

Cohen, J. "On the project of a universal character," *Mind* 63, 1954.

Edwards, P., ed. *The Encyclopaedia of Philosophy,* 8 vols. New York, 1967.

Frege, G. "Über den Briefwechsel Leibnizens und Huygens mit Papin," *Jenaische Zeitschrift für Naturwissenschaft,* 15, 3, 1881.

Begriffsschrift, eine der Arithmetischen nachgebildete Formelsprache des reinen Denkens. Halle, 1879.

Grundlagen der Arithmetik, 1884. Translated as *Foundations of Arithmetic* by J. A. Austin. Oxford, 1950.

Grundgesetze der Arithmetik. Jena, Bd. 1, 1893, & Bd. 2, 1903. Partially translated into English as *Basic Laws of Arithmetic,* by M. Furth. Oxford, 1975.

"Der Gedanke," *Beiträge zur Philosophie des deutschen Idealismus.* 1910. Translated by A. and M. Quinton, as "The Thought: A Logical Inquiry," *Mind,* 65, 1956. Reprinted in *Philosophical Logic.* Edited by P. F. Strawson. Oxford and New York, 1967.

Translations from the Philosophical Writings of Gottlob Frege. Translated by P. Geach and M. Black. Oxford, 1952.

Geach, P. Posthumous Writings: *Reference and Generality.* Ithaca, 1962.

Husserl, E. *Logische Untersuchungen,* 2d ed. Halle 1900, 1913. Translated as *Logical Investigations* by J. N. Findlay. London, 1970.

John of St. Thomas. *Cursus Philosophicus I: Ars Logica.* Translated as *Outline of Formal Logic* by F. C. Wade. Milwaukee, 1955.

Jungius J. *Logica Hamburgensis.* 1638. Edited with annotation as *Joachimi Jungii Logicae Hamburgensis additamenta,* by W. Risse. Göttingen, 1977.

Kant, E. *Selected Pre-critical Writings and Correspondence with Beck.* Translated by Kerferd and Walford. Manchester, 1968.

Kaplan, D. "Quantifying in" in D. Davidson and J. Hintikka, eds., *Word and Objections* (essays on the work of W. V. Quine). Dordrecht, 1969.

Kneale, W. and M. *The Development of Logic.* Oxford, 1962.

Kretzmann, N. "History of Semantics" in P. Edwards, ed., *Encyclopedia of Philosophy.* Vol. 7, p. 365.

Kripke, S. "Semantical Analysis of Modal Logic," *Zeitschrift für mathematische Logik und Grundlagen der Mathematik,* 9, 1963.

"Semantical Considerations in Modal Logic," *Acta Philosophica Fennica* 16. Helsinki, 1960.

"Naming and Necessity" in D. Davidson and G. Harman, eds., *Semantics of Natural Language,* 2d ed. Dordrecht, 1972.

Lambert, K. and van Fraassen, B. "Meaning Relations, Possible Objects and Possible Worlds" in K. Lambert, eds., *Philosophical Problems in Logic.* Dordrecht, 1970.

Lewis, C. I. *A Survey of Symbolic Logic.* Berkeley, 1918. Reprinted by Dover. New York, 1960.

Lewis, D. "How to Define Theoretical Terms," *Journal of Philosophy,* 67, 1970.

"Counterpart Theory and Quantified Modal Logic," *Journal of Philosophy,* 65, 1968.

Counterfactuals. Oxford, 1973.

Locke, J. *An Essay Concerning Human Understanding.* 1689.

Long, P. "Modality and Tautology," *Proceeding of the Aristotelian Society,* LX, 1959–60.

Lully, R. *Raymundi Lulli Opera ea quae ad adinventam ab ipso artem universalem . . . pertinent*. Strasbourg, 1617.

MacDonald, M., ed., *Philosophy and Analysis*. Oxford, 1954.

Marcus, R. B. "Essentialism in Modal Logic," *Nous,* I, 1967.

Montague, R. "The Proper Treatment of Quantification in Ordinary English," in R. Thomason, ed., *Selected Works*. 1976.

Moody, E. A. *Truth and Consequence in Medieval Logic*. Amsterdam, 1953.

Ockham, W. *Philosophical Writings*. Edited and translated by P. Boehner. Edinburgh, 1957.

Peano, G. *Arithmetices Principia Nova Methodo Exposita*. Rome, 1899.

Peter of Spain *Summulae Logicales*. Edited by I. Bochenski. Rome, 1947.

Putnam, H. "Red, Green and Logical Analysis," *Philosophical Review,* 65, 1956.

"On Properties," in N. Rescher, ed., *Essays in Honour of Carl G. Hempel*. Dordrecht, 1969.

"Meaning and Understanding," *Mind, Language and Reality: Collected Papers,* Vol. 2. Cambridge, England, and New York, 1975.

Quine, W. V. O. *From a Logical Point of View*. Cambridge, Mass., 1953.

Word and Object. New York, 1960.

Ontological Relativity and other Essays. New York, 1969.

Ramsey, F. *Foundation of Mathematics*. London, 1926.

Russell, B. "On Denoting," *Mind* 14, 1905.

Principles of Mathematics. London, 1903.

Lectures on the Philosophy of Logical Atomism. London, 1918.

Introduction to Mathematical Philosophy. London, 1919.

(with Whitehead) *Principia Mathematica,* 1st ed. Cambridge, England, 1910–13. 2d ed. Cambridge, 1925–7.

Schopenhauer, A. *Über der Wille in der Natur.* 1835. English translation in *Two Essays by Schopenhauer.* London, 1889.

Scott, D. "Advice on Modal Logic" in K. Lambert, ed., *Philosophical Problems in Logic*. Dordrecht, 1970.

Strawson, P. F. "On Referring," *Mind,* 59, 1950.

Swift, J. *Gulliver's Travels,* 1726.

Van Fraassen, B. *Introduction to the Philosophy of Time and Space*. New York, 1970. (See also under Lambert, K.)

von Wright, G. H. *Logical Studies*. London, 1959.

Wiggins, D. *Identity and Spatio-temporal Continuity*. Oxford, 1968.

William of Shyreswood. *Introductiones*. Translated as *Introduction to Logic* by N. Kretzmann. Minneapolis, 1966.

Wittgenstein, L. *Tractatus Logico-Philosophicus*. Translation by C. K. Ogden. London, 1922. Translation by D. Pears and B. McGuiness, 1961.

Index